REDISCOVERING GANDHI

VOLUME 6 : Gandhi and Jesus: The End of Fundamentalism

Series Editor: ***Prof. R.P. Misra***

Vol. 1. Hind Swaraj: *Gandhi's Challenge to Modern Civilization*
—R.P. Misra

2. Ahimsa: *The Way to Peace*
—Jonathan K. Crane & Jordi Agusti-Panareda

3. Satyagraha: *Gandhian Approach to Conflict Resolution*
—Jainarain Sharma

4. Consensual Democracy: *Gandhi on State, Power, and Politics*
—Ashu Pasricha

5. Humanizing Science and Technology: *Some Case Studies*
—Vinnie Jauhari and Parul Goyal

6. Gandhi and Jesus : The End of Fundamentalism
—Wolfgang Sternstein

ABOUT THE AUTHOR

Wolfgang Sternstein, Born on March 12, 1939 in Brunswick, Germany received his D. Phil. degree at the University of Frankfurt am Main (1975). He was research associate of the Berghof Foundation for Conflict Research in Berlin; (1976-80) and board member of the Federal Association of Citizens' Initiatives for the Protection of the Environment (BBU) (1982-84). Since 1979 he was research associate of the Institute of Environmental Science and Rights to Life. He is active as a peace researcher and peace worker in the resistance movement against atomic power plants as well as in the peace movement ever since 1975. He participated in several campaigns, was on trial more than a dozen times for acts of civil disobedience, and nine times in jail.

Publication: *My Way between Violence and Non-Violence: An Autobiography.*

Dr. Wolfgang Sternstein, Hauptmannsreute 45, 70192 Stuttgart, Germany. E-mail: sternstein@uwi-ev.de

REDISCOVERING GANDHI

Series Editor
Prof. R.P. Misra

Volume 6

Gandhi and Jesus : The End of Fundamentalism

Wolfgang Sternstein

Translated by
Birgit Bruckhoff and Werner Haiges

Published for
Centre for Gandhi and Peace Studies
Indira Gandhi National Open University, New Delhi
by
CONCEPT PUBLISHING COMPANY, PVT. LTD.
NEW DELHI-110059

ISBN-13: 978-81-8069-374-0 (Set)
ISBN-13: 978-81-8069-985-6 (Vol. 6)

First Published 2014

Published and Printed by

Concept Since 1974

Concept Publishing Company Pvt. Ltd.
A/15-16, Commercial Block, Mohan Garden
New Delhi-110059 (India)
T: 25351460, 25351794, *F*: 091-11-25357109
E: publishing@conceptpub.com, W: www.conceptpub.com
Editorial Office: H-13, Bali Nagar, New Delhi-110 015, India.

Cataloging in Publication Data--*Courtesy:* D.K. Agencies (P) Ltd. <docinfo@dkagencies.com>

Sternstein, Wolfgang.
[Gandhi und Jesus : das ende des fundamentalismus. English]
Gandhi and Jesus : the end of fundamentalism / Wolfgang Sternstein ; translated by Birgit Bruckhoff and Werner Haiges.
p. cm. — (Rediscovering Gandhi ; v. 6)
Translated from German.
Includes bibliographical references and index.
ISBN 9788180699856
ISBN 9788180693740 (series)

1. Gandhi, Mahatma, 1869-1948. 2. Jesus Christ. 3. Judaism. 4. Fundamentalism. 5. Religious absolutism. 6. Religious tolerance. 7. Bible—Criticism, interpretation, etc. I. Bruckhoff, Birgit. II. Haiges, Werner. III. Title. IV. Series: Rediscovering Gandhi ; v. 6.

DDC 954.035 23

Editor's Foreword

Mahatma Gandhi had answers to many of the problems humanity faces today. On religious intolerance, he said, "I believe in *Sarvadharamsamanvatva* having equal regard for all faiths and creeds". "Religions are not for separating men from one another, they are meant to bring them together. It is a misfortune that today they are so distorted that they have become a potential cause of strife and mutual slaughter." To Gandhi Rama, Krishna, Mahavira, Buddha, Zoroaster, Jesus Christ and Mohammad were equally great spiritual leaders. They all asked their followers to be truthful, non-violent, and charitable. No wonder then that he considered it "intolerance to believe that one's religion was superior to others".

Gandhi distinguished *dharma* from religion. *Dharma* encompasses all ethical, moral, social and other values or principles, code of conduct and behaviour which contribute to the well-being, sustenance and harmonious functioning of individuals, societies, nations and the world and which prevent their disintegration. In a wider sense it is *dharma* which sustains and supports the whole world. "Eating, sleeping, fearing and mating—human beings have these in common with animals. What distinguishes them from animals is *dharma*. Those devoid of *dharma* are no better than animals."

Dharma comes from one's inner self; it consists of the basic human values like truth, *ahimsa* (non-violence), love and sacrifice as propounded by the spiritual leaders at different times and in different parts of the world. Religion connotes a set of dogmas and beliefs, a code of conduct, a Founder, a Sacred Book and a Church, Temple, Mosque, Synagogue or similar institution. Religion is ritualistic; *dharma* is spiritualistic. Being ritualistic, religions at times become self-centric and go against the *dharmic* values expounded by their originators to fit them to space, time and social context. Gandhi showed reverence to the *dharmic* values of all religions. He remained a Hindu which accommodates within its fold people with widely differing beliefs and dogmas and proclaimed himself a "*Sanatani* Hindu", thus distancing from Hinduism as a religion.

Gandhi stopped going to Hindu temples when he saw the lowest caste Hindus not allowed to enter temples. He called these people *Harijans* (God's people) and the upper caste Hindus who made the rules to debar them from their *dharmic* rights to enter temples *durjans* (wicked people). And if today, all Hindus can enter a temple in India, it is to a great extent because of Gandhi. Realizing that there was no religion in the world which adhered to the values for whose preservation it was organized Gandhi distinguished Hindu *dharma* from Hindus; Islam *dharma* from Muslims; Christianity from Christians. In response to a question on Christianity, he said: "I like your Christ; I do not like your Christians. Your Christians are so unlike your Christ." One can find similar comments of Gandhi on other religions. Gandhi had respect for all religions but he believed, and rightly so that they were not perfect.

The book *Gandhi and Jesus* by Dr. Wolfgang Sternstein reveals the true meaning and mission of Christianity, as propounded and practiced by Jesus Christ himself over 2000 years ago. It focuses on Gandhian philosophy and its concurrence with Christian philosophy as propounded by Jesus in *Sermon on the Mount* and his own life. Gandhi altered his life to conform to the basic principles of Hinduism and in the process realized that Christianity too was based on the same principles. He thus ventured to study *Bible* and *Sermon on the Mount* and came to the conclusion that the two religions, even though they originated in different geographical, social and temporal settings were basically the same.

Gandhi's reverence to Jesus and the Sermon on the Mount brought a number of practicing Christians close to him. Among them, Henry Polak and his wife Millie Graham Polak were in his innermost circle in South Africa. Polak introduced *Unto This Last* by John Ruskin to Gandhi. The book helped Gandhi to know the common spiritual currents that flowed through Hinduism and Christianity. John Newman's *Lead Kindly Light* became a favourite prayer of Gandhi. How these Christian associates of Gandhi helped him understand religions other than Hinduism has been beautifully presented by Ms. Millie in her book *Mr. Gandhi—the Man.*

Seeing Gandhi referring to Christian scriptures especially the *Sermon on the Mount* so often, a lady asked Millie, "Is Mr. Gandhi a Christian" ? Millie asked for further clarification whether she meant one converted to Christianity or one who believed in the teachings of Christ. The visitor emphatically told that, she meant the former. She was talking about him with some friends and they were wondering that Gandhi knew Christian scriptures so well and fond of quoting words of Christ frequently and hence her friends thought he must be a Christian.

Ms. Millie brooded over. What the visitor said was true. To Gandhi the *Sermon on the Mount* was so inspiring that he not only kept it constantly in his mind but also quoted from it quite often while conversing with visitors or delivering talks. In the centre of his office room was a beautiful picture of Jesus Christ. The other pictures in the room were those of Justice Ranade, the great social reformer of India *Annie Besant*, who denounced injustices of the British rule; and Sir William Wilson Hunter, the editor of the *Imperial Gazetteer of India* who denounced in his writings the system of Indian indentured labour as 'semi-slavery'. And at home, was the photograph of Dadabhai Naoroji, the grand old man of India who was fighting for liberation of the oppressed and was so close to Gandhi's heart.

When *asked "why he did not embrace Christianity"*, Gandhi said that he was tremendously attracted when he studied the scriptures but he found nothing really special there which were not in Hinduism and thus "to be a good Hindu also meant that I would be a good Christian. There was no need for me to join your creed to be a believer in the beauty of the teachings of Jesus or try to follow His example" When Gandhi asked Millie, "What do you think is the essential lesson for man in the teaching of Christianity?" Millie replied: "I could think of two or three. But one that stands out strongest "One is your Master Christ and all ye are brethren". And Gandhi was quick to respond: "Yes, and Hinduism teaches the same great truth and Mohammedanism and Zoroastrianism too".

"To live the gospel is the most effective way; most effective in the beginning, in the middle and in the end. Not just preach but live the life according to the light. If, therefore, you go on serving people and ask them also to serve, they would understand. But you quote instead John 3:16 and ask them to believe it and that has no appeal to me, and I am sure people will not understand it. The Gospel will be more powerful when practiced and preached." remarked Gandhi. Vincent Sheehan had rightly said about Gandhi: "The most Christ-like man in history was not a Christian at all".

Look at what James said in *Bible* (1:22-25). "Do not deceive yourselves by just listening to His word; instead, put it into practice.

If you listen to the word, but do not put it into practice you are like people who look in a mirror and see themselves as they are. They take a good look at themselves and then go away and at once forget what they look like. But if you look closely into the perfect law that sets people free, and keep on paying attention to it and do not simply listen and then forget it, but put it into practice, you will be blessed by God in what you do".

Mahatma Gandhi was one of truest followers of Christ but he did no see Christ in Christianity as practiced in South Africa in his time. That is why Gandhi told the missionaries, "I like your Christ; I do not like your Christians. Your Christians are so unlike your Christ". When asked why he did not embrace Christianity, Gandhi said it offered nothing he could not get from his own religion, observing, "...to be a good Hindu also meant that I would be a good Christian. There is no need for me to join your creed to be a believer in the beauty of the teachings of Jesus or try to follow his example". The death of Gandhi on January 30, 1948 was described by the legendary missionary E. Stanley Jones as, "the greatest tragedy since the Son of God died on the Cross". Gandhi greatness lay in the fact that he took the ideas of Christ and applied them faithfully adhering to Hinduism, thus proving that *truly knowing Christ has nothing to do with Christianity.*

More often than not, Christianity like other institutionalized religions bears no resemblance to its original mission. It is man-made. If Christ brings peace and harmony, how can Christianity generate conflict and hatred? Yet, many a people feel safe in organized beliefs and call themselves Christian, Hindu, Muslim or Buddhist, to name a few.

The idea that the God who appears to Gandhi as Cosmic Law can be bribed with good work, piety, rituals and traditions is widely accepted and millions of followers of various religions are mesmerized and shackled by the idea. All religions proclaim loudly that it is the God who chose and sent each of us to earth. Whether we see God in one form or the other, it makes no difference to Him and hence we cannot bribe our way to God through religious practices. To reach God, we have to free ourselves of the religious rut and realise the truth. That is what Gandhi did all through his life. And when his mortal end came, he uttered *He Ram* (Oh God).

Dr. Wolfgang Sternstein's book relates Gandhi's journey through the labyrinth of religions to applied spirituality. Although it focuses on Christianity, the conclusion he has drawn are applicable to all religions and all those who claim to be religious.

I fully concur with the conclusion the author has drawn that to bring peace and harmony in the world, humanity has to return to Jesus' life and teaching. In his own words: What is essential is a reformation of head and limbs of Christianity. What is essential is the dialogue of the denominations, religions and philosophies while abandoning any absolute truth claim. What is essential is following Jesus' call: "*The time has come; the kingdom of God has dawned*".

What unites Gandhi and Jesus despite their distance in time, space and cultural background? I know no better answer than the five principles that Gandhi recommended as the subjects of daily prayers or daily meditation:

> "I want to adhere to the truth.
> I do not want to bow to injustice.
> I want to be free of fear.
> I do not want to use force.
> I want to see, first of all, the good in everyone."

Let me take this opportunity to thank the Centre for Gandhi and Peace Studies, Indira Gandhi National Open University (IGNOU), New Delhi for sponsoring the publication of the series (volume V) onwards especially its coordinator Prof. D. Gopal and Sri Ashok Mittal, Concept Publishing Company Pvt. Ltd. for publishing the series. I am quite sure the volume would be as popular as the earlier ones.

Allahabad
January 30, 2013

R. P. Misra
Series Editor

Preface

This book was published in Germany in 2009. It was a challenge not only for Christianity, but equally for Judaism and Islam, generally called the Abrahamic religions, because all three of them, though enemy brothers, refer to Abraham as their common ancestor. It questions the absolute truth and superiority claim of these religions, Christian and Islamic missionary activities as well as Christian dogma. So it is not surprising that the book, if it was noticed in the first place, met with rejection.

This very reason may make it of interest to the Indian reader, because Hinduist India, whose most convincing spiritual representative is, in my opinion, Mahatma Gandhi, saw itself confronted twice in her history with the Abrahamic truth and superiority claim. This claim of Islam and Western civilisation has moulded the more recent history of India more strongly than anything else.

The first wave of conquest reached India from the North West in the form of the Mogul regime, beginning in the sixteenth century and reaching its climax under Emperor Aurangzeb (1658-1707). It consisted, first and foremost of a religious and political expansion of Islam. The second wave of conquest took place in the second half of the eighteenth century in the form of the East India Company. It reached its climax in the Indian Empire (1858-1947). It failed as a religious conquest, because Hinduism proved to be largely immune against dogmatic Christianity.

All the more successful was the conquest by Western civilisation, predominantly based on science, technology and industry. It was an economic and political conquest, which had far reaching consequences: the disintegration of the subcontinent into India, Pakistan and Bangladesh, the Hindu-Moslem conflict that remains virulent even today, the pauperisation of these countries due to the destruction of their local textile and cottage industries by the British as well as the cultural alienation by Islam and later by Western civilisation.

In view of this history of blood, sweat and tears it may be surprising that there should have been a "brother in spirit" of the Hindu Mohandas K. Gandhi in the form of the man standing in the centre of the Christian religion, namely Jesus of Nazareth. This is, nevertheless, the main thesis of this book. For the last approximately 240 years the Life-of-Jesus Research endeavoured to reconstruct from the texts of the New Testament the life and the teaching of the "historical" Jesus, the man who lived during the reign of the Roman emperors Augustus and Tiberius in Palestine, the small strip of land between the Eastern shore of the Mediterranean Sea and the Jordan Valley, and who was convicted to death and executed around the year 30 A.D. by the Roman Governor Pontius Pilate. This work has been largely completed today, even though not all details of his life and teaching have been clarified with absolute certainty.

The historical Jesus of Nazareth has little in common with the Jesus Christ of the Christian dogma, the only and only begotten Son of God standing in the centre of the Christian preaching. There are all the more similarities between him and Mohandas K. Gandhi in spite of the enormous distance in space, time and cultural sphere that separates them. This is particularly true for their rejection of any kind of fundamentalism, that highly poisonous plant flourishing on the root basis of the absolute truth and superiority claim of the Abrahamic religions.

The Hindu religion knows the *avatar* figure, the incarnated God who descends to Earth in times of world crisis in order to show a path of salvation to mankind. I believe that both Gandhi and Jesus were *avatars*. They have shown us a path of salvation. But we do have to walk it ourselves, after all.

I am deeply grateful to the publisher, Concept Publishing Company Pvt. Ltd. for making the release of the book possible. Professors Rameshwar P. Misra and Cherian Kurian as well as my friend Peter Ruhe have substantially contributed to its publication. To them, I extend my words of thanks, but also to the translators Birgit Bruckhoff and Werner Haiges for their excellent work done.

Wolfgang Sternstein

Contents

PART II
JESUS OF NAZARETH

1
Introduction

> If I were to ask myself from what literature we here in Europe, we who have been nurtured almost exclusively on the thoughts of Greeks and Romans, and of one Semitic race, the Jewish, may draw that corrective which is most wanted in order to make our inner life more perfect, more comprehensive, more universal, in fact more truly human, a life, not for this life only, but a transfigured and eternal life — again I should point to India.
>
> —*Friedrich Max Muller*

Religion stands for the highest and the lowest in man. It enables to render selfless service to one's fellow human beings, active help to the weak and sick, to love one's enemies, and even to sacrifice one's life for one's conviction and for others. It enables, however, also to commit the most horrific crimes and most inhuman atrocities, because it gives the perpetrators a good conscience, since God is presumed to stand on their side or might even order them to commit such actions.

Such ambiguity seems to be a characteristic of all religions. Nevertheless the question arises if that has to be necessarily so, based on the nature of religion itself. In my opinion, this is not at all the case, as I hope to be able to demonstrate using the example of two exceptional religious figures — Gandhi and Jesus. Religion, as I understand it, is not only free from hate and violence, lies and deception, but is, on the contrary, in the position to overcome such behaviour poisoning our coexistence and to create a world in which we deal with one another and the surrounding nature in a humane manner. This is not as self-evident as it may sound for many. Even a short glance into the *Bible*, which is by many Christians still taken as the *Holy Scripture* and the *Word of God*, shows, that almost every human rights violation and every crime can be justified and was indeed justified in the history of Christianity with reference to the *Bible*. Whoever does not allow himself to be lulled by the varied churchly language regimes recognises a shocking amount of *unholiness* in the *Holy Scripture.*

Nevertheless this book is spread in the millions by the Christian churches and denominations around the world without any critical commentary. Long overdue is, however, a *Bible* edition, which incorporates the findings of historical-critical *Bible* research, religious science, religious sociology and religious psychology. Without question, such an undertaking would trigger a veritable surge of controversies among theologians and laymen. But that does not matter. Controversies do not harm as long as they find their place within the framework of a constructive debate. Differences of opinion are the salt of life, since there is neither progress in knowledge nor in belief without disputes. There is an indispensable precondition, however, for the fruitful work at a *critical edition of the Bible*: there must be no taboos; there must be no absolute truth claim for Christianity, the *Bible*, the Dogmas or the Creeds. It is self-evident that the outcome of such a discussion will always be temporary. The progress of the findings will continue and result in further critical releases. This would be the sign of a living religion.

It is a serious shortfall that there has not been a critical edition of the *Bible* up to now. It is one of the main reasons for the growing alienation between theology and church communities, and it is one of the reasons for the amount of mischief carried out with the *Bible*. Ever since the seventies of the past century, religious fundamentalism[1] in the Abrahamic[2] religions is on the rise. Pious Jews, Christians and Moslems are taking the Hebrew *Bible* (the *First Testament*)[3] and the *Second Testament* as well as the *Koran* literally, and correlate doomsday prophecies contained therein with the present time in the way the messianic apocalypticists[4] of earlier days had already done. For them the *Bible* or the *Koran* is God's timelessly valid word, which must not be doubted.

Their attention is spellbound by the Palestine of our days, that tiny piece of land at the east coast of the Mediterranean, where, according to their conviction, the events of the last days predicted by the *Bible*, namely in the Revelation of John, would begin. They interpret the Middle East conflict in the light of the *Bible* and come to the conclusion, that the final battle at Armageddon,[5] a mythical place in the North of Israel mentioned in the Apocalypse of John, is imminent. For them, the signs that are supposedly obvious everywhere, indicate that the Islamic peoples arm themselves to destroy God's "chosen people". This way, they allegedly force God to interfere with the course of history and to let the world perish in a cosmic catastrophe in order to replace it with a new one, in which His chosen ones enjoy a life of paradisiacal abundance in the kingdom of the Messiah. The same applies for the Islamic fundamentalists, albeit with inverted sign. For them, the USA represent the great, and Israel the small Satan, whom Allah will destroy in the already soon-to-come final days.

As an enlightened contemporary, one is tempted to dismiss such speculations as absurd delusions of sectarians. This, however, would be a disastrous misjudgement, since they influence massively the election of political office-bearers and the government policies in the USA, Israel, Iran, and increasingly also in other countries due to their potential in votes as well as their intensive lobbying and missionary activities.

As weird as the fundamentalist doomsday speculations may seem, they do have a concrete core: the Middle East conflict that is steadily intensifying and expanding since the foundation of the state of Israel in the year 1948, and the threat to the existence of mankind by the gigantic potential of destruction that was amassed by the nuclear powers since Word War II. A down-to-earth analysis of the global political situation comes, therefore, to similar results as the religious fundamentalists, albeit with the "small" difference that after an atomic world war there will not be the recreation of the world in the offing, but an atomically contaminated blue planet will continue to circle the sun as sung in a peace song of the eighties of the past century. This, however, does by no means rule out a "recreation" of the world. Nature has an infinite amount of time. For it, a million years are as much as a day for us. Radioactivity on Earth will have died down that much after a few million years that a new evolution will set in, since algae and bacteria survive even the strongest radiation.

Religious fundamentalism thus has quite a concrete basis. Above all, it is so dangerous because, instead of mobilising people's energy to avert the impending catastrophe, religious fundamentalism brings about the catastrophe by way of a self-fulfilling prophecy, probably even actively advancing it in order to become part of the eternal bliss. In short, it is the *escape from the existence-threatening reality in a collective religious delusion.*

Without question, the threat to our existence by atomic armament and environmental catastrophes is real. If we understand the nineteenth century as the century of the fight between the European nations for world dominance and the twentieth century as the century of the fight of the capitalist, communist and fascist ideological communities for world dominance, then the twentyfirst century emerges as a new paradigm in the "fight of the cultures" for world dominance. To the players in this global game belong the USA, Europe, Russia, the Islamic World, China and India. We are dealing with such profane things as the access to mineral resources, markets and secure transport routes. The present situation differs from the battles of the past mainly by the fact that the most important players in this field are atomic powers, which makes the use of these weapons in regional and global wars foreseeable. It is the knowledge of the atomic threat to mankind and all higher developed life forms on Earth that gives such an immense boost to doomsday speculations.

Samuel Huntington[6] rightly points out the central role of religion in the emergence of cultural identity. At the same time, it turns out to be an inexhaustible arsenal to get weapons for the propaganda war inside and outside of warring countries.

The moderate forces of Judaism, Christianity and Islam should rise to the challenge of fundamentalism. Fortunately a number of initiatives do exist today which tend to bring the inter-religious dialogue forward instead of the "war of religions". Among them are the "World Ethos Project" of Hans Küng or the "World Conference of Religions for Peace" and many more. It is up to us to develop a broad movement for inter-denominational, inter-religious and inter-cultural dialogue from there that can defy fundamentalism.

Viktor and Viktoria Trimondi[7] have come up with an analysis of the messianic-apocalyptic movements in the Abrahamic religions from the point of view of a science committed to enlightenment and humanism. This has my unqualified approval. However, I regard it as desirable or even as essential to attempt such an analysis from a religious point of view. This is what this book is about. One of its results is: Religious fundamentalism is not a peripheral phenomenon in the Abrahamic religions. It rather has its roots in the *absolute truth claim* of these religions. This means, it is not a matter of fundamentalism alone, it is also the matter of the *absolute truth claim* of the Abrahamic religions.

The first chapter outlines the positions of several well-known authors regarding the *absolute truth claim* of the Abrahamic religions. This is followed by a First Part dealing with Gandhi's perception of

God against the background of the *Bible's* image of God, and its consequences for his life and work. Gandhi's religious thinking results in a completely new view of the life and teaching of Jesus of Nazareth. It coincides widely with the results of historical-critical *Bible* science, but exceeds it in essential points. This is demonstrated in the Second Part of the study.

REFERENCES

1. A definition of fundamentalism is offered by Thomas Meyer: "Fundamentalism is an arbitrary secluding movement, that is meant to bring back absolute certainty, a firm hold, reliable security and unquestionable orientation by irrational condemnation of all alternatives as an immanent countertendency towards the modern process of general opening of thinking, acting, the ways of life and the society." Thomas Meyer: *Fundamentalismus. Aufstand gegen die Moderne*, Hamburg, 1989, 18.
2. Judaism, Christianity and Islam are summarised as Abrahamic religions, because all three base themselves on Abraham as their ancestor. In total more than half of the 7 billion inhabitants of the Earth belong to them.
3. I use the term *First* and *Second Testament* instead of *Old* and *New Testament* to avoid any semblance of discrimination.
4. "Messianic apocalypticists" are Christians expecting the end of the world and the appearance of Jesus Christ as the ruler of all (pantocrator) over a new kingdom created by God.
5. Apocalypse of John, chapter 16, verse 16 (16:16).
6. Samuel P. Huntington, *The Clash of Civilizations,* Simon & Schuster, New York, 1996.
7. Krieg der Religionen. Politik, Glaube und Terror im *Zeichen der Apokalypse*. München, 2006, Kap. 12-17.

2
The Absolute Truth Claim of the Abrahamic Religions

> Whoever claims to be in the final possession of truth, can talk no more with the other, — he breaks off genuine communication in favour of his believed contents. —*Karl Jaspers*

In this chapter, the absolute truth claim of the Abrahamic religions is up for discussion. By that we mean the claim raised by Jews, Christians and Moslems, that their respective religion is the only true religion because God revealed it. This claim differentiates the Abrahamic religions from the religions of the East, Hinduism, Buddhism, Confucianism and Taoism. In the era not only of economic, but also of social and cultural globalisation, it remains to be brought forward only cautiously by most Christians, but there are minorities "of strong faith", i.e., those with a tendency to fundamentalism and fanaticism, who still assert the claim resolutely. Even the major churches do not want to do without it, in spite of their efforts towards inter-religious dialogue. The suffering this claim has brought about in history, and continues to do up to today, exceeds any imagination. There were wars waged in its name and crusades undertaken, people of other faiths converted by force, tortured and burned as heretics. The number of humans sacrificed on the altar of this bloodthirsty idol goes into the millions upon millions.

The topic is by no means new. It is as old as the age of enlightenment, if not even older. It was then when the clash between followers of the religion of revelation and the followers of the religion of reason broke out. The former invoked the *Bible* as the source of absolute truth, the latter referred to reason as the source of a religion that regards God as the creator of the Universe. They said that God had arranged the World according to the rules of reason, that He had created it like a watchmaker creates the clockwork that, once put in motion, followed its prescribed course according to the Laws of Nature.

Essential components of the religion of reason were the encouragement of tolerance towards those who were different-minded and of different beliefs, as well as the strong turn against obscure belief in the superstitions and in miracles, which was prevalent in the Europe of the Middle Ages until far into modern times, and which can partially be found up to today — if we think of the doomsday belief of religious fundamentalists or the rejection of Darwin's theory of evolution by American "creationists".

The clash between religion of revelation and religion of reason has now-a-days become largely outdated, whereas the open or concealed absolute truth claim for one's own religion has not. To deal with it remains as necessary today as it did ever before. The religions raising this claim protect themselves from critical questions by regarding them as a result of sin or even by cursing them as blasphemous. Whoever does not want to attract these anathema remains silent.

As we know, it is the children whose unspoilt souls let them exclaim what everyone sees, but does not dare to say: "But the Emperor does not wear anything"![1] To this kind of queries belongs also this one: There are three religions that do differ, after all, but of which each raises the claim to be the absolute truth revealed by God. Something cannot be correct there: Either only one of them is absolutely true and the others are untrue, or all three are, irrespective of their claim, untrue, or, as a third possibility, we say goodbye to reason and declare: with God everything is possible, why then not this also? The experts fear nothing as much as this kind of childlike queries. They have long since come to the understanding that their respective own religion is the true one, and that's it! This is why they answer the childlike questions like head teachers answer the questions of bright students: 'Wrong! Sit down! Failed!'

GOTTHOLD EPHRAIM LESSING

Lessing (1729-1781) was one such rebellious bright mind. He liked it to get at loggerheads with the theologians of his times, among whom Hamburg's Main Pastor Goetze stood out. The conflict escalated, resulting in Duke Karl von Braunschweig, who was Lessing's highest-ranking master, decreeing a publication ban on his sharp-tongued librarian from Wolfenbüttel. Lessing found himself obliged to return to his trade as a poet, in order to test, as he confided in Elise Reimarus, "if they would not allow me, at least, to preach without hindrance on my old pulpit, in the theatre". Much more has come out of that than a sermon in the theatre, namely the dramatic poem called "Nathan The Wise".

The heart of this drama is "The Parable of the Three Rings". Of the story, playing during the time of the crusades, only this much needs to be known for our purpose: The generous, if not to say lavish Sultan Saladin is once again in financial troubles, because he intends to make the beggars in his country rich. He undertakes to lure a Jew, who is known among the people not only for his extreme wealth but also not any less for his wisdom, into a trap, in order to get at his money. He poses him the question, which of the religions Judaism, Christianity and Islam, all three of which claim to be revealed by God and thus absolutely true, is in effect the true one. Nathan is in an awkward position. If he said Jewish, then he would be regarded by the Moslem as blasphemous and lose his wealth, may be even his life. The same applied if he declared Christianity to be the only true religion. If, however, he declared Islam to be the only true one, then he would betray the belief of his forefathers, could subsequently no more be regarded as wise and would be expelled from his religious community. During the short time to think it over granted to him by the Sultan, the life-saving idea comes to his mind: "Not only children can be quieted with stories". — This is Lessing! Instead of storming up the pulpit or the lectern to declare pompously the be-all and end-all, the truth he has to convey comes in the pauper's guise of a little story by which an old Jew saves his neck.

> "In days of yore", he begins the talk with the sultan
> "there dwelt in east a man
> Who from a valued hand received a ring
> Of endless worth: the stone of it an opal,
> That shot an ever-changing tint: moreover,
> It had the hidden virtue him to render
> Of God and man beloved, who in this view,
> And this persuasion, wore it."

So it is not only the magic power of the ring that makes the wearer beloved by God and man. He also has to contribute something himself by wearing it with this confidence.

"Was it strange
The eastern man ne'er drew it off his finger,
And studiously provided to secure it
For ever to his house. Thus—He bequeathed it;
First, to the MOST BELOVED of his sons,
Ordained that he again should leave the ring
To the MOST DEAR among his children—and
That without heeding birth, the FAVOURITE son,
In virtue of the ring alone, should always
Remain the lord o' the' house
From son to son,
At length this ring descended to a father,
Who had three sons, alike obedient to him;
Whom therefore he could not but love alike.
At times seemed this, now that, at times the third,
—Accordingly as each apart received
The overflowings of his heart — most worthy
To heir the ring, which with good-natured weakness
He privately to each in turn had promised."

When the good father feels his end come near, he grows embarrassed. What to do? Finally he has a brilliant idea. He orders a jeweller to manufacture two additional rings with the design of the first one. The jeweller fulfils the request so expertly that even the father is unable to differentiate the true from the fake rings. He summons each of his sons for a confidential talk, and gives each of them his blessing and a ring. Just shortly after the father has passed away, each son appears to show his ring, and claims to be the lord of the house. Since it is not possible to find out the real ring, the matter is brought before the judge. He declares himself not to be in charge, but then he remembers that the real ring had the "secret power to make the wearer beloved by God and man". So he asks the brothers, whom of them the other two loved. They remain silent, so that the judge declares that the real ring has obviously lost its power, or that, possibly, none of their rings is the real one. He gives the advice that each of them should regard his ring as the real one, and live accordingly:

"Let each feel honoured by this free affection.
Unwrapped of prejudice; let each endeavour

To vie with both his brothers in displaying
The virtue of his ring; assist its might
With gentleness, benevolence, forbearance,
With inward resignation to the godhead,
And if the virtues of the ring continue
To show themselves among your children's children,
After a thousand thousand years, appear
Before this judgment-seat—a greater one
Than I shall sit upon it and decide.
So spake the modest judge."

No further words are needed to explain what Lessing wants to tell us through Nathan: The fight for truth is fruitless, even destructive. What is important is the implementation of the love for God and man in day-to-day life. An old hat? – Not at all! Lessing's "sermon" of a belief, that stands the test of life by understanding, love and kindness towards those who are different-minded, of different belief and of different ways of life, is as relevant as ever before. Looking at religious fundamentalism in all its forms is sufficient to demonstrate that. This applies in particular to the situation in Palestine, where the followers of these religions have fought and continue fighting for the "Holy Land". During all times, religions have served as an arsenal, from which weapons are taken for the war against the "infidels" and, not seldom, for the enforcement of concrete power and economic interests. In times of globalization, in which "The Clash of Civilizations" (Samuel Huntington) and the "War of Religions" (Victor and Victoria Trimondi) are imminent, the danger increases that religion degenerates into ideology.[2]

KARL BARTH

Even after Lessing and the proponents of the Enlightenment, the absolute truth claim was not at all restricted to fundamentalist circles only. Karl Barth (1886-1968), a renowned theologian, who shaped, together with Rudolf Bultmann (1884-1976), the protestant theology of the post-war era of the German Federal Republic, went to the extent of claiming in his monumental fragmentary work "Church Dogmatic Theology": "No sentence is more dangerous, more revolutionary than the one that God is One, that Nobody is equal to Him!.... If this sentence is pronounced in a way that it is heard and grasped, it always tends to cost instantly the joint lives of 450 Baal's shavelings."[3]

Karl Barth was an important theologian with undoubted, great merits as one of the leading men of the Confessing Church in their resistance against National Socialism, but you ask yourself instinctively, what was, after all, so overwhelmingly new and Christian in the message "that God is One, and that Nobody is equal to Him", when Judaism and Islam have advanced this thought far more convincingly, accusing Christianity, not without reason, of latent polytheism.

But worse is to come. The reference to the scripture with the 450 "Baal's shavelings" shows unmistakenly, which kind of spirit is speaking here. The biblical story tells of Prophet Elijah, who, in the name of the "true" God Yahweh, proclaims and executes the death sentence for 450 Baal's priests on Mount Carmel. This horrific bloody deed — if it was in fact historical, which is doubtful — is supposedly justified by a judgement of God. Elijah speaks to the people on Mount Carmel: "Give us two bulls. They (the Baal's priests) shall choose one, cut it, and lay it onto the wood, but without lighting a fire. I shall choose the other one, cut it, and lay it on the wood without lighting a fire. Then you shall call the name of your God, and I shall call the name of the Lord. The God who answers with fire shall be the true God. There, the whole people shouted out: the proposal is good."[4] Of course, the 450 Baal's priests do not succeed in lighting the fire by magic power. They are even made fun of by Elijah. He, however, succeeds easily with Yahweh's help. The fire consumes not only the sacrifice, but also the wood, the stones and the earth, and it even licks the water up that had been poured, at his behest, onto the altar and the trench around the altar. Yahweh seems to be unusually hungry and thirsty on this particular day. Thus, the subsequent end of the story is: "The whole people saw it, threw themselves down on their faces, and shouted: Yahweh is God, Yahweh is God! But Elijah ordered them: Seize the prophets of Baal! None of them shall escape. They were seized, and Elijah let them be brought down to the Kishon stream, and get them killed there".[5]

This way, Barth justifies in a sloppy formulation (going for them) the murder of 450 priests of another religion, whom, on top of it, he calls, derogatively, "Baal's shavelings", in the name of the true God! For him, there is only the one God who reveals himself in the *Bible*. It is irrelevant, in this respect that Barth differentiates between "natural theology" and Revelation. He finds religion in terms of "natural theology" not only in the form of other religions, but also within

Christianity. To it he contrasts and confronts the Revelation as God's word in the Holy Scripture and in the person of Jesus Christ that has to be accepted unconditionally.

Dietrich Bonhoeffer (1906-1945) rightfully criticises Barth's theology as "Revelation positivism".[6] Critical questions are forbidden. Whoever points at contradictions and inconsistencies in the biblical scriptures only manifests his disbelief by that. He should beware not to meet the fate of the 450 Baal's priests! Here, religious fundamentalism and fanaticism, insisting to be in the possession of the absolute, revealed truth, raises its ugly head. Barth: "There can be no room at all any more for precisely what modern age calls tolerance. Apart from God only His creatures exist, or just false Gods, and therefore, apart from the belief in Him, only religions that are religions of superstition, of misbelief and ultimately of faithlessness."[7]

CONCLUSION: *Karl Barth smashes with a huge mallet all non-Christian and vast sections of the Christian religions.* His notion that God and not he himself is swinging this hammer makes little difference. At the end, he still hits the "Baal's shavelings" and those of different faith.

JOSEPH RATZINGER/POPE BENEDICT XVI

On the Catholic side, Joseph Ratzinger/Benedict XVI belongs to those congenial with Karl Barth. Whoever thinks of himself as being in the possession of the absolute truth thinks feels and acts with fundamentalist tendency. It does not matter how this truth is defined, be it by religion, by philosophy, or "scientifically" in the sense of a pseudo-science such as social Darwinism, the Nazi's racial ideology or the "scientific socialism" of the communists. Seen from that angle, the Jesus book by Ratzinger/Benedict XVI is also of fundamentalist tendency, because for him it is certain: *God, the absolute truth has incarnated himself in Jesus Christ.* Accordingly, the teachings of Jesus, his life, his death and his resurrection are the absolute truth, which he entrusted to this Church — which is the Catholic one. The believers of other denominations and religions as well as the faithless come into view, for him, only as the addressees of mission, if at all. They are to be returned to — or incorporated into — the womb of Holy Mother Church by patient and persistent work of persuasion. Only this way they gain the full share of salvation in the belief of God the Father, God the Son and God the Holy Ghost: "To ask for God's Kingdom means to tell Jesus: Let us be yours, Lord! Penetrate us, live in us; gather the dispersed mankind in your body, so that everything be subordinated to God in you, and that you can pass the Universe to the Father, then, so that "God be all in all' ".[8]

Regarding the people, who have neither in the past nor in the presence heard anything about Jesus, let alone have been educated about the Christian belief to a point that they were or are able to make a decision either in favour or against it — and this is the vast majority of mankind in the past and now — their fate remains in the dark of the unfathomable will of God. That much is sure, anyway: The Christians, especially the Catholic ones, are, according to Church father Aurelius Augustine (354-430) God's chosen people roaming through history.

For the long serving Prefect of the Congregation for the Doctrine of the Faith, the successor organisation of the Holy Inquisition,[9] particular concern is required for those persons and communities within the Catholic Church who are in danger of succumbing to the insinuations of the Anti-Christ or Devil. In connection with the interpretation of Jesus' temptation in the desert he comes to talk about Marxism. Those familiar with the background know that here he aims particularly at the Latin American liberation theologians and their followers all over the world. He links up their involvement for the poor, their demand for social justice with the Anti-Christ. For this, he refers to the small work of Vladimir Solowjev (1853-1900): *Tale of the Anti-Christ*.[10] This *Anti-Christ* writes, among others, a book with the significant title: "The open road to peace and welfare of the world".[11] Whoever perceives hunger, misery and hardship of countless people in all parts of the world, who recognises it as a crime against God and mankind and demands social justice instead of charitable care, can only be the Anti-Christ! No, Ratzinger/Benedict XVI brings something much more important to the people. He brings them God. How could it be different for a man of the Church who knows hunger, misery and hardship from hearsay only, if at all? Just the opposite to Gandhi, who experienced firsthand the hardship of the working population of South Africa and India: "For the poor the economical is the spiritual. One cannot appeal to these hungry millions in a different way. But bring them something to eat, and they will regard you as their God. They are not capable of thinking of anything else".[12]

Besides the liberation theology, which he regards as Marxist inspired, Ratzinger/Benedict XVI uncovers yet another field of activity of the Anti-Christ: *the historical-critical theology*. He does not reject it right away. He says it has some validity, after all. As soon as it questions Christian dogmas, however, it turns into devilish temptation. No wonder then, that the University of Tübingen, this hotbed of historical-critical *Bible* exegesis, bestows the honorary doctorate upon the Anti-Christ. Ratzinger/Benedict XVI: "*Bible* interpretation can indeed become the instrument of the Anti-Christ. This is not just told us by Solowjew; this is the core testimony of (Jesus') temptation history itself. The worst books to destroy the figure of Jesus and to dismantle the belief have been concocted through the presumed results of the scientific exegesis." And a bit later he continues. "Then the *Bible* speaks no more of God, the living God, and then it will be only us to speak and to determine what God can do, and what we want to or ought to do. And the Anti-Christ tells us then with the gesture of high scholarly standards, that an exegesis that reads the *Bible* in the belief of a living God and thereby listens to him, will be regarded as fundamentalism; and that only his own exegesis, which is claimed to be purely scientific, where God himself does not say anything and has nothing to say, is at the height of time."[13]

What must have pleased Ratzinger/Benedict XVI very much in Solowjev's tale, is that therein a Protestant theology professor named Pauli installs at the end of times, in agreement with John, the Patriarch of the Russian-Orthodox Church, the Pope Peter to the Head of the whole of Christianity, citing the biblical Jesus with the words: "Thou art Peter".[14] The "Tale of the Anti-Christ" combines all the components of Christian fundamentalism: the absolute truth claim, messianism and apocalypticism.

Who was Jesus of Nazareth? Of course, Ratzinger/Benedict XVI knows this. We mere mortals, however, are not really sure of it. As a result, we depend on reconstructions, which can claim only relative validity. We do not know, how he looked like, we do also not know for sure what he said and did. In a word, we do not know who he was. Even the testimony of the Holy Ghost in the scripture of the Second Testament does not help us any further, because this testimony contains extreme differences, in part even contradictions.

HANS KÜNG

It is only rare, now-a-days that the absolute truth claims is raised as openly as done by Barth und Ratzinger/Benedict XVI. Yet, it is not at all abandoned, as I believe to be able to show using the example of the prominent Catholic theologian Hans Küng.

Küng's outstanding merits regarding the inter-religious dialogue do not need to be commented here. They are well known. Küng leaves the antique and medieval: "There is no salvation outside the Church" miles behind him. He also leaves behind him the point of view still taken by many Christians up to today: "There is no salvation outside Christianity". For him, salvation exists also outside Christianity. He even accords followers of other religions the right to be equally convinced that they are in possession of the absolute truth. Consequently, claim is facing claim here, without allowing to derive any kind of compulsion from it to convert people of other faiths to one's own religion. Küng makes an emphatic and passionate case for renouncing compulsion and violence in religious matters. Instead of confronting the followers of other religions with his own truth claim, he emphasizes the priority of self-reflection. The Church should become conscious of how often and how horribly Christians have failed when measured with the yardstick of their own message. He admits that there is truth in other religions and untruth in the Christian religion: "Because every unbiased person knows: The borderline between truth and untruth is not necessarily identical with the borderline between one's own and the respective other religion. Whoever keeps things in perspective, will concede: *The borderlines between truth and untruth* go also *through one's respective own religion*".[15] He considers being open for self-criticism an indispensable precondition for a constructive inter-religious dialogue.

In the second part of his book Project Global Ethic, Küng deals with the question of truth. There he starts with the following question: "Is a path theologically justifiable, which allows Christians as well as believers of other religions to accept the truth of the respective other religions without abandoning the truth of one's own religion and consequently one's own identity"?[16] To answer this question, he refers to general ethical principles, which he thinks he can make out, emphasised to a higher or lower degree, in all religions. In the sphere of Christianity, however, they do not originate predominantly from Christian tradition, but from antique Humanism, which implemented them only in the course of the modern Enlightenment-driven emancipation process in the form of the freedom of belief, of conscience, and of religion. Its presumably most convincing manifestation he found in the postulation of human dignity and the human rights derived therefrom, which do however require, in Küng's opinion, the religious substantiation in order to claim absolute validity.

The decisive question remains, however: How do you deal with the absolute truth claim of Christianity such as in form of the dogma, that Jesus is the only and only begotten son of God, *true* man and *true* God, meaning totally man and totally God? In the words of Küng: "If one believes in Jesus as the Path, the Truth and the Life, can one also accept then, that there are other paths, other truths, other life out of transcendence? *The Torah*? *The Qoran*? *The Eightfold Path of the Buddha*"?[17] In order to escape this dilemma, he proposes to differentiate between an outer and an inner perspective: "Seen from the *outside*, from the theological point of view, so to say, there are, of course, *different true religions:* religions that in principle conform, with all their ambivalence, to certain general (ethical as well as religious) criteria. There are different paths of salvation (with different saviours) to that one end, which can partly even overlap, and, in any case, cross-fertilise each other.

Seen from *inside*, which means from the point of view of the faithful Christian oriented at the *New Testament*, for me as the affected, challenged man, for that matter, there is only *the one true religion*: "Christianity, in so far as it bears witness to the one true God, as revealed in Jesus Christ. The one true religion does, however, not necessarily exclude truth in other religions, but can accept others as *conditionally true*. religions. Other religions may well supplement, correct and deepen the Christian religion, as long as they do not directly contradict the Christian message".[18]

Küng asks: "Is this possibly a contradiction"? and answers in the negative. I do, however, recognise a contradiction there. What does count then, after all, the outer or the inner perspective? As it is, both do not match. And when he finally concludes: "A maximum of theological opening towards the other religions does not require at all the suspension of one's own religious conviction. As if one demanded from participants of a religious dialogue to abandon, for a start, their religious conviction".[19] To abandon "one's religious conviction" is just not the point, the sole point is the abandoning of the *absolute truth claim*, which has, however – I do not dispute that – serious consequences for the Christian dogmas. The crux of the matter is ultimately to deal with the question: *Is the absolute truth claim an indispensable part of Christianity as well as of Judaism and Islam?* My answer is: No, never ever! It belongs neither to Christianity nor to any other religion. Nor does it belong to the concept of religion either. The Eastern religions do not raise it, but no one would disqualify them from being religions because of that.

I concede that the step to abandon the absolute truth claim is of paramount significance. It is almost as if one requested from the Catholic Church to abolish the institution of the Pope. However, this depends on the perspective. One may take this abandonment, in anticipation of the truly revolutionary consequences resulting from it, as a blatantly unacceptable impertinence, as a demand to abandon one's own belief and one's own identity because one sees the absolute truth claim as a part of one's own belief. This is why one shies away even from the very thought of it. But one may also perceive the abandonment of the absolute truth claim as an act of liberation from the narrow, stifling prison of Christian dogmatism. One may experience it as a gate that, once opened, allows us to step out from the narrow and gloomy prison of dogmatism into the vast, blooming world of inter-denominational and inter-religious dialogue. One and the same request, to abandon the absolute truth claim, can have such a different effect on people! Most Christians shy away from overstepping this threshold. Nevertheless I would like to encourage them to do this step. They lose nothing, and gain all. Expressed differently, they lose something wrong, bad and hostile to life, and gain something right, good and life promoting.

Is the claim of absolute truth an indispensable part of Christianity, so that whoever gives it up abandons likewise with it "the truth of one's own religion and thus one's own identity"?[20] Küng and with him most Christians answer this question in the affirmative. Others negate it. For me, I do not take the absolute truth claim for an integral part of Christianity. Quite the opposite, I am convinced that it is not a blessing but a curse to Christianity and should be abandoned, the sooner the better. The same applies, by the way, to Judaism and Islam, as far as they raise such a claim. Küng sees only *a lack of steadfastness*[21] in one's confession to the own belief in that, the impertinence to put other beacons of revelation and saviours such as the Roman Emperor or Gautama Buddha[22] on a par with Jesus Christ the Lord. I am not aware of anyone, now-a-days, who would still want to put Jesus of Nazareth on a par with the Roman Emperor as a beacon of revelation. The question is rather, whether all those, who see Jesus indeed as a son of God but not as the only and only begotten Son of God, have to be "designated as *non-Christian* from the point of view of the *New Testament*".[23] If this definition is applied, I am not a Christian. I doubt, however, that this is an applicable definition, since we have to remember that the dogmatic formula "true Man and true God" pretending to describe the nature of Jesus Christ has nothing to do with the historical Jesus of flesh and blood, but that it represents the result of three hundred years of development in Christian theological history.

It is, however, correct that whoever gives up the absolute truth claim has to give up also the contents of this claim and these are the dogmas. As it is, Hans Küng has raised to question, with good reasons, the infallibility of the Pope when he talks "ex cathedra", which means with the highest apostolical authority. According to Catholic teaching, the dogmas are revealed absolute truth. Whoever questions them is leaving the Catholic religious community. But, does someone who questions the validity of even only *one* dogma not question the whole system? Aren't there also good reasons to doubt the validity of the dogmas of Mary? Where does this start, where does it end? Does whoever questions the infallibility dogma and the dogma of Mary's bodily entry into heaven not release a domino effect, at the end of which the domino stones of the Christ and Trinity dogmas will collapse, too? Seen with the eyes of the Pope, the Curia, most of the priests and possibly even the majority of Catholic believers this is the case. This is why Hans Küng's theological teaching licence had to be withdrawn.

I admire Küng's courage while questioning the Papal infallibility dogma. I would wish him wholeheartedly the courage to go further and raise all the other remaining dogmas of the Church to question. I admire even more his tireless commitment to the inter-denominational and inter-religious dialogue. But I wish him, beyond that, the courage to abandon the mental reserve of the absolute truth claim for Christianity in order to create therewith the precondition for a truly fruitful inter-religious dialogue. Of the essence of Christianity absolutely nothing is given away, neither, as incarnated by Jesus of Nazareth, the spirit of love for God, neighbour, and enemy, nor anything of his engagement for the poor, the humiliated and ostracized, for justice and peace. On the contrary, we recognise now that the dogma had blocked our view at the historical Jesus, the man of flesh and blood, and his message.

There are three verbal guns named indifferentism, syncretism and relativism that are preferably aimed at and fired against such a position. They make a lot of noise, but do not hit. *Indifferentism* describes an attitude that regards all religions as equally valid, thus indifferently valid and ultimately indifferent. The indifferent keeps an attitude of sceptical distance towards all religions. For him, everything is possible and everything allowed in the religious sphere. *Syncretism* is the term used for a procedure where, bluntly spoken, all religions are thrown into one pot, stirred forcefully and then given away as a unified mush to everyone interested. *Relativism* is an attitude that does not permit anything absolute, but declares all and everything as relative, i.e., depending on other factors.

The allegation of indifferentism does not hit, since nobody is hindered to pursue, in Lessing's sense, "his unbridled love", be it Jewish, Christian or Islamic, Hindu or Buddhist. The allegation of syncretism does not hit any better, since this has nothing to do with abandoning one's own religion, but with putting into practice in our daily lives what we recognise as being true in our and other religions. But what about the allegation of relativism? Is it not ultimately justified as soon as we give up the absolute truth claim? The answer: not at all. Absoluteness does exist, even though people have, from time to time, called it differently: God, Reason for Being, *Nirvana*, First Reality, or Eternal, Indestructible Being. All these words have in common, that they evade the grasp of *sense perception* and *intellectual comprehension*. The absolute is not available to us human beings. *No man and no institution can claim to be in possession of the absolute truth.* Of those who affirm that about themselves, we only know for sure one thing: They do not possess it.[24] This is no world-shattering news. And yet, if followed through consistently to the end, this results in altogether revolutionary consequences regarding the Abrahamic religions. *The absolute truth has its place solely in the relation of God or the First Reality to the individual, nowhere else!* If it is asserted over others by people or institutions, such as the demand for absolute obedience under reference to a God given authority, it changes into its opposite, turns from a blessing into a curse and, as such, becomes the source of boundless suffering. At the same time, this recognises the biblical priority: "One must obey God more than man".[25]

Whoever asserts an absolute truth claim for his own religion, places with that, he may want it or not, those representing a deviating teaching inevitably into the absolute untruth. The followers of other religions become infidels; the followers of deviating teachings within the own religion become heretics, even though Küng keeps quiet about that. What they represent is "superstition, misbelief and disbelief" (Barth) or *"conditionally true"* religion (Küng). One may indignantly deny this conclusion. In view of the efforts of the Christian churches for the inter-religious dialogue, I reiterate nevertheless: They remain hypocritical, as long as the absolute truth claim for the own teaching is not given up. Those of different faiths meet the efforts of the Catholic Church for inter-religious dialogue, therefore, with unabashed reservation, if not even scepticism. They suspect therein what Küng wrongly accuses the religions of Indian origin of, a kind of embracing strategy. The Protestant churches, however, do hardly any better than the Catholic in this respect.

One of the most important consequences of abandoning the absolute truth claim is the *renunciation of mission.* If the world religions are substantially equivalent, it makes no sense to convert those of other faiths to the "only true" religion. It is rather more important to improve oneself in one's own religion and to work at its perfection. Henceforth we meet people of other faiths as brothers and sisters, not as pagans or infidels. As such, it is no coincidence that the main characters in Lessing's play, except for Nathan, finally turn out to be members of the same family, irrespective of their different religious convictions. Humaneness linking all human beings triumphs over the discord of the religions.

No matter how you look at it, mission replaces, when directed at the followers of other religions, cooperation with rivalry, open and unprejudiced dialogue with the ambition to save those of different faiths from their being lost to untruth.

MAHATMA GANDHI

"Religions are different roads converging to the same point. What does it matter that we take different roads so long as we reach the same goal"?[26] "All religions are divinely inspired, but they are imperfect because they are products of the human mind and taught by human beings. The one Religion is beyond all speech. Imperfect men put it into such language as they can command and their words are interpreted by other men equally imperfect. Whose interpretation is to be held to be the right one? Everybody is right from his own standpoint, but it is not impossible that everybody may be wrong. Hence the necessity for tolerance, which does not mean indifference towards one's own faith but a more intelligent and pure love for it. Tolerance gives us spiritual insight, which is as far from fanaticism as the North Pole is from the south. True knowledge of religion breaks down the barriers between faith and faith. Cultivation of tolerance for other faiths will impart to us a truer understanding of our own."[27]

Even though Gandhi does not raise an absolute truth claim, I am not able to discover the slightest hint of indifferentism, syncretism, relativism or lack of steadfastness. He rather combined a *high degree of tolerance* with *a high passion of belief.* He committed himself to Hinduism, even called himself on occasions an orthodox (*sanatani*) Hindu, because he accepted all essential elements of Hinduism. This did not stop him from rejecting a lot of what his fellow countrymen regarded as part of the religious tradition of Hinduism such as untouchability, the excesses of the caste system,[28] temple prostitution, child marriage and animal sacrifices, while accepting much of what he found as being true during the study of other religions. And nothing was further from him than relativism in the above sense. He rather dedicated his life without compromise to the commitment to truth as far as he could recognise it. He saw himself as recipient of inexhaustible love, which he, in turn, passed on to all living beings. He saw the collective pursuit of truth as the basis of a fruitful inter-religious dialogue. That united him with the adherents of other religions and with the philosophers. This search for the truth, this *pursuit* of the absolute truth that we, as long as we live, will never reach, replaces the *possession* of the absolute truth.

In "Christianity and World Religions", authored by Hans Küng and others, the orientalist Josef van Ess writes: "According to the female Islamic theologian Riffat Hassan, each of the three great Middle Eastern religions has a certain neuralgic point, which is for this particular religion not 'negotiable', but for the other two not acceptable: For Judaism this is the unrivalled choice of Israel as *God's People* (with the promised land), for Christianity the teaching of Christ as *God's Son*, whereas for Islam it is the teaching of the *Koran* as *God's Word*. But…it must be allowed to talk about these questions".[29]

The analogue sequence is noteworthy: *God's People, God's Son God's Book*. If we take Lessing's or Gandhi's point of view when we look at these truths that have been determined as being absolute, that stand in the centre of the teaching of the respective religions mentioned, thus making them, in a way, the focus and heart of their belief, we arrive at conclusions as follows:

God's People? Why not? But why not the other peoples also? It may well be that the people of Israel has a particularly intensive religious history. But that is no reason to regard oneself as *chosen.* Even though it is flattering our vanity to consider ourselves as chosen, this is even less a reason for that assumption. And how does the idea of chosenness agree with the one of God's Justice? The objection that we are dealing with God's unfathomable resolution is not convincing for me. Where then remains God's Justice? No, *God is the God of all peoples as much as he is the God of all human beings and of all of creation.*

The Jewish scholar Schalom Ben-Chorin (1913-1999), in his book: *Die Erwählung Israels* (The choosing of Israel),[30] held the view that Israel's chosenness was not a privilege, but was counterweighted by the commitment to observe strictly Yahweh's commandments and thus contribute to the salvation of other peoples. I cannot agree to this assertion since I think that the one as well as the other constitutes a discrimination of other peoples. I cannot believe that my salvation as well as the salvation of my people depends on the conduct of another people, no matter if it satisfies or fails the obligation imposed on it by God. Both privilege and obligation are incompatible with God's justice. I know my conclusion will meet the fierce protest of many Jewish and Christian fundamentalists. As one example among many, the anathema should be mentioned that the German Jewish theologian Martin Buber (1878-1965) cast against those who raise the chosenness claim and the claim of the Jews over the "holy land" to question: "Who denies that the land of Israel is holy land and that Israel is God's people acts like Hitler, serves Hitler's god – and will perish together with him".[31] The trouble with the belief in being the chosen people is that it is highly contagious. Not only Christianity adopted it in form of the *New Covenant*, after God had allegedly discarded the people of the Old Covenant, Israel, for murdering his "son". Even the Islamic peoples consider themselves in the role of the "true believers" chosen by Allah. Even worse, Adolf Hitler, too, took the German people to be chosen. The same even applied to the pious Boers in South Africa, who, armed with *Bible* and rifle, started their trek to the North. Finally, many North Americans consider themselves up to today as God's chosen people, and the USA as "God's own country".

God's Son? Sure enough, why should Jesus of Nazareth not be a son of God? But then, why the only and only begotten one? Undisputedly he was an outstanding religious figure, but are there not other ones: Abraham, Moses, Gautama, Zoroaster, Kung-Fu-Tzu,

Lao-Tzu, Rama, Krishna, Socrates, Mohammed, to name just a few? Are they not also God's sons, not to mention His daughters? And are we not all God's children, even though it is so rare that we live up to this title of honour? Though it flatters our vanity to regard ourselves as being redeemed by Christ as opposed to all non-Christians, this should rather be a reason not to believe that.

God's Word? The *Koran* is undoubtedly a book of God, a Holy Scripture, as much as the *Bible*, the *Bhagavad Gita*, the discourses of Buddha and others. But why the only authentic one? For the historical-critical research this is a totally unfounded and unproven assertion, since, after all, quite some body of thought flowed from the *Bible* into the *Koran*. Of course, the belief that we are in possession of the pure and unadulterated Word of God flatters human vanity. But that should be the very least reason for this presumption.

Whoever takes the step of abandoning the absolute truth claim for the own religion as a Jew, a Christian or a Muslim, joyfully experiences the walls of strangeness and enmity between the religions coming tumbling down, and we meet each other the way we are according to Lessing's and Gandhi's opinion: *children of God, brothers and sisters*.

REFERENCES

1. In a fairy tale of the Danish poet Hans Christian Andersen (1802-1875) a vain emperor was taken for a ride by two swindlers who offered to make the finest garments for him.

   They claimed that these garments were not visible to people who were unsuitable for their office or inexcusably stupid. He ordered the robe and the swindlers set to work. They imitated dressmakers, although there was nothing at all in their hands. The whole court and the emperor himself played their game for fear to be revealed as unsuitable for their office or inexcusably stupid. In a festive street procession the emperor wanted to present his new robe and even the people gave him a big cheer until a little child called out: "But the emperor does not wear anything"! This is how the emperor was exposed to ridicule.
2. I regard ideology as the instrumentalisation of religion, philosophy or science for material interests.
3. Karl Barth, *Kirchliche Dogmatik* II 1, 500.
4. I Book of Kings, Chapter 18, verse 23.
5. I Book of Kings, 18:39, see also II Book of Kings 10:18-30.
6. Dietrich Bonhoeffer, *Widerstand und Ergebung*, München 1990, 173.

7. Karl Barth, *Kirchliche Dogmatik* II 1,500.
8. In reference to First Letter to the Corinthians (1 Cor 15:23-28), Ratzinger/ Benedikt XVI: *Jesus von Nazareth*, Erster Teil, Freiburg 2007, 181.
9. Papal office during the 13th to 15th century with the task to track down and interrogate (often under torture) people holding views that deviated from the official teaching, and to hand them over, in the case of a confession, to the secular authorities for execution (mostly by being burnt alive).
10. Translated and commented by Ludolf Müller, München
11. Ratzinger/Benedikt XVI., *Jesus von Nazareth*, Freiburg 2007, 73.
12. *Young India*, 5.5.1927.
13. Joseph Ratzinger/Benedikt XVI, *Jesus von Nazareth*, Freiburg 2007, 60 ff.
14. Solowjev, *Anti-Christ*, translated and introduced by Ludolf Müller, München, 64 f.
15. Hans Küng, *Projekt Weltethos*, München 1991, 109.
16. *Ibid*, 105.
17. *Ibid*, 125.
18. *Ibid*, 129.
19. *Ibid*, 130.
20. *Ibid*, 105.
21. *Ibid*, 123 f.
22. *Ibid*, 131.
23. *Ibid*,
24. Based on the absolute truth claim the Catholic Church derives the absolute obedience claim that the apostolic authority of the Pope demands from clerics and laymen.
25. Acts of Apostles, chapter 5, verse 29 (5:29)
26. *Hind Swaraj,* 11.12.1909; CWMG 10, 271.
27. *Young India*, 2.10.30; CWMG 50, 79.
28. Gandhi did not reject the caste system altogether. He rather pleaded for keeping the four main castes – Brahmins, Kshatriya, Vaishya and Shudra – while replacing the *vertical* caste classification by a *horizontal* one. Untouchability was, however, to disappear completely. Of course, the path to the highest spiritual accomplishment should be open to all castes. After all, Gandhi, a member of the third caste, had also pursued this for himself.
29. Hans Küng and others, *Christentum und Weltreligionen*, München 1984, 72.
30. Hans Küng and others, *Christentum und Weltreligionen*, München 1993, 41
31. Fritz May, *Die Wahrheit über Israel*, CFI-Service, 35576 Wetzlar, 72.

PART I

MAHATMA GANDHI

3
Gandhi and Christianity

> Religion can be defended only by the purity of its adherents and their good deeds, never by their quarrels with those of other faiths.
>
> — *Mahatma Gandhi*

Let us recapitulate: An essential precondition for a fruitful inter-religious dialogue is the abandonment of the absolute truth claim for one's own religion. This applies to the three Abrahamic religions in equal measure. We have to accept that all human thinking, feeling and acting is imperfect. *Perfection is only with God*. He is the *absolute* truth. In this world, however, there is only *relative* truth. Yet, we can come closer to the absolute truth. We will still deal with how this is possible. The claim of being in possession of the absolute truth revealed by God will then be replaced by the collective aspiration for truth.

The term tolerance derives from the Latin verb *tolerare*, which means to endure, to put up with something, to hold out. When Gandhi speaks of tolerance, he means much more than that. His concern is not just the enduring of other religions, but rather the sympathetic *devotion* to them, with the desire to understand. Sooner or later we will then harvest the fruits of such efforts, not only in form of a better understanding of other religions, but also of our own.

Whoever has abandoned the absolute truth claim for his own religion and turns with caring interest towards other religions, will initially experience, that he does not understand them, and that quite some of it appears strange, maybe even repulsive. Only a long, patient and thorough engagement with them will open up our understanding. In social science, this process of gradual understanding is known as the 'hermeneutic circle', and the studies dealing with it as hermeneutics or the studies of interpretation.

What is meant with this shall be explained with the help of the translation of a foreign language text as an example: Provided we are dealing with a text in a foreign language, probably even in a foreign script, it will appear as a complete mystery to us at the beginning. If we want to understand it, we will have to find out first, in which language and script it is written. After that, we will have to learn the meaning of the characters, and then, in the following step, get some idea, with the help of a dictionary, of what the text is about. But a literal translation is only possible when we manage to acquire the grammar of the foreign language. A meaningful translation requires a vast knowledge of the foreign language and its phrases. However, to fully understand the text, it is still necessary to get to know the foreign mentality and culture, too. In the mirror of the foreign language and culture we do understand our own one better, then.

Gandhi is himself a living example for the fruitfulness of *inter-religious dialogue*, even though the term did not even exist in his days. Born on the 2nd of October 1869 in Porbandar, a small town at India's west coast, he grew up in the most colourful and varied world of Hinduism, which influenced him deeply, namely in the form of his pious mother Putlibai. His family belonged to the Vaishya, the third caste. In his father's house the members of the different religious faiths congregated as equal and respected conversation partners of his father: Hindus of all castes, Jain monks, Sikhs, Moslems and Parsees. All this worked together to inculcate tolerance for all religious faiths in him.

His first encounter with Christianity as a student in Rajkot was, however, anything else than inviting. In his autobiography he recounts: "In those days Christian missionaries used to stand in a corner near the high school and hold forth, pouring abuse on Hindus and their gods. I could not endure this. I must have stood there to hear them once only, but that was enough to dissuade me from repeating the experiment. About the same time, I heard of a well-known Hindu having been converted to Christianity. It was the talk of the town that, when he was baptized, he had to eat beef and drink liquor, that he also had to change his clothes, and that thenceforth he began to go about in European costume including a hat. These things got on my nerves. Surely, thought I, a religion that compelled one to eat beef, drink liquor, and change one's own clothes did not deserve the name. I also heard that the new convert had already begun abusing the religion of his ancestors, their customs and their country. All these things created in me a dislike for Christianity".[1]

Gandhi does not only manifest his intuitive rejection of missionary Christendom, he also relates the gossip stories circulating in the small town of Rajkot about Hindus that converted to become Christians. Later, during his studies in London and during his twenty years of residence in South Africa, he came to know staunch Christians who put his prejudice towards Christianity into perspective. Nevertheless he withstood their efforts to convert him to Christianity. He told them that he wanted to learn to know his own religion first before taking a conversion into consideration. This is why he dealt with the *Bhagavad Gita* only when he was in London. It is part of the *Mahabharata* epic, written in the fourth century B.C., and it was to influence his life in a substantial way. Regardless of that, he acquired everything he recognized as good and true in other religions.

He had promised a pious Christian, who took great pains to "save his soul", to read the whole *Bible*. He did not find much liking in the First Testament. The reading, so he admits, made him fall asleep. He only held out because he did not want to break his promise. The Second Testament appealed much more to him; namely the *Sermon on the Mount* filled him with enthusiasm since he found a lot in it that he was familiar with from his religion. Even though the life and teaching of Jesus filled him with admiration, he nevertheless rejected Christian dogmatics decidedly. His conclusive verdict about it is found in his jail memories from 1926. I am quoting the full length of it, not only because of its content, but also because of its form.

Before that, a few words to the situation in which it came into being. Gandhi had been convicted to six years of jail in March 1922 for his role in the resistance movement against the British colonial regime. He was, however, released ahead of time in February 1924 due to an appendicitis that brought him to the brink of death. He used the time in jail for the study of religions. He writes:

"Many Christian friends were most attentive to me. I received books from them from America, England and India. I must confess that whilst I recognized their kind motive, I could not appreciate the majority of the books, they sent. I wish I could say something of their gifts that would please them. But that would not be fair or truthful if I could not mean it. The orthodox books on Christianity do not give me any satisfaction. My regard for the life of Jesus is indeed very great.

"His ethical teaching, his common sense, his sacrifice command my reverence. But I do not accept the orthodox teaching that Jesus was or is God incarnate in the accepted sense or that he was or is the only Son of God. I do not believe in the doctrine of appropriation of another's merit. His sacrifice is a type and an example for us. Every one of us has to be "crucified" for salvation. I do not take the words 'Son' 'Father' and 'the Holy Ghost' literally. They are all figurative expressions. Nor do I accept the limitations are sought to be put upon the teaching of *The Sermon on the Mount*. I can discover no justification in the *New Testament* for wars. I regard Jesus as one among the most illustrious teachers and prophets, the world has seen. Needless to say I do not regard the *Bible* as an infallible record of the life and teachings of Jesus. Nor do I consider every word in the *New Testament* as God's own word. Between the Old and the New there is a fundamental difference. Whilst the Old contains some very deep truths, I am unable to pay it the same honours I pay the *New Testament*. I regard the latter as an extension of the teaching of the Old and in some matters rejection of the Old. Nor do I regard the New as the last word of God. Religious ideas like everything else are subject to the same law of evolution that governs everything else in this universe. Only God is changeless and as His message is received through the imperfect human medium, it is always liable to suffer distortion in proportion, as the medium is pure or otherwise. I would, therefore, respectfully urge my Christian friends and well-wishers to take me as I am. I respect and appreciate their wish that I should think and be as they are even as I respect and appreciate a similar wish on the part of my Mussalman friends. I regard both the religions as equally true with my own. But my own gives me full satisfaction. It contains all that I need for my growth. It teaches me to pray not that others may believe as I believe but that they may grow to their full height in their own religion. My constant prayer, therefore, is for a Christian or a Mussalman to be a better Christian and a better Mahomedan. I am convinced, I know, that God will ask, asks us now, not what we label ourselves but what we are, i.e., what we do. With Him *deed* is everything, *belief* without deed is nothing".[2]

Let us summarize the relevant testimonies of this fundamental text :

1. Gandhi rejects the Christian dogmas.
2. He also rejects the cross and atonement theology (died for our sins). For him, what applies instead is: "His sacrificial death is a role model and example for us".

3. Gandhi sees in Jesus one of the greatest prophets and teachers ever given to the world.
4. He contradicts the fundamentalist teaching, which takes every word of the *Bible* as a word of God. He is also unable to see an infallible record of the life of Jesus in the *Second Testament*.
5. He cannot approve of the restrictions imposed on the *Sermon on the Mount*. He does not find any justification for war in the *Second Testament*.
6. He recognizes an essential difference between the *First* and *Second Testament*, but cannot see God's last message in the *Second Testament* either.
7. The religious ideas are, in his opinion, subject to the rule of evolution, like everything on Earth.
8. The "purity of the medium" decides about the measure by which the teaching of the unvarying God is distorted or not.
9. For Gandhi, other World religions are as true as his own.
10. He rejects mission in the sense of conversion to one's own religion.
11. God does not ask what we believe, but what we do. Belief and deed are one and the same for Him.

Due to my preoccupation with the life and work of Gandhi I have come to the conviction that we have in him a 'mediator' of particular purity before us. We can learn from him what religion is, or what it is supposed to be. I even think that he came with his unbiased study of the world religions close to the unwritten "religion behind the religions" (metareligion): "In theory, since here is one God, there can be only one religion. But in practice, no two persons I have known have had the same and identical conception of God. Therefore, there will, perhaps, always be different religions answering to different temperaments and climatic conditions. But I can clearly see the time coming when people belonging to different faiths will have the same regard for other faiths that they have for their own. I think that we have to find unity in diversity. ... We are all children of one and the same God and, therefore, absolutely equal".[3]

The present part of the book deals with this religion, in particular with Gandhi's perception of God and his relation to God. However, Gandhi's religion, and this cannot be emphasized strongly enough, must not be equated with Hinduism. I neither have the intention nor the ability, let alone the professional knowledge to represent Hinduism in its myriad forms. I will limit myself to the sketchy illustration of Gandhi's religion, which also incorporated elements of Christianity, Buddhism and Islam. It is thus also indicative for the width and openness of his religion that he included lyrics and songs of other religions in his prayer assemblies in the *ashram*, the community of those who were striving for the realization of truth, non-violence and abstinence.

When Gandhi writes: "So I, therefore, pray for a Christian that he may become a better Christian, and for a Moslem to become a better Moslem", he will, understandably, meet the determined objection of most of the Christian missionaries. Otto Wolff, who had been active in the service of the Gossner Mission in India for a length of time, therefore, pulls Gandhi's religious thoughts mercilessly to pieces in his book *Gandhi und Christus*, which was published in 1955. A sample from the preface: "The holy man becomes a trailblazer for communism. The helper of the poor, suppressed and ostracized becomes their suppressor in the name of a cold orthodoxy. The fighter for unity prepares tenaciously the division among the Indian sister nations that is taking place with hate and blood. The unique, great preacher of non-violent love, in front of whom one bows respectfully in the East as in the West, is the secret ally of physical as well as moral violence".[4]

Wolff recognizes, correctly, that Gandhi rejects the Christian absolute truth claim, and insinuates, therefore, a Hindu universality claim by him: "The ... barrier, with which Gandhi deliberately distinguishes himself from the Christians, is the universality claim he directs against Christianity in the name of Hinduism. Gandhi's universality claim raised for Hinduism is a superiority claim. With this superiority claim he counters the Christian absolute truth claim, the essence of which never dawns on him, but which he conceives at any time rather as a blow to the cultural self-confidence of the Asian". And he continues: "It has become sufficiently obvious that the so-called absolute truth claim of Christianity is that trigger for Gandhi that makes, first of all, Christianity personally unacceptable for him, that, secondly, makes him reject the spiritual part of mission work as not serving any real purpose, and that, thirdly, makes him rehabilitate the life's values of his own Hinduism *vis-à-vis* Christianity. The rehabilitation ends in the postulation of one's own superiority".[5]

It is true that Gandhi did not like the Christian missionaries, with the exception of the Anglican missionary Charles Andrews, whom he called affectionately Charly. He, however, had, under the influence of Gandhi, abandoned proselytising the Indians anyway. What Gandhi thinks about the Christian mission in India, he makes clear in a speech in Colombo (Sri Lanka), directed at Christian missionaries:

> "Confuse not Jesus' teachings with what passes as modern civilization, and pray do not do unconscious violence to the people among whom you cast your lot. It is no part of that call, I assure you, to tear the lives of the people of the East by its roots. Tolerate whatever is good in them and do not hastily, with your preconceived notions, judge them. Do not judge lest you be judged yourselves. In spite of your belief in the greatness of Western civilization and in spite of your pride in all your achievements, I plead with you for humility, and ask you to leave some little room for doubt, in which, as Tennyson sang, there was more truth, though by 'doubt' he no doubt meant a different thing. Let us each one live our life, and if ours is the right life, where is the cause for hurry? It will react of itself. ... By all means drink deep of the fountains that are given to you in the *Sermon on the Mount*, but then you will have to take sackcloth and ashes. The teaching of the *Sermon* was meant for each and everyone of us. You cannot serve both God and Mammon."[6]

Gandhi is in principal not against mission. However, he does not understand it as a conversion of those with other faiths to one's own religion, but as *selfless deed in the service of your neighbour*. This kind of "mission" equals the picture and fragrance of a rose delighting our heart. The famous humanist, theologian, doctor and musician Albert Schweitzer (1875-1965) originally wanted to become a missionary in Africa, but was rejected as being too liberal. So he became a doctor and cured sick natives. This kind of mission surely would have pleased Gandhi. The same applies to the "mission" of Jesuit padre Michael Windey, who, inspired by Gandhi's writings, set up a village development programme. Under his management and with the help of donation money from Europe, more than 400 villages destroyed by natural disasters were rebuilt, 109 kindergartens with an average of 50 children, 6 secondary schools with different numbers of children, as well as 4 school centres against child labour with an average of 175 children were set up. Padre Windey too, like Charly

Andrews, abstained from converting Indians to Christianity, but did his mission in the best meaning of this term by "converting" people to truth, love, tolerance and solidarity.

> I think that Otto Wolff is wrong by insinuating that Gandhi raised a universality claim for Hinduism, which was also a superiority claim *vis-à-vis* Christianity. That cannot be the case at all. I have only a depth psychological explanation for Wolff's claim: We are dealing with the classical case of projection: The enemy is assumed to do exactly what one is doing oneself.
>
> Subsequently, a fruitful inter-religious dialogue requires two things: firstly, abandoning the absolute truth claim. The alleged ownership of the absolute truth is replaced by the *collective aspiration for truth.* Whoever claims to be in possession of the absolute truth only proves that he does not possess it. Secondly, it amounts to *conversion to one's own religion.* By this, the competitive relationship between the religions changes into a relationship of cooperation in the collective search for truth and the efforts of its implementation.

REASON AND BELIEF

At times, Gandhi calls himself a *Sanatani Hindu*, which means an orthodox Hindu, for having accepted all basic teachings of Hinduism. He is, however, not less critical towards his inherited religion than towards other religions. He rejected firmly the intolerable discrimination of the untouchables, the discrimination of women in Indian society, the excesses of the caste system, child marriage, temple prostitution, goat sacrifices for goddess Kali and quite some more, he even risked his life, repeatedly, to fight the "cancerous evil" of untouchability. With the same attitude, he also faced other religions. During his talk with the American cleric Dr. Crane, who had resigned from his office as a pastor in abhorrence of the orgy of violence of the First World War, he names three criteria that he slots in ahead, so to say, as three filters when reading the holy scriptures of the World Religions. These are: *satya* (truth), *ahimsa* (non-violence) and *reason* in matters which can be reasoned out.[7] He only admits to his religion what these three filters allow to pass. I have purposely maintained the Sanskrit words *satya* and *ahimsa*, often used by Gandhi, because the further course of the study will show that they can be described only inadequately by the English words truth or love or "non-violence". Since I shall still refer to these two terms in detail later on, I will limit myself, at this point, to the third criterion, reason, in matters that can be reasoned out.

To Dr. Crane's question: "in matters which can be reasoned out"? he replied: "Yes, there are subjects where Reason cannot take us far and we have to accept things on faith. Faith then does not contradict Reason but transcends it. Faith is a kind of sixth sense which works in cases which are without the purview of Reason. Well then, given these three criteria, I can have no difficulty in examining all claims made on behalf of religion. Thus to believe that Jesus is the only begotten son of God is to me against Reason, for God can't marry and beget children. The word 'son' there can only be used in a figurative sense. In that sense everyone who stands in the position of Jesus is a begotten son of God. If a man is spiritually miles ahead of us we may say that he is in a special sense the son of God, though we are all children of God. We repudiate the relationship in our lives, whereas his life is a witness to that relationship".[8]

The intellectual history of the occident is, for long periods, dominated by the conflict between reason and belief, rationalism and irrationalism, whereby the last-named term is not meant to be derogative. Rationalism has its roots in Greco-Roman philosophy, irrationalism in Oriental-Jewish religion. These two cultures intermingle in Hellenism and in Hellenist shaped Christianity; but they also fight each other to the bitter end as soon as they raise an absolute truth claim. We became acquainted with the absolute truth and validity claim of the Abrahamic religions, already. However, in response to that, there is also an absolute truth and validity claim by some rationalists. *For Gandhi, there is no such contradiction.* Reason has its justification in the realm of sense perception and intellectual comprehension, but has no universal validity. The same applies to belief. Whoever denies man's descent from animals due to his belief only makes a fool of himself. To claim, that only exists what is accessible to sense perception and intellectual comprehension, would be no less ridiculous. Fortunately the scientists, who respond to the narrow-minded totality claim of some Christians with an equally narrow-minded totality claim of the scientific world explanation, become increasingly rare. Gandhi already said: "Rationalists are admirable beings; rationalism is a hideous monster when it claims for itself omnipotence. Attribution of omnipotence to reason is as bad a piece of idolatry as is worship of stock and stone believing it to be God. ... I plead not for the suppression of reason, but for a due recognition of that in us which sanctifies reason itself".[9] Albert Schweitzer argues along the same lines, when he says that all truly religious thinking was reasonable and all truly reasonable thinking religious.

The most important conclusion of this paragraph is: There are no miracles in the sense of breaking the laws of Nature. Gandhi, too, sees it the same way: "The laws of Nature are changeless, unchangeable, and there are no miracles in the sense of infringement or interruption of Nature's laws. But we limited beings fancy all kind of things and impute our limitations to God. We may copy God, but not He us. We may not divide Time for Him, Time for Him is eternity. For us there is past, present and future. And what is human life of a hundred years but less than a mere speck in the eternity of Time"?[10]

The *Bible* is full of tales of miracles. It would fill many pages just to list them. It is high time to say goodbye to them, as far as they contradict the laws of nature. The same applies to the prophecies presumably inspired by God, because they have all too often turned out to be questionable or false. The tales of miracles and prophecies of the *Bible* are, therefore, caught in the filter of reason. Are there no miracles then? — Surely there are! The Universe with its 15 billion galaxies, each of which consists, in turn, of billions of suns, most of which are likely to be orbited by several planets, is a miracle beyond compare. Yet, this also applies to both the living and inanimate nature in its overwhelming beauty and boundless diversity. *The omnipotence of God is manifest in the laws of nature, not in their violation!*

The belief in miracles is based on a very particular image of God, namely the concept of an "almighty", that is to say absolute ruler, who is not bound to his own laws, but who can interfere at any time powerfully in nature and history. We have to bid farewell to this concept. Countless people have, under the influence of the biblical texts, beseeched God for such a miracle, to no avail. Here, God is created after the image of man — in fact, after the image of a very certain man: the *Oriental despot* — but not, as it says in the creation myth, man after the image of God. This God, worshipped as their common tribal, war, desert and mountain God by the twelve nomadic tribes united in a covenant, had demonic traits. He was a draconic ruler, demanding unconditional obedience, who tended to rage, was bigoted and jealous, patriarchal, militant, gruesome, punishing, judging and destroying, choosing and quashing individuals and peoples at will: "I accord grace to whom I want, and I grant mercy to whom I want." He is a God who demands the sacrifice of the first-born among humans and animals, but who generously forgoes the human sacrifice of the first-born son once it is redeemed, i.e., replaced by an animal sacrifice.

The image of God in the biblical scriptures has gone through a profound transformation during its one and a half thousand years of history of origin, which I cannot deal with in detail. It ranges from the anthropomorphic image of God in the second creation account of the Book of Genesis to the image of a demonic tribal and war God, the "Lord of the Armies" to the almighty, omnipresent and all knowing God who calls the Universe into being by His Word; an image of God that found its expression in the first creation account of the *Bible*.

Before I turn to Gandhi's image and experience of God, I find it indispensable to chart the Judeo-Christian conception of God, at least in broad outline, in order to make the differences clearly apparent.

REFERENCES

1. Mahatma Gandhi, *Autobiography*, CWMG, 44, 116 f.
2. *Collected Works of Mahatma Gandhi (CWMG)*, Vol. 29, page 90 (29:90)
3. *Harijan*, 2.2.1934; *CWMG*, 63, 85.
4. Otto Wolff: *Mahatma und Christus*, Berlin: Lettner 1955, 11.
5. *Ibid.*, 259.
6. *Young India*, 8.12.1927; *CWMG*, 40, 374
7. *Harijan*, 3.6.1937; *CWMG*, 71, 1-5.
8. *Ibid.*, 2.
9. *Young India*, 14.10.1926; *CWMG*, 36, 401 f.
10. *Harijan*, 17.4.37; *CWMG*, 71, 132.

4
Bible Review

> The Biblical-Christian image of God is inacceptable to the standards of critical reason and enlightened-human ethics.
>
> — *Franz Buggle*

It is a gloomy world that we enter by reading the Holy Scripture. Seen as a whole, it is a terrible, cruelly inhuman book. I can only agree with the Freiburg psychologist Franz Buggle when he states that this fact is not generally known because religious teachers, preachers and theologians do a selective reading and interpretation of the *Bible* by trivialising it.[1] Who as a Christian does not remember the colourful stories in his religious education about the creation of the world, about Noah and the Deluge, about Abraham, Isaac and Jacob? Do we not like remembering the stories about Joseph and his brothers, the exodus of the Israeli people from Egypt and their migration through the desert, Moses on Mount Sinai, Saul's melancholy and David's heroism? Children and youngsters are very susceptible to this kind of stories. They do not ask about their truth. Later, when a critical consciousness emerges, they turn to a scientific explanation of the world and abandon the religious explanation as myths and legends, usually together with the ideas attached to it. However, what we assimilate in this pre-critical level of development of our psyche forms our character and our vision of the world far more than what we acknowledge from a critical distance. Nonetheless the churches still claim that the *Bible* contains the unrestricted *Word of God*. In the following you get a "florilegium" of the cruelties delivered to posterity through the *Bible*. It could be continued almost at random.

The account of the exodus of the people of Israel from Egypt in the Book *Exodus* relates that Yahweh hardened the heart of the Pharaoh in order to render his power over him, his people and his gods. It is repeatedly stated that Yahweh makes a difference between the Egyptians and the Israelites.[2] As a result, the Pharaoh becomes guilty without being guilty because Yahweh has hardened his heart. Yahweh punishes him and the people of Egypt, who are twice innocent, with the most terrible plagues in order to demonstrate his power.

Furthermore, Israel is a stubborn, obstinate people whom Yahweh tries to submit by punishment, like a wayward son or a disloyal bride, which, however, fails repeatedly.[3] He threatens them with complete extermination if they forget the Lord, their God, and follow other gods, serve them and prostrate themselves before them.[4] In the *Song of Moses* it says: "The LORD is a warrior. Your right hand, O LORD, is glorious in power. Your right hand, O LORD, smashes the enemy. In the greatness of your majesty, you overthrow those who rise against you. You unleash your blazing fury; it consumes them like straw".[5] Yahweh expresses himself even more cruelly in the second version of the *Song of Moses* in Deuteronomy: Now I raise my hand to heaven and declare, "As surely as I live, when I sharpen my flashing sword and begin to carry out justice, I will take revenge on my enemies and repay those who reject me. I will make my arrows drunk with blood, and my sword will devour flesh — the blood of the slaughtered and the captives, and the heads of the enemy leaders".[6]

The Book of Joshua reports in detail about the annihilation campaigns lead by Joshua on behalf of Yahweh against the kingdoms of Canaan; he even takes part in the fights himself. When the Amorites are fleeing after a lost battle, "the LORD destroyed them with a terrible hailstorm from heaven that continued until they reached Azekah".[7] The hail killed more of the enemy than the Israelites killed with the sword.

I am aware of the fact that the *Book of Joshua* is regarded by historical-critical research as a text of much later origin glorifying the time of the occupation retrospectively. Having said that, though, this Book is still considered as a part of the Holy Scripture and has had its fatal effect as a model for the 'occupation' of land in the West of the USA by pious settlers, by pious Boers in their 'occupation' of Northern South Africa and eventually as a religious justification of the occupation and colonisation policy of the State of Israel in Palestine. We should also not forget, that the findings of historical-critical science are relatively young, and that this text has been taken by many generations of pious Jews and Christians at face value, even as God's unquestionable word, and is to some extent today still taken as that.

Even some of the psalms, for many Jews and Christians a centrepiece of the *Bible*, are full of vengeance fantasies.[8] The frequently cited second psalm, of which the seventh verse: "You are my son. Today I have become your Father", is often referred to Jesus, contains the cruelly inhuman sentences: "Only ask, and I will give you the nations as your inheritance, the whole earth as your possession. You will break them with an iron rod and smash them like clay pots".[9] And what beats everything in inhuman cruelty, not justifiable by anything, especially not in a Holy Scripture: "The LORD said to my Lord: Sit in the place of honour at my right hand until I humble your enemies, making them a footstool under your feet. The Lord stands at your right hand to protect you. He will strike down many kings when his anger erupts. He will punish the nations and fill their lands with corpses; he will shatter heads over the whole earth".[10]

This God who reveals himself by word and by deed, who seeks to enforce unconditional obedience, who judges with wrath over the peoples — foreign as well as his own — and who carries out the sentence on them merciless, dominates almost the whole of the First Testament.

YAHWEH AND HIS CHOSEN PEOPLE

To his own chosen people, Yahweh is hardly less atrocious and cruel than to other people. He takes revenge for the errors of the fathers on their sons up to the third and fourth generation. He demands the death penalty by stoning for all those who incite apostasy, even if they are their own next of kin. They are explicitly commanded: "You shall not nurture pity".[11] The principle of retaliation is firmly established: "He who spills human blood shall have his own blood spilled by man".[12] He is quick at hand with the death penalty. It is not only demanded for manslaughter and kidnapping, which would still be understandable, but also for those who beat or curse father or mother, who work on Sabbat, who eat sacrificial meat on the third day after the sacrifice or those who eat leavened bread on the festival of the unleavened bread.[13] In the Book of Leviticus, the list is enlarged by child sacrifice, conjuration of the dead and fortune-telling, adultery, crime of fornication and sex with a menstruating woman.[14] In the Book *Deuteronomy*, the people are requested nine times: *You shall purge the evil from among you!* As if a community that intends to do away with evil in this manner would not contaminate itself with evil just because of that! In the Second Testament, this terrible word reappears with Paulus, although there he apparently only means the exclusion from the community and not the death penalty.[15] For the unconditionally obedient, Yahweh has blessings in store, for the disobedient a curse. If you. meet me with hostility, I will also meet you with hostility and beat you seven-fold for your sins".[16] Here, it is Yahweh himself who invalidates the commandment of moderation of "an eye for an eye and a tooth for a tooth".

All Israelites that protested against the Lord on their migration through the desert are punished by perishing in the desert and by not seeing the Promised Land.[17] The following *Bible* text, too, bears witness to exceptional cruelty: The involvement of the people with Baal-Peor made the Lord furious against Israel, and the Lord said to Moses: "Seize all the ringleaders of the people and impale them before the LORD in broad daylight, so that his fierce anger will turn away from the people of Israel. So, Moses said to the judges of Israel 'each of you must put to death the men under your authority, who joined in worshipping Baal of Peor".[18] To the priest Pinchas, who committed the "heroic deed" of spearing a twosome of an Israelite and a Midianite on their bed, he grants his peace alliance.[19] In the first Book of Kings he talks to the prophet Elijah: "Yet I will preserve 7,000 others in Israel who have never bowed down to Baal or kissed him"![20] Another eloquent testimony of Yahweh's sadistic cruelty is the following quote:

> "Just as the LORD has found great pleasure in causing you to prosper and multiply, the LORD will find pleasure in destroying you".[21]

I could go on with this line-up for a long time, but will leave it at that.

WHERE IS THE POSITIVE?

Rightly, you could object, that my account is one-sided and contorted because I omit the positive features of Yahweh. You may find it no less selective that the one of most theologians. Without doubt, there are also positive features in Yahweh's biblical image. They are, however, in most cases inextricably linked with the dark and atrocious ones, they form, in a way, the bright side as a contrast to the dark side of Yahweh. Even the oriental despot is not only an angry, cruelly punishing monster. He usually possesses likeable streaks, too, is good-natured, generous and merciful, provided that his orders are carried out without delay. In that case he rewards his servants with prosperity, power and privileges. The same can be said about the God of the First Testament. Out of the numerous evidences, I choose just one example: In Psalm 44, the singer celebrates Yahweh as the helper of Israel: "O God, we have heard it with our own ears — our ancestors have told us of all you did in their day, in days long ago. You drove out the pagan nations by your power and gave all the lands to our ancestors. You crushed their enemies and set our ancestors free. They did not conquer the land with their swords; it was not their own strong arm that gave them victory. It was your right hand and strong arm and the blinding light from your face that helped them, for you loved them. You are my King and my God. You command victories for Israel. Only by your power can we push back our enemies; only in your name can we trample our foes. I do not trust in my bow; I do not count on my sword to save me. You are the one who gives us victory over our enemies; you disgrace those who hate us".[22] That is followed by a complaint, because Yahweh denies his people the fortunes of war without any obvious reason.

You don't have to be a psychologist to realise that the dreams of the singer are presented here as deeds of Yahweh. Yahweh's blessing for his people corresponds to his judgement on the peoples who do not bend to his will or who are antagonistic against his chosen people: "Who is this who comes from Edom, from the city of Bozrah, with his clothing stained red? Who is this in royal robes, marching in his great strength? It is I, the LORD, announcing your salvation! It is I, the LORD, who has the power to save! Why are your clothes so red, as if you have been treading out grapes? I have been treading the winepress alone; no one was there to help me. In my anger I have trampled my enemies as if they were grapes. Their blood has stained my clothes. For the time has come for me to avenge my people to ransom them from their oppressors. I was amazed to see that no one intervened to help the oppressed. So I myself stepped in to save them with my strong arm, and my wrath sustained me. I crushed the nations in my anger and made them stagger and fall to the ground, spilling their blood upon the earth".[23]

Reward and *punishment, promise of salvation and threat of destruction* belong inextricably together in the preaching of the priests and prophets of Israel. They create that atmosphere of fear of punishment and destruction that is present in the Scriptures of the *First Testament* like a dark shadow, but also, partially, in those of the *Second Testament*, as we will see later on.

Besides the threat of punishment we will, however, find the imperative of love: "Listen, Israel! Yahweh, our God, stands alone. Therefore, you shall love the Lord, your God with all your heart, soul and strength".[24] But the question is if obedience enforced by means of threat of punishment loses its coercive nature through the imperative of love. A love enforced by threat of punishment is no love, because love cannot be demanded or, even worse, ordered. Only the one who is *lovable* will receive love. This can hardly be said of the God of the *First Testament*. It is a God that you can fear, but not love, and the demand to love him does not make the matter any better, but worse. It is, as if a husband who beats his wife, would require, on top of that, to be loved by her.

Even the *Ten Commandments*, this core of the *First Testament*, do not change anything there. Many theologians celebrate the monotheism that we find in the *First Commandment* as an outstanding achievement of religio-historical value of Judaism. Gandhi, however, questions this conclusion: "I dispute the description that Hindus believe in many gods and are idolaters. They do say there are many gods, but they also declare unmistakably that there is One God, God of gods. It is, therefore, not proper to suggest that Hindus believe in many gods. They certainly believe in many worlds. Just as there is a world inhabited by men and another by beasts, so also is there one inhabited by superior beings called gods, whom we do not see but who nevertheless exist. The whole mischief is created by the English rendering of the words *deva* or *devata* for which you have not found a better term than 'god'. But god is Ishwara, Devadhideva, God of gods. So you see it is the word 'god', used to describe different divine being that has given rise to such confusion. I believe that I am a thorough Hindu but I never believe in many gods. Never even in my childhood did I hold that belief, and no one ever taught me to do so".[25]

Even though monotheism may be regarded as a significant religio-historical achievement of Judaism, I consider it, nevertheless, wrong to degrade the polytheistic religions in comparison. In my opinion, Socrates was not only an important philosopher but also a deeply religious person subservient to the Delphic god Apollo, who paid with his life for defending the truth he had discovered. It is, therefore, possible to follow the highest ethical and religious principles in a polytheistic religion, too.

I see a far more serious shortcoming of the monotheism of the *First Testament* in Yahweh's desire to destroy other gods and their cults. He poisons the image of God in the *First Testament*, because his behaviour towards other gods also characterises his behaviour towards other peoples and towards his own 'chosen' people. It also characterises the behaviour of the people of Israel towards other peoples as being told by the Hebrew *Bible*.

Another problem is the prohibition of images. It forbids not only any depiction of Yahweh as an idol, but also the pictorial representation of the world in general.[26] Islam adopted this dictate, as well as many other things, from Judaism. The prohibition of images, however, does not protect at all against dogmatism and fanaticism as forms of idolatry, while the worship of images does not necessarily need to be a symbol of idolatry. The same can be said about the *Second Commandment*, as far as it is based on an identification of God with his name. After all, believers of all religions pray to the same God, irrespective of the different names they use to address him. In this general form, the commandment of not misusing the name of God is justified. However, I also see such misuse, when war and violence, oppression, exploitation and injustice are justified in the name of God, or when, again in the name of God, people are threatened with heavy penalties, annihilation, or even eternal torment in hell.

Although the Commandment of observing the Sabbath as holy may have a certain right to exist, its strict enforcement by threatening with the death penalty in case of infringement can under no circumstances be justified. The remaining Commandments codify general ethical rules that can be found in almost all religions, as Hans Küng proved convincingly in his meritorious "World Ethos Project". This does not, however, affect the criticism of the draconic punishments for the infringement of the Commandments mentioned in the Decalogue.

I cannot claim to be an expert of Islam, but in my opinion there is a close relationship between Yahweh and Allah as well as between the *First Testament* and the *Koran*. The figure of a god who demands unconditional adherence to his commandments, and who tries to enforce compliance to them by threatening with terrible punishment and by applying this punishment, who rewards obedience generously and who punishes disobedience dreadfully, is common to both religions. While reward and punishment in the texts of the Hebrew *Bible* are, however, mostly limited to mundane life, Prophet Mohammed gathers the idea of eternal pleasure in paradise and eternal agony in hell from the *Second Testament*. With that, our existence on earth becomes the place of decision between good and evil, God and Satan, heaven and hell.

THE "HOLY REST" OF THE IMAGE OF GOD IN THE *FIRST TESTAMENT*

The dialectics of the day and night side of Yahweh's image, however, is not everything. There remains a 'holy rest' of positive characteristics that cannot be disregarded. Among the unquestionably positive characteristics of Yahweh is his advocacy for the poor and weak, strangers, widows and orphans. The 'commandment' of altruism, which becomes the centre of Jesus' ethics, can already be found in the *First Testament*: "You shall love your neighbour as yourself. I am the Lord".[27] From the context we can deduct that neighbour here means mainly family, clan or tribal members. But even in this limited form it is opposed by the repeated request: "You shall not nurture pity", referring, in particular, to relatives who commit a crime of idolatry or other offences. In the *Book of Exodus* we can even find a rudimentary form of love of the enemy.[28] The introduction of the Sabbath,[29] the sabbatical year[30] and the jubilee year[31] that are supposed to serve the recovery of man and nature, as well as, although only to a limited degree, to social balancing, are also to be valued positively.

In this context it goes without saying that the often-cited 'gems' from other writings of the *First Testament* must not be left out. But they are all too often imbedded in between punishment and revenge fantasies. The principle of revenge is, in general, firmly established in the whole of the First Testament, frequently even in the form of seven-fold revenge or in revenge on children and grandchildren. This reveals a fundamental difference to some of the doctrines of the *Second Testament*, after all.

In the following only a few examples of what cannot be explained from the dialectics of the day and night side of Yahweh: Magnificent in its linguistic strength and visual beauty is the peoples' pilgrimage to the mountain of the Lord: "In the last days, the mountain of the LORD's house will be the highest of all the most important places on earth. It will be raised above the other hills. People from all over the world will stream there to worship. People from many nations will come and say, 'Come, let us go up to the mountain of the LORD, to the house of Jacob's God. There he will teach us his ways, and we will walk in his paths'. For the LORD's teaching will go out from Zion; his word will go out from Jerusalem. The LORD will mediate between nations and will settle international disputes. They will hammer their swords into ploughshares and their spears into pruning hooks. Nation will no longer fight against nation, nor train for war anymore".[32] "Some nations boast of their chariots and horses, but we boast in the name of the LORD our God".[33] "Turn away from evil and do good. Search for peace, and work to maintain it".[34] "He causes wars to end throughout the earth. He breaks the bow and snaps the spear; he burns the shields with fire".[35] "Unfailing love and truth have met. Righteousness and peace have kissed"![36]

A tone that is completely different from the one in most of the texts of the *First Testament* can also be found in the "Songs of the Servants of God" in Deutero-Isaiah. One of the most famous passages of these songs that were already referred to Jesus by the early Christian community says: "Look at my servant, whom I strengthen. He is my chosen one, who pleases me. I have put my Spirit upon him. He will bring justice to the nations. He will not shout or raise his voice in public. He will not crush the weakest reed or put out a flickering candle. He will bring justice to all who have been wronged ... I, the LORD, have called you to demonstrate my righteousness. I will take you by the hand and guard you, and I will give you to my people, Israel, as a symbol of my covenant with them. And you will be a light to guide the nations. You will open the eyes of the blind. You will free the captives from prison, releasing those who sit in dark dungeons".[37]

Conclusion: Even if we take into account the last mentioned passages of the *Bible*, the image of God in the *First Testament* remains sullen. Yahweh is presented as an incalculable, wrathful despot who claims unconditional obedience, who punishes disobedience cruelly and who judges and destroys. The quantitative distribution of *blessing for obedience* and *curse for disobedience* in the Book Deuteronomy is characteristic for the spirit that rules in the *First Testament*: 47 lines of blessings face 204 lines of curse, which is more than four times![38]

THE SECOND TESTAMENT

Theologians and laymen often oppose the God of the Second Testament, who through the figure of Jesus of Nazareth reveals himself as full of light, loving, kind-hearted, merciful and forgiving, to the sullen, strict, angry, threatening and retaliatory God of the *First Testament*. This contrast is, however, much too nice to be true. Franz Buggle is absolutely right when he indicates that the *Second Testament* is dominated in most parts by the idea of reward and punishment, too, that it partially even outdoes the *First Testament*.[39] While in the far more extensive *First Testament*, eternal condemnation is only mentioned twice,[40] the threat of eternal torment in hell for sinners and non-believers appears more than thirty times in the Second Testament. As a matter of fact, the affirmation of life for obedience and the threat of death for disobedience against Yahweh's commandments are replaced in the Second Testament by the promise of eternal blissfulness for the "saints" who believe in Jesus Christ the Redeemer and who confess to him, and the threat of eternal condemnation for the sinners and non-believers. There is however one considerable reservation. From the *First Testament*, Paul adopts the divine omnipotence doctrine, which manifests itself in the fact that God takes pity on and gives grace to whom he wants.[41] Therefore, exclusively God brings about even faith. The Reformer John Calvin developed this concept into the doctrine of predestination, by adding, however, that the one, who is faithful, virtuous and successful in this world, may take this as a sign of belonging to the redeemed. In Calvinism, this doctrine unfolded unexpected consequences because it became the foundation of capitalism with a Puritan touch.

Let us return to the threat of eternal condemnation. Is a worse cruelty imaginable than the punishment for temporary crimes, no matter how terrible they might be, by an eternal, that is to say never-ending, agony? The fear of the torment of eternal condemnation or the timely limited torment of purgatory (in the Catholic doctrine) overshadowed and poisoned the life of uncountable Christians. It is an excellent instrument of domination of the souls, and contributed considerably in the bringing up of pious Christians with an attitude of unconditional obedience towards clerical and worldly authorities.

The *Second Testament* strikes, without question, a new note, with Jesus of Nazareth spreading the "Good News" of God's love towards men, especially the poor, victims of persecution, the humiliated and disdained, where Jesus could build on the positive sides of Yahweh's character. But even the *Biblical Christ*[42] is generously threatening with eternal punishment in hell (16 times). Not even the *Sermon on the Mount*, which is rightfully the heart of the *Second Testament*, is free of threats. We will deal later on with the question if these comments refer to the *historical Jesus.* To come to the point: I do not consider it probable. In view of the *Bible* text from the *Gospel of Mark* that Franz Buggle mentions repeatedly: "Anyone who believes and is baptized will be saved. But anyone who refuses to believe will be condemned",[43] the authorship of Jesus can definitely be excluded, because the annexe to the *Gospel of Mark* is an addition by an unknown author of the second century.

The close connection between the *First* and *Second Testament* is obvious even to the theological layman. Prophecies of the Messiah from the *First Testament* are referred to Jesus. He is declared to be a descendant of David and hence is the 'anointed one' (Messiah, Christ) of Yahweh. Jesus' death on the cross is interpreted as an expiation and sacrificial death, taking recourse to the *Songs of the Servants of God* in Deutero-Isaiah. Behind that stands the concept of a just God whose wrath about disobedient men has to be pacified temporarily by an animal sacrifice and by the human sacrifice of his only begotten son once and for all, at least for the people who believe in Jesus Christ. There is no doubt that this is a relapse into the way of thinking of the *First Testament*, connected with the Gnostic teaching of the Saviour and Redeemer.

A dark chapter in the history of Christianity is the anti-Judaism in the *Second Testament* which is responsible for the centuries-long discrimination of Jews and for uncountable pogroms, and which sowed the seeds for the racialist "Final Solution of the Jewish Question" by the National Socialists. From very early on, we can see in the Gospels the tendency of exculpating the Romans from any kind of culpability for Jesus' death and of blaming "the Jews" for it. In the *Gospel of Matthew*, Pilate says, after having washed his hands: "I am innocent of this man's blood. The responsibility is yours"![44] It is said that in reply to that, "all the people", incited by the high priests and elders, shouted: "We will take responsibility for his death — we and our children"![45] This sentence belongs to the most terrible of the whole *Bible*, having the gravest of consequences. Ineffable are also the words put into Jesus' mouth in the Gospel according to John: "If God were your father you would love me; because I have come to you from God. I am not here on my own, but he sent me. Why can't you understand what I am saying? It's because you can't even hear me! For you are the children of your father, the devil and you love to do the evil things he does. He was a murderer from the beginning".[46]

Conclusion: If we look at the Second Testament as a whole, it strikes us that the reform movement in Judaism that began with Pharisaism around 125 B.C. and reached its climax with the "Rabbi and Prophet"[47] Jesus of Nazareth, declined in the first century after Christ to touch bottom (for the time being) far below the level of the *First Testament* in the Revelation of John with its sadistic orgies of torture and violence.

OBJECTIONS

With quite some reason one can object towards my presentation, that the results of the historical-critical biblical science identified a considerable part of the cruel-inhuman stories of the *Bible* as myths and legends and, therefore, alleviated them. The recent historical-critical biblical science even reaches the conclusion that substantial parts of the Hebrew *Bible* are myths because the related events could not in the slightest be confirmed by archaeological findings. This can be said especially for the exodus of the Israelites from Egypt, the migration through the desert, the conquest of Canaan and the Empire of David and Salomon. While the far older Epic of Gilgamesh and the Homeric Epics were long ago recognised as myths, the Christian churches and religious communities claim, up to this day, that the biblical narrations are, though mythically exaggerated, still historical events. Nevertheless the scriptures of the *First Testament* as well as of the whole *Bible* in its present form had their impact for centuries since the historical-critical *Bible* investigation is little more than two hundred years old and restricted to a small circle of experts. The *Bible*, this cannot be emphasised enough, has had its historical effect in the form that we preserve until today. There is almost no cruelty, no war or injustice that cannot be justified by making reference to the *Bible*.

Another objection against the critical *Bible* reading is: We may not take the *Bible* word-for-word. We must separate its time-conditioned style from its timelessly valid content. This point is not satisfying because the criticism, as convincingly exposed by Franz Buggle, is directed against the timelessly valid content of the biblical texts: the day and night side of Yahweh, the reward and punishment scheme, the ethical damnability of Yahweh's deeds as reported in the *Bible*, etc. The depth psycholcgical finding is obvious: What is presented as Yahweh's commandments and discourse with divine authority in the *Bible*, are mostly idle dreams, fantasies and projections of priests and prophets.

One can further hear occasionally that for many people, the *Bible* keeps on hand wonderful words of comfort in situations of illness, distress and mortal danger. Against that, the questionable parts of the text are supposed to be ignored. This cannot be valid because these are exactly the text parts that countless fundamentalists refer to and use them, with the same right for orientation of their personal as well as public life.

Occasionally we can find the opinion that Yahweh became lonely after His destruction of the world of gods. It is said that He needs man to overcome His loneliness. This is why the devotion of man is so important to Him. This is why the turning away of man from Him fills him with feelings of jealousy, wrath and revenge. In my opinion, this is an anthropomorphisation of God, which can only be explained in one way: Man imputes God with his thoughts and feelings but God's thoughts are not our thoughts and His ways are not our ways !

Eventually there is another point that shall be mentioned: In the times of the making of the *Bible*, there was no separation between fiction and truth in historical narrative, they were both inseparable in myth. That may be right. But now-a-days we do not live in an era of mythical worldview any more. This is why the *Bible* can largely be considered only a myth today, but not as truth manifested by God in a circulation of approximately 50 million copies printed and distributed yearly. The Catholic Church put a stop to all intents of figurative understanding of *Bible* texts or of elimination of parts of the *Bible* because of its inhuman cruel content. It was, ironically, the reform-minded Second Vatican Council (1962-1965) that declared in the "Dogmatic Constitution about the Divine Revelation", among other things: "What was revealed by God, what is contained and available in the Holy Scripture, was written under the afflatus of the Holy Spirit; because of the apostolic belief, to our holy Mother, the Church, the Books of the *Old* as well as the *New Testament* are holy and canonical as a whole *in all its parts*, because they were written under the influence of the Holy Spirit ..., have God as their origin, and were given like this to the church. For the composition of the Holy Books, God chose men who were meant to serve him through the use of their own abilities and power to deliver in writing as true authors all that and *only* what He wanted to see in writing — in them and effective through them. As, therefore, everything that is said by the inspired authors or hagiographers must be taken as having been said by the Holy Spirit, we are to acknowledge that the Books of the Scripture teach surely, faithfully and *without error* the truth that God wanted to be written in the Holy Scriptures for our salvation."[48]

Though it does not appear to be so gloomy in Protestantism, things do look similar among evangelical movements, not to mention 'bible-abiding' sects. Through the principle of scripture (sola scriptura), originally directed against the rich traditional body of the Catholic Church, Martin Luther gave a special position to the *Bible* as the word of God that provided it with an almost untouchable status.

Conclusion: Religious fundamentalism can virtually be understood as the intent to restore the irretrievably lost world of myth in the era of scientific explanation of the world. It is reactionary.

A RELIGIO-HISTORICAL NOTE

For a better understanding of the Biblical texts I find a religio-historical analysis helpful. The Yahweh-cult of the nomadic tribes obviously went into a deep crisis with their immigration into the "promised land" Canaan. The Israelites mixed with the local population and started worshipping their gods, namely the fertility cults around Baal, Astarte, Milkom, Kemosch, among others. The more the Yahweh priests and prophets were threatened in their existence, the more bigoted and jealous, furious and cruel became their God with his "chosen" but now unfaithful people. His 'burning wrath' was no more only directed against his own people, now, but also against the foreign people and their gods. The relationship between the threat to the survival of the Yahweh priests and the increasing power of Yahweh is palpable. It applies to the whole period from the time of colonisation up to the destruction of the Northern Empire by the Assyrians in 722 B.C. and the Southern Empire by the Babylonians in 586 B.C. While his people is defeated or goes into exile, Yahweh ascends from tribal, war, mountain and desert god to the mightiest among the gods and eventually to autocrat and creator of Heaven and Earth.

However, instead of becoming the God of *all* men and people, what would have been the logical consequence, Yahweh remains the God of Israel, the God of Abraham, Isaac and Jacob. Thus, the Israelites *universalised* God but *privatised* the relationship towards Him. From a religio-scientific point of view, this is an *atavism*, a conservation of a long overcome religious idea. The teaching of the chosen people, with whom Yahweh concludes a treaty (covenant), is the central theme of the whole First Testament. It is inherited by Christendom as the new covenant, with catastrophic consequences not only in form of the absolute claim of truth towards pagans and heretics, but also by turning against its own roots, Judaism.

The problem here is not the development of monotheism, which is, on the contrary, a significant religio-historical achievement — though not restricted to Judaism — but the adherence to a collective relationship to God from the early times of history when Yahweh was still the tribal god of Israel. The well-being of Israel was from then onwards interpreted as a reward for its obedience towards Yahweh and his commandments; the downfall of the two microstates Israel and Judah that were literally pulverised between the superpowers of the antique world was considered as Yahweh's punishment for religious unfaithfulness and the moral corruption of the "chosen" people. Among the prophets, the suffering from the rottenness of the world releases the utopia of a kingdom of God at the end of the days. In this kingdom of justice, peace and joy, the Messiah reigns as a sovereign figure elevated into the superhuman along the lines of King David, as a representative of Yahweh on earth over the "holy rest"[49] of Israel. The Prophet, known as the third Isaiah (Trito-Isaiah) dreams of a world in which the relationship between Israel and the peoples turns around, thanks to the powerful intervention of Yahweh, provided that Israel fulfils its determination of being Yahweh's chosen people and obeys his will unconditionally. Then, the peoples of the earth will serve the priestly people of Israel:

> "Arise, Jerusalem ! Let your light shine for all to see. For the glory of the LORD rises to shine on you. Darkness as black as night covers all the nations of the earth, but the glory of the LORD rises and appears over you. All nations will come to your light; mighty kings will come to see your radiance. Look and see, for everyone is coming home ! Your sons are coming from distant lands; your little daughters will be carried home. Your eyes will shine, and your heart will thrill with joy, for merchants from around the world will come to you. They will bring you the wealth of many lands. Foreigners will come to rebuild your towns, and their kings will serve you. For though I have destroyed you in my anger, I will now have mercy on you through my grace. Your gates will stay

open day and night to receive the wealth of many lands. The kings of the world will be led as captives in a victory procession. For the nations that refuse to serve you will be destroyed."[50]

If we include the historical background into the analysis of these texts, it becomes clear that it is a question of compensation, even overcompensation of a sad reality. The small people of Israel, additionally weakened because of its division into northern and southern empire, was ground between the superpowers of the antique world — Assyria, Babylonia and Egypt, later Greece and Rome — like grains between millstones. The prophets interpreted this painful experience as judgement of Yahweh for the sins of "unfaithfulness", i.e., of idolatry. The prophets tried to bring the people to a change of mind by threats and promises in the name of Yahweh. As this failed, they announced the judgement of Yahweh over Israel and the sinful world in the form of the Apocalypse (Day of the Lord). Only the just will be saved.

In similar situations of major distress during the times of the Roman occupation, the Jewish Wars 66-70 and the persecution of Christians under Emperor Domitian at the end of the first century A.D., the apocalyptic visions of the *First Testament* resurge in Christian guise in the early Christian community and with Paul, the synoptic Gospels as well as the Revelation of John. John dreams of a thousand-year-long kingdom in which Christ as the Messiah reigns together with the resurrected martyrs. At the end of the thousand-year-old kingdom, there is a final battle of Satan after having been released from his prison and of the peoples of the world seduced by Satan against the camp of the Saints and God's loved city. "But fire from heaven came down on the attacking armies and consumed them. Then the devil, which had deceived them, was thrown into the fiery lake of burning sulphur, joining the beast and the false prophet. There they will be tormented day and night forever and ever."[51]

The *Book of Revelation* and with it the *Bible* ends with the vision of the New Jerusalem. But the author of this holy scripture remains faithful to himself because this masterpiece of biblical literature is followed by a curse: "And I solemnly declare to everyone who hears the words of prophecy written in this book: If anyone adds anything to what is written here, God will add to that person the plagues described in this book. And if anyone removes any of the words from this book of prophecy, God will remove that person's share in the tree of life and in the holy city that are described in this book. He who is the faithful witness to all these things says, 'Yes, I am coming soon' " ![52] Apparently, he was not in such a terrible hurry, or should "soon" have been measured in terms of eternity in this case?

THE *BIBLE* — A HOLY BOOK?

Who reads the *Bible* without bias from beginning to end can only be horrified by this most printed and most widespread book of world literature. It is not the inhuman cruelties as such, which are described in it, that account for the scandal — the classical world was a brutal and cruel world in which individuals but also communities and whole people went easily to rack and ruin, — it is the claim that they were performed upon the command of God or, in parts, even by God's own hand. If it were like that, I would immediately become an atheist. The *Bible* does contain, no doubt about that, divine revelation, too. But for long periods it is not a *holy,* but an extremely *unholy* scripture. If we take into consideration that this book has intellectually shaped a whole cultural circle, then we are no more surprised about the history of the Western World, characterised by intolerance and force, war and violence, conquest, suppression and exploitation, wherewith I do not want to say that the *Bible* alone is responsible for that. The "sharp intolerance"[53] of the Judaeo-Christian religion that it shares with fundamentalist Judaism and Islam, its absolute truth claim towards other religions, which became the basis of the superiority claim of the Christian culture over the non-Christian cultures or the white race over the non-white respectively, the unscrupulous exploitation of man and nature, all that is, if nothing else, a consequence of the spirit that dominates in most parts of the *Bible*. I do not demand to lock it into the "poison cabinet" of the forbidden books, like the Catholic Church did with books put on the index, I rather make a plea that the main churches let it circulate only in a commented edition which summarises the most important results of the historical-critical research. At the same time, it should be preceded by a prologue that clarifies that large parts of the *Bible* are not holy, many of them even downright unholy. Undeniably there would be a severe argument about what should in the future be considered holy in the Holy Scripture. But that does not matter; such an argument could definitely be fruitful and bring some life into the stiff and obsolete church congregations. I am afraid that the critic of

Christianity Franz Buggle is right, when he attributes the incapability of the churches to reform first and foremost to its powerful position in politics and society.[54]

I am well aware of the fact, that some of the observation I have just made will be considered as blasphemy by Christian, Jewish and Islamic fundamentalists – because the same applies basically to the *Koran*. But I only write about what I am convinced to be true, whereas the possibility of error can never be categorically excluded. Disagreements in ideological questions are a blessing, not a curse, because they present an opportunity to make progress in a "discourse that is free of domination" (Jürgen Habermas) on the way towards the recognition of truth and its implementation. The aberration of Christianity began, when the common striving for truth was abandoned, and when, instead, it was believed that what was deemed right and wrong had to be fixed by an institution.

REFERENCES

1. Franz Buggle, *Denn sie wissen nicht, was sie glauben*, Reinbek 1997, 245 und 248.
2. *Exodus*, the Second Book of Moses, 8:19; 9:4; 11:7.
3. *Exodus*, the Second Book of Moses, 32:9; 39:9; *Deuteronomium*, the Fifth Book of Moses,8:2-3; 8:16.
4. *Deuteronomium*, (Fifth Book of Mose) 8:19.
5. *Exodus* (Second Book of Mose) 15:6.
6. *Deuteronomium*, (Fifth Book of Mose) 32:40-42.
7. Jos, 10:11.
8. Psalms, 59, 79, 83, 94, 109, 110, 137.
9. Psalms 2:8. Such words have, without doubt, inspired the author of the Revelation of John in his violence and destruction phantasies.
10. Psalms, 110:1.5, see also Prophet Isaiah, 24.
11. *Deuteronomium*, (Fifth Book of Mose), 13:7-12.
12. Genesis, First Book of Mose, 9:6.
13. Exodus (Second Book of Mose) 12:15; 21:12-19; 35:2; Leviticus, (Third Book of Mose) 19:8.
14. Leviticus (Third Book of Mose), 20:1-18.
15. First Letter to the Corinthians, 5:13.
16. Leviticus (Third Book of Mose), 26:23
17. *Numeri*, Fourth Book of Moses,14:22-38.
18. *Ibid.*, 25:4
19. *Ibid.*, 25:6-15.
20. First Book of Kings, 19:18.

21. *Deuteronomium* (Fifth Book of Mose), 28:63.
22. Psalms, 44:1-8.
23. Prophet Isaiah, 63:1-6.
24. *Deuteronomium* (Fifth Book of Mose), 6:4.
25. *Harijan* 13.3.37; *CWMG* 71, 25.
26. *Exodus* (II Book of Mose), 20:4.
27. Leviticus (III Book of Mose), 19:18.
28. *Exodus* (II Book of Mose), 23:4
29. *Ibid.*, 20:8-11.
30. *Ibid.*, 23:10-12.
31. Leviticus (III Book of Mose), 25:8-31.
32. Prophet Isaiah, 2:2-4, see also Prophet Isaiah 11:1-16; Prophet) Isaiah, 60-62; Prophet Micah, 4:1-5, Ez 34:23-31. The opposite opinion is, however, found in Prophet Joel (4:9).
33. Psalms, 20:8.
34. *Ibid.*, 34:15.
35. *Ibid.*, 46:10
36. *Ibid.*, 85:11.
37. Prophet Isaiah, 42:1-7.
38. *Deuteronomium*, 28, *see* also Lev 26:3-38.
39. Franz Buggle: Denn sie wissen nicht, was sie glauben, Reinbek 1997, 131.
40. Prophet Isaiah, 66:22 und Dan 12:2, cited by Buggle 1997, 98.
41. Letters to Romans (Röm) 9:6-29, *see* also Apocalypse of John, 13:8.
42. With this I mean the Christ appearing in the scriptures of the Second Testament as opposed to the historical Christ the historical-critical *Bible* research attempts to reconstruct.
43. Gospel according to St. Mark, 16:16.
44. Gospel according to St. Mathew, 27:24.
45. St. Mathew, 27:25.
46. Gospel of John 8:42-44.
47. Rudolf Bultmann: Theologie des Neuen Testaments, Tübingen 1961 (4. Auflage), 19.
48. Quoted in Franz Buggle: Denn sie wissen nicht, was sie glauben, Reinbek 1997, 21 (emphasis by Franz Buggle).
49. Prophet Micah, 5; Prophet Zakariah, 13:7-9.14.
50. Prophet Isaiah, 60:1-12, see also Is 61:5-9 and Prophet Zakariah, 8:23.
51. Apocalypse of John, 20:9.
52. *Ibid.*, 22:18-20.
53. Gerhard von Rad, *Theologie des Alten Testaments*, München 1957, Bd. 1, 203, 207.
54. Franz Buggle: Denn sie wissen nicht, was sie glauben. Reinbek 1997, 399 ff.

5

Gandhi's Way to God

After a study of those religions to the extent it was possible for me, I have come to the conclusion that, if it is proper and necessary to discover an underlying unity among all religions, a master key is needed. That master key is that of truth and non-violence. . . . Religion can be defended only by the purity of its adherents and their good deeds, never by their quarrels with those of other faiths.

—*Mahatma Gandhi*

If we now turn towards Gandhi's religious thinking, we enter a completely different, a light, fearless and life-affirming world. But let us be careful! We tend too much to pass from one extreme to the other, which means to the dark, angry, furious and jealous, judging and destructive God whom we encounter in many parts of the *Bible* we contrast a loving, generous, merciful and forgiving God. It is, however, correct that for Gandhi, God is love (whereas is it yet necessary to clarify his concept of love), but He is not a sweet God. This is why Gandhi can say about Him: "He is patient but He is also terrible. He is the most exacting personage in the world and the world to come. He metes out the same measure to us that we mete out to our neighbours — men and brutes. With Him ignorance is no excuse. And withal He is ever forgiving for He always gives us the chance to repent. He is the greatest democrat the world knows, for He leaves us "unfettered" to make our own choice between evil and good. He is the greatest tyrant ever known, for He often dashes the cup from our lips and, under cover of free will, leaves us a margin so wholly inadequate as to provide only mirth for Himself at our expense. Therefore, it is that Hinduism calls it all His sport — *lila*, or an illusion — (*maya*). We are not, He alone is. And if we will be, we must eternally sing His praise and do His will. Let us dance to the tune of His *bansi* (lute), and all would be well".[1]

It is this radical devaluation of all the things that make life worth living for us normal human beings: money, possession, power, enjoyment, reputation and entertainment that frightens and repels us. We do not only find it with Gandhi but also with Jesus, Francis of Assisi and many saints. What frightens us most is the absoluteness claim that God raises towards man. He does not claim less than the complete devotion to His great law that He is Himself. *In the relationship to God, this absoluteness claim has its place and nowhere else.* If it is raised by men towards men, truth becomes untruth, good becomes evil, salvation disaster.

What is it that Gandhi tells us about God? Before we bring out attention to this question, it is absolutely necessary to clarify where his knowledge about God comes from. If we ask a Jew about the source of the revelation, he will answer: In the first place the *Torah* (the five Books of Moses); and secondly the remaining texts of the *Tanakh* (the Hebrew *Bible* or the *First Testament*), and the *Talmud*. If we ask a Christian, he will answer: The *Bible*. If we ask a Muslim, he will answer: In the first place the *Koran* and secondly the *Hadiths* (sayings of the Prophet Mohammad). With Gandhi this is different, for him there are three sources of revelation: at first, the holy scriptures of Hinduism (the *Vedas*, the *Upanishads*, the *Mahabharata* and therein especially the *Bhagavad Gita*, as well as the *Ramayana* of the poet Tulsidas), in the second place there are the holy scriptures of other religions and finally the direct revelation of God expressed through the voice of conscience. From that we can deduce that for Gandhi, revelation is not limited to a certain time, a certain geographical space or a certain people, instead it is possible anytime and everywhere.

Gandhi is aware of the danger that is associated with such an extension of the concept of revelation. Again and again there emerged people, in all parts of the world, who claimed that they had received divine messages or revelations which turned out to be baseless or a result of mental illnesses. The First Testament already knows about false prophets. Nevertheless, it is Gandhi's opinion that these facts do not invalidate the possibility of an authentic revelation.

"Nobody has to my knowledge questioned the possibility of the inner voice speaking to some, and it is a gain to the world even if one person's claim to speak under the authority of the inner voice can be really sustained. Many may make the claim, but not all will be able to substantiate it. But it cannot and ought not to be suppressed for the sake of preventing false claimants. There is no danger whatsoever if many people could truthfully represent the inner voice. But, unfortunately, there is no remedy against hypocrisy. Virtue must not be suppressed because many will feign it. Men have always been found throughout the world claiming to speak for the inner voice. But no harm has yet overtaken the world through their short-lived activities. Before one is able to listen to that voice, one has to go through a long and fairly severe course of training, and when it is the inner voice that speaks it is unmistakable. The world cannot be successfully fooled for all time. There is, therefore, no danger of anarchy setting in because a humble man like me will not be able to substantiate it. But it cannot and ought not to be suppressed for the sake of preventing false claimants. There is, therefore, no danger of anarchy setting in because a humble man like me will not be suppressed and will dare to claim the authority of the inner voice, when he believes that he has heard it."[2]

I cannot share Gandhi's optimism that no harm has been done to the world by its own way of acting. If we think about the harmful legacy of fundamentalists, especially the messianic apocalypticists in the Abrahamic religions, one is more inclined to assume the contrary. Some of the holy scriptures of the world religions were certainly written by people who claimed that they had received divine revelations. The author of the Revelation of John is one of them, the prophets of the *First Testament* and Prophet Mohammed are also among them. On the other hand, there are texts in the *Bible* whose authors never raised that claim. These are the authors of the History Books of the *Old Testament*, the *Psalms* and the *Song of Songs* as well as the *Books of Teaching*. In the *Second Testament*, the Gospels and the epistolary literature are among them. The decision, if a text is declared holy or is included in a collection of holy texts (Canon), is ultimately a decision made by humans. There is no objective criterion, based on which a text can be recognised as "holy", i.e., as a source of divine revelation. This is also the reason why it is no offence and much less blasphemy if we consider that the holy scriptures of the world religions contain some unholy texts, no matter if the author raised a claim of revelation or not. To Gandhi, however, it is clear: Not everybody can claim without hesitation having heard God's voice, the inner voice or the voice of conscience.

What does Gandhi mean when he talks about a long and fairly severe course of training that we have to go through successfully before we may claim that we are able to hear the voice of conscience as God's voice within us? He means the study of the holy scriptures of the world religions, fasting and prayer. The study of the holy scriptures of other religions should not be characterised by prejudices and general denial, but should be done to a certain extent from the point of view of those who confess to that religion. Fasting is meant as an act of self-control and self-purification, as turning away from the material world towards the spiritual world. By prayer, Gandhi does not mean so much a pleading, but an establishing of contact with God. Gandhi wrote beautiful words about praying, of which I can only reproduce one here: "The Divine Mind is unchangeable, but that Divinity is in everyone and everything — animate and inanimate. The meaning of prayer is that I want to evoke that Divinity within me. . . . I beg it of myself, of my Higher Self, the Real Self with which I have not yet achieved complete identification. You may, therefore, describe it as a continual longing to lose oneself in the Divinity, which comprises all. . . . I am part of that Infinite, and yet such an infinitesimal part that I feel outside it. Though I give you the intellectual explanation, I feel, without identification with the Divinity, so small that I am nothing. Immediately I begin to say I do this thing and that thing, I begin to feel my unworthiness and nothingness, and feel that someone else, some Higher Power, has to help me. . . . I pray to God who exists somewhere up in the clouds, and the more distant He is, the greater is my longing for Him and I find myself in His presence in thought. And thought as you know has a greater velocity than light. Therefore, the distance between me and Him, though so incalculably great, is obliterated. He is so far and yet so near.[3]

FIVE MONASTIC VOWS OF ASIAN RELIGIONS

According to Gandhi's understanding, studying the Holy Scriptures, fasting and praying are not enough to complete successfully what he calls a "long and fairly severe course of training". There is a further precondition, which is the incessant effort to put into practice the five monastic vows of the Asian religions. These are: *satya, ahimsa, brahmacharya, aparigraha and asteya*. We will analyse these terms explicitly later on. In this place, a short explanation that cannot be more than a first approach must suffice:

Satya (truth, truthfulness)

It is a central term in Gandhi's religious and philosophical thinking. It refers to what the catholic mystic and Zen master Willigis Jäger calls the 'first reality', or what Hans Küng calls the "first and last reality". To Gandhi, the word has the same meaning as God: "Devotion to this Truth is the sole justification for our existence. All our activities should be centred in Truth. Truth should be the very breath of our life".[4]

Ahimsa (non-violence, love)

It is a combination of the negative prefix a (non) and *himsa* (violence in the sense of harmful behaviour). *Ahimsa,* therefore, means abandonment of life harming behaviour. Gandhi gave this term, which is understood in Hinduism and Jainism mainly as a negative, i.e., abstinence from violence, a positive meaning: "I accept the interpretation of *ahimsa*, namely, that it is not merely a negative state of harmlessness but it is a positive state of love, of doing good even to the evil-doer. But it does not mean helping the evil-doer to continue the wrong or tolerating it by passive acquiescence — on the contrary, love, the active state of *ahimsa*, requires you to resist the wrong-doer by dissociating yourself from him even though it may offend him or injure him physically".[5]

The term *ahimsa*, as understood by Gandhi is, therefore closely related to the Christian concepts of love of one's neighbour, love of foreigners and love of one's enemies.

Brahmacharya

The literal meaning of *brahmacharya* is striving for the divine. To Gandhi the word means: renunciation of all kind of sensual enjoyment, i.e., abstention, chastity, ascesis: "*Brahmacharya* means control of all the organs of sense. He who attempts to control only one organ, and allows all the others free play, is bound to find his effort futile. To hear suggestive stories with the ears, to see suggestive sights with the eyes, to taste stimulating food with the tongue, to touch exciting things with the hands, and then at the same time to expect to control the only remaining organ is like putting one's hands in the fire, and expecting to escape being burnt. He, therefore, who is resolved to control the one must be likewise determined to control the rest. I have always felt that much harm has been done by the narrow definition of *brahmacharya*. If we practise simultaneous self-control in all directions, the attempt will be scientific and possible of success. Perhaps the palate is the chief sinner. That is why in the *ashram* we have assigned to control of the palate a separate place among our observances."[6]

Concerning *brahmacharya*, Gandhi was of an almost frightening radicalism and uncompromisingness: "Realisation of God is impossible without complete renunciation of the sexual desire."[7]

Aparigraha (Non-possession, Voluntary Poverty)

Possession is a main obstacle on the way to God.[8] "It is easier for a camel to go through the eye of a needle, than for a rich man to enter the Kingdom of God!" says Jesus, and Francis of Assisi, one of his most convincing followers, replied to the comment of the Bishop of Assisi: "Your life seems hard to me, not to own anything on earth is difficult". "Lord, if we wanted to own something we would also need weapons for our defence. This is why the quarrelling and fights come up, that prevent our love to God and to our neighbours. That is the reason why we do not want to own anything mundane in this world."[9]

Asteya (Non-stealing)

The word means not taking more than one needs for life. The idea behind it is: There is enough for all of us but not more. If somebody takes more than he needs for his life, he takes it away from other people and becomes guilty of their misery.

The monastic vows of monks and nuns of the Asian religions can be found in a more or less distinct form in all world religions. According to Gandhi, not only monks and nuns should strive for their realisation but all people within their possibilities. I am aware of the fact that they are diametrically opposed to the life style of the Western industrial societies. That does not prove, however, that they are unreasonable or wrong. Gandhi strived all his life for the realisation of these principles, to which a few more can be added such as tolerance, humility, altruistic serving, physical work, and preference of local products (*swadeshi*).

THE ONTOLOGICAL PARADOX

To Gandhi, the statement: God exists, is an axiom, i.e., an assumption that can neither be proven nor refuted. He thinks, though, that the existence of God can, up to a certain level, be explained by reason. On a trip through the Southern Indian Principality Mysore, he met poor village people who did not know who reigned over Mysore. They thought some kind of god was reigning over Mysore. Such as these poor village people did not know anything about the government of Mysore, we human beings do not know anything about God who reigns over the world. But we can understand, "that there is orderliness in the Universe, there is an unalterable Law governing everything and every being that exists or lives. It is not a blind law; for no blind law can govern the conduct of living beings. . . . That Law then which governs all life is God. Law and the Law-giver are one. I may not deny the Law or the Law-giver, because I know so little about It or Him. Even as my denial or ignorance of the existence of an earthly power will avail me nothing, so will not my denial of God and His Law liberate me from its operation; whereas humble and mute acceptance of divine authority makes life's journey easier even as the acceptance of earthly rule makes life under it easier. I do dimly perceive that whilst everything around me is ever changing, ever dying, there is underlying all that change a living Power that is changeless, that holds all together, that creates, dissolves and recreates. That informing Power or Spirit is God. And since nothing else I see merely through the senses can or will persist, He alone is".[10]

Gandhi was well aware of the fact that this is no "proof" in the sense of modern science: It is, however, also correct that every religion, every philosophy and every science is based on such positing or axioms. Therefore, Gandhi's statement is trivial. This fact is unfortunately passionately disputed by dogmatists, fundamentalists and fanatics of all times who raise an absolute truth claim for their ideology.

I still say that the assumption that God exists is an axiom. It is up to the free decision of each individual if he sets this axiom. Gandhi set it. To him, God exists. With that, a dramatic change of his life and his social environment began under the influence of that mysterious power that he called God or the truth. Over the years, what originally was to him not more than an arbitrary positing, meaning something simply unreal, became more and more real, while what originally seemed as simply real to him became more and more unreal. I call this phenomenon the ontological paradox. What is meant by this bulky term? Everything that is accessible to our sensual perception proves to be destructible, frail and perishable when measured by eternity. It emerges and vanishes. This can even be said about our home planet Earth, which will one remote day be absorbed by the expanding sun, unless it collides already earlier on with a celestial body straying in space. Gandhi believed to recognise a reality that is indestructible, imperishable and eternal behind this reality that under closer scrutiny turns out to be unreal, because it is perishable. This reality that seemed to him completely unreal in the beginning is what he calls God: "There is an indefinable mysterious Power that pervades everything. I feel It, though I do not see It. It is this unseen Power which makes Itself felt and yet defies all proof, because It is so unlike all that I perceive through my senses. It transcends the senses. . . . . I do dimly perceive that whilst everything around me is ever changing, ever dying, there is underlying all that change a living Power that is changeless, that holds all together, that creates, dissolves and recreates. That informing Power or Spirit is God. And since nothing else I see merely through the senses can or will persist, He alone is."[11]

We are thus dealing with two diametrically opposed concepts of reality. To the modern, scientifically educated man, the world that is palpable by the senses — either directly, or indirectly through instruments — reaches the highest level of reality; a weakened reality is, however, assigned to the norms and moral concepts, because they are based on convention that can turn out one way or the other. These are 'soft' concepts in contrast to the 'tough' facts. The lowest level of reality is found in general ideas like God or the platonic ideas of the True, the Good and the Beautiful, because their existence cannot be proven at all. With Gandhi it is exactly the other way round. The highest level of reality is assigned to God, even more, only He is real. In Hinduism, He is understood as world soul (*atman*) and world spirit (*Brahman*). To norms and values, reality is only assigned insofar as they are an emanation of the divine law (*dharma*). The world of the visible, sensually palpable objects possesses the lowest level of reality (*maya*). Reality is assigned to it only to the extent it participates in the reality of God.

According to Gandhi, the meaning of our life consists in freeing ourselves from the addiction to the material world in order to adopt that "first reality". Metaphorically said, it is like moving out from the house of bondage to the material world, just like the Israeli people moved out from the "house of bondage of Egypt", in order to reach, finally, after a migration through the desert, the praised land of freedom, identical with becoming one with God or the truth.

EXISTENTIAL HERMENEUTICS

Let us stay for a while with the relationship between man and God. It is our responsibility as humans to implement in our life what we have recognised as true. By doing that we will discover a new and deeper truth that must now, in turn be implemented existentially. Let us think about a wanderer in an unknown terrain. As long as he remains on the spot, for example on an observation point, he will see the landscape up to the horizon line. If he begins moving, the landscape will start changing. In front of him, a new, unknown terrain will arise above the horizontal line, and behind him, the terrain already known will sink below the horizontal line. The same thing happens, when a person starts implementing the truth as he understands it in his daily life. He sets himself in motion in an existential sense, with the result that he now understands a new truth, up to then unknown to him, which, in turn, must be implemented if he wants to proceed on the way of understanding the truth. I call this process of gradual approach to the absolute truth that never, as long as we live, reaches its goal, existential hermeneutics because it can be understood as a parallel to the humanistic method of hermeneutics that I described in detail using the example of the translation of a foreign language text. The difference is that the existential hermeneutics — another bulky word monster — plays a role in the field of existence and consciousness while the humanistic hermeneutic only refers to the field of consciousness.

What distinguished Gandhi from us "common" humans are his will and the energy with which he put immediately into practice what he believed having recognised as true. For us, there is normally a long way between the recognition of a truth that challenges us to change our life and its implementation, and often enough, the attempt to reach the goal remains just an attempt. With Gandhi that was different. An example may illustrate that. In South Africa, Gandhi had already risen to be the political leader of the Indian minority and dedicated his time intensively to questions of religion and life reform. For a long train trip, one of his colleagues gave him John Ruskin's

(1819-1900) book *Unto This Last* as reading material. He writes about that in his autobiography:

> "The book was impossible to lay aside, once I had begun it. It gripped me. Johannesburg to Durban was a twenty-four hours' journey. The train reached there in the evening. I could not get any sleep that night. I determined to change my life in accordance with the ideals of the book. ...
>
> The teachings of *Unto This Last* I understood to be:
>
> 1. That the good of the individual is contained in the good of all.
> 2. That a lawyer's work has the same value as the barber's, inasmuch as all have the same right of earning their livelihood from their work.
> 3. That a life of labour, i.e., the life of the tiller of the soil and the handicraftsman is the life worth living.
>
> The first of these I knew. The second I had dimly realised. The third had never occurred to me. *Unto This Last* made it as clear as daylight for me that the second and the third were contained in the first. I arose with the dawn, ready to reduce these principles to practice."[12]

It is fascinating to observe how, under the influence of the truth that he called God, the shy boy, addicted to sensuality because he had been married at the age of thirteen, became the political leader, social reformer and religious ascetic whom we know from history and about whom Albert Einstein (1879-1955) wrote: "Generations to come will scarcely believe that a one as this ever in flesh and blood walked upon the earth". Who wants to study this process of change may read Gandhi's autobiography.

About God as the driving force of this change he writes: "God to be God must rule the heart and transform it. He must express Himself in every the smallest act of His votary. This can only be done through a definite realisation more real than the five senses can ever produce. Sense perceptions can be, often are, false and deceptive, however, real they may appear to us. Where there is realisation outside the senses it is infallible. It is proved not by extraneous evidence but in the transformed conduct and character of those who have felt the real presence of God within".[13]

The change in behaviour and character of those who have felt the presence of God inside them is accessible to experience and consequently also to scientific research. God is in a way the invisible power whose actions become visible in the world. In this context, Gandhi used a comparison with electricity that, although invisible, performs visible actions by turning an electrical motor, heating a cooking plate or lighting a bulb: "God is not a person. He is the all-pervading, all-powerful spirit. Anyone who bears Him in his or her heart has access to a marvellous force or energy as effective in its results as, say, steam or electricity, but much subtler".[14]

In that, one could see an indirect proof of God, because from the change in character of those who have felt the presence of God inside them we can deduce that there must be a power that triggers this change. It is obviously not a conclusive proof. It could just as well be the result of autosuggestion. With reference to his own experience, Gandhi is well aware of this possibility: "I know that I have no other resource as a *satyagrahi* than the assistance of God in every conceivable difficulty, and I would like it to be believed that what may appear to be inexplicable actions of mine are really due to inner promptings. It may be a product of my heated imagination. If it is so, I prize that imagination as it has served me for a chequered life extending over a period of now nearly over 55 years, because I learned to rely consciously upon God before I was 15 years old".[15]

The following question makes us be careful: Into which direction does the character of a religious person change? Quite a few religious fundamentalists and fanatics consider themselves as chosen by God and use this belief to justify hatred and violence against people of other faiths. In my opinion, Gandhi is too optimistic with regard to human nature when he considers that by its short-lived action no harm has been done to the world.

The intimate relationship that ties Gandhi to God is expressed by the constant repetition of the divine name Ram. He writes about that: "Although my mind and my heart have long since recognised that the truth is the highest aspect of God, that truth is his highest name, I do, however, know this truth under the name of Ram. In the darkest hours of my trials, this name saved me again and again and still saves me today. When I was a child, my *nanny* told me to pronounce the name Ram whenever I was afraid or felt pain. And as time went on and my knowledge grew, it became something like my second nature. I can even say that his word is, though not constantly on my lips, twenty-four hours a day in my heart. It has become my redeemer and I stay with it all the time".[16]

Gandhi makes use of a daring comparison when he describes his relationship to God as "slavery": "My claim to hear the voice of God is no new claim. Unfortunately there is no way that I know of proving the claim except through results. God will not be God if He allowed Himself to be an object of proof by His creatures. But He does give His willing slave the power to pass through the fiercest of ordeals. I have been a willing slave to this most exacting Master for more than half a century. His voice has been increasingly audible as years have rolled by. He has never forsaken me even in my darkest hour. He has saved me often against myself and left me not a vestige of independence. The greater the surrender to Him, the greater has been my joy".[17]

This comment is highly capable of being misunderstood because the term 'slavery' refers to the most extreme level of human bondage and is, therefore, a fundamental offence against human dignity and human rights. Gandhi, however, wants to say something different, namely the relationship to God or to the truth chosen in freedom, in other words the conscious abandonment of freedom, independence and autonomy. To him, the unconditional relationship to God constitutes the only freedom worth having. It is our destiny as men to be slaves, either voluntary "slaves" of God or slaves of our passions, addictions and fears. The departure into freedom in the sense of independence and liberty mostly ends in slavery towards people, be it as recipients of orders or as subordinates, even if we have the small freedom of choosing our masters ourselves. The same can be said about the slaveholders or masters. They are dependent on the services of their 'slaves' and, more than that, only all too often on their passions, addictions and fears. The most frightening example of this kind of voluntary slavery are elite soldiers. Their "free will" merges completely with the will of their commanders, because they are drilled to execute every order obediently, even the most inhuman and criminal one. To them, the meaning of their life consists exclusively in being a functioning wheel of gigantic military machinery. The same can be said about the commanders, because they only pass on the orders they receive from above to their subordinates; they are consequently masters and slaves at the same time. One should suppose that the supreme commander is free. But even this is wrong because he is subject to numerous influences and factual constraints. Slaveholder and slave are both un free just because of their mutual dependence.

The term slavery used by Gandhi to characterise his relationship to God reminds us of the term of voluntary subjugation created by the short-lived Frenchman Etienne de la Boethie (1530-1563) in his *Discourse about the voluntary servitude.*[18] To Boethie, voluntary servitude means the willing submission to a tyrant in order to execute his orders and to be rewarded for this service with power and privileges. Tyranny, therefore, builds a pyramid of domination with the tyrant on the top, numerous sub-tyrants in the middle and the servants or slaves at the base. Without the voluntary servants who support the tyrant, and without the involuntary servants who execute the sub-tyrants' orders, the system of tyranny could not survive for a single day. Thus, the massive refusal of cooperation with the oppressors puts an end to any kind of tyranny. It requires, however, the mental strength to tolerate the sanctions used by the oppressors in their efforts to enforce obedience, no matter how cruel they might be. In the end, Gandhi's method of a non-violent struggle is based on the idea of bringing into life this mental strength of the oppressed, and of organising it in the common struggle.

If we compare the voluntary servitude of Etienne de la Boethie with Gandhi's, a fundamental difference becomes obvious. The voluntary subjugation of the sub-tyrants means participation of power and privileges for the price of subjugation and exploitation of other people. The voluntary servitude, according to Gandhi's understanding means, on the contrary, "service to God" and, therefore, service to our neighbours: "Not until we have reduced ourselves to nothingness can we conquer the evil in us. God demands nothing less than complete self-surrender as the price for the only real freedom that is worth having. And when a man thus loses himself, he immediately finds himself in the service of all that lives. It becomes his delight and his recreation. He is a new man never weary of spending himself in the service of God's creation".[19]

REFERENCES

1. *Young India*, 5.3.1925; CWMG 30, 334 f.
2. *Harijan*, 18.3.1931; CWMG 60, 76 f.
3. *Harijan* 19.8.1939; CWMG 76, 165 f
4. *From Yervada Mandir*, SWMG 4, 213.
5. *Young India* 25.8.1920; CWMG 21, 199.
6. *From Yervada Mandir*; SWMG 4, 222 f.

7. *Young India,* 24.6.1926; CWMG 35, 358.
8. *Gospel According to St Matthew*, 19:24.
9. Franz von Assisi: *Geliebte Armut*, Freiburg 1977, 50.
10. *Young India*, 10.11.1928; CWMG 43, 95 f
11. *Ibid.*
12. *Autobiography*, SWMG 2, 445 f.
13. *Young India*, 10.11.1928; CWMG 43, 96.
14. *Harijan*, 14.7.1946; CWMG 91, 228.
15. *Harijan*, 11.3.1939; CWMG 75, 136.
16. *Harijan*, 18.3.1933; CWMG 61, 15.
17. *Harijan*, 6.5.1933; CWMG 61, 86 f.
18. Etienne de la Boethie (1530-1563), *The Politics of Obedience: The Discourse of Voluntary Servitude*, translated by Harry Kurz and with an introduction by Murray Rothbard, Montrèal/New York/London: Black Rose Books, 1997. ISBN.
19. *Young India*, 20.12.1928; CWMG 43, 417.

6
God is the Truth

God as the truth has always been for me a treasure of indescribable value and I wished he were it for each of us.
—Mahatma Gandhi

We have now learned enough about Gandhi's sources of revelation and his relationship with God in order to be able to turn to the question, what he has to tell us about God. I have tried to summarise his findings in eight items:

1. God is different from us;
2. God is not a person and is a person;
3. God is neither male nor female nor neuter;
4. God is existence, knowledge and bliss;
5. God is omnipresent, omniscient and omnipotent;
6. God is one, there is no second;
7. God is truth and love; and
8. Once again: Who or what is God?

GOD IS DIFFERENT FROM US

The *Vedas* describe God as "*neti-neti*" (not that, not that), and in the *First Testament*, Yahweh says: You must not make for yourself an idol (of me). This means that God is the absolutely different, the strange, inscrutable, shapeless and nameless. He escapes perception by the senses and access of the knowing mind. As Gandhi says, He is only visible to the eye of faith and He can only be perceived by those who approach Him in the right way.

From the religio-historical point of view, there are two different types of religious orientations: hostile to images and image-friendly. The image-friendly — Hinduism, Buddhism and Catholicism are not inferior to the ones that are hostile to images. Wooden or stone statues, images and symbols only become idols or fetishes, if they are put on a level with God or supernatural beings. On the other hand, as the scholar of the *First Testament* Gerhard von Rad (1901-1971) observed rightly in view of the ban on images of Judaism, "the rejection of images of worship of God is in itself no obvious phenomenon;. it can express a very deep fetishistic and a very high idea of God".[1]

The disdain of Yahweh's priests for the cults of the Canaanites, who worshipped gods of wood and stone, is not justified in this generality. The portrait is, like the house of God (temple, synagogue, mosque or church), merely a means to communicate with the invisible God. On the other hand, the imageless worship of God, that in Judaism and Islam includes even banning the depiction of living beings, includes absolutely no guarantee of a purer form of worship. The commandment: "You must not make for yourself an idol" is also violated if we form God according to the image of man, especially to the image of the oriental despot, the Greek tyrant or the modern dictator. Gandhi about that: "I am both an idolater and an iconoclast in what I conceive to be the true sense of the terms. I value the spirit behind idol worship. It plays a most important part in the uplift of the human race. And I would like to possess the ability to defend with my life the thousands of holy temples which sanctify this land of ours. My alliance with the Mussalmans presupposes their perfect tolerance for my idols and my temples. I am an iconoclast in the sense that I break down the subtle form of idolatry in the shape of fanaticism that refuses to see any virtue in any other form of worshipping the Deity save one's own. This form of idolatry is more deadly for being more fine and evasive than the tangible and gross form of worship that identifies the Deity with a little bit of a stone or a golden image".[2]

In the second chapter of this book, I already dealt with the fatal tendency of the biblical authors to shape God according to the image of man, more specifically according to the image of the oriental despot. The angry, vindictive, threatening, judging and annihilating God who makes an appearance there does not really exist. He has actually never existed. This can be said about the negative but also about the positive human qualities that we ascribe to God, as far as they refer dialectically to the negative. Nor does the arbitrarily selecting, gracious, merciful and loving God exist. He has also never existed. These are, as Ludwig Feuerbach (1804-1872) already explained with convincing arguments, projections of human qualities onto God.

It is true that God is love, benevolence, truth, non-violence, but in a very different way from what we, who can only think in opposites (polarities) and contradictions (antagonisms), usually imagine. God is, as the medieval mystic Nicholas of Cusa (1401-1464) realised, the coincidence of opposites (coincidentia oppositorum). What he meant may be explained using the example of the notion of love. The word is sometimes used synonymous with sexuality. We mostly understand it however as the amorousness of a young couple, the affection for the own family, for the own community or for the own people. But that is, on closer consideration, nothing else than an extended egotism. Love in this sense is always dialectically referred to hatred as well as friendship is referred to enmity and affection to aversion. Most people can only think and feel in just these opposites. Nevertheless, there is a : *love* beyond the opposition of (selfish) love and hatred, goodness beyond good and evil, a *truth* beyond truth and untruth. All these are names of God. He is this love, goodness, beauty and truth without opposites. The word "beyond", in this context, does not mean the often cited "perfect balance" between extremes. "Beyond" rather means a qualitative jump into a world that exceeds our cognitive capacity. That is what Nicholas of Cusa bears in mind when he speaks about God as the coincidence of opposites. The love of God includes not only all people, regardless of which gender, race, social class, religion or philosophy they belong to, but also extra-human nature. It is the duty of man to realise this all-embracing love. It is basically nothing more than a reflection of God's love to the world. "Let us resolve that we will never give up the pursuit of truth. To follow truth, the only right path in this world is that of non-violence. Non-violence means an ocean of love, whose vastness no one has ever been able to measure. If it fills us we would be so large-hearted that we would have room in it for the whole world. I know this is difficult to achieve, but not impossible."[3]

The differentness of God can best be illustrated with the difference between the earthly and heavenly love. While the earthly love is always conditional, the heavenly love is always unconditional. Being conditional means that when we love we expect to be loved back and when we give we expect to receive. To what extent that is the case can easily be seen when the loved one turns her or his love to another person. All of a sudden, a maniac jealousy comes alive. We feel cheated of the reward for our love — being loved in return. God's love is completely different. It is unconditional. It does not expect being returned. Thus it does not turn into jealousy and hatred when not reciprocated. Who accepts it will be so full of it that he or she cannot do anything else than passing it on to his or her fellow human beings — the neighbour, the stranger, even the enemy — and the extrahuman nature. For the one who declines it, the all-embracing love will be replaced by the differentiation between love and hatred, friend and foe.

The parable of the prodigal son in Luke's Gospel is an impressive metaphor for God's love to the world — inasmuch as God and the world can be separated. It does not matter if the story is based on the historical Jesus or originates from the early Christian community, because it was created, should the latter be the case, entirely in the spirit of Jesus. A son demands his inheritance from his father and spends it in the company of false friends. His situation gets worse and worse, he is hired as a swineherd, eats the waste from the pig's trough in order to appease his biting hunger. When he finally came to his senses, he said to himself, "At home even the hired servants have food enough to spare, and here I am dying of hunger"! I will go home to my father and say, "Father, I have sinned against both heaven and you, and I am no longer worthy of being called your son. Please take me on as a hired servant". So he returned home to his father. And while he was still a long way off, his father saw him coming". Filled with love and compassion, he ran to his son, embraced him, and kissed him. His son said to him, "Father, I have sinned against both heaven and you, and I am no longer worthy of being called your son". But his father said to the servants, "Quick! Bring the finest robe in the house and put it on him. Get a ring for his finger and sandals for his feet. And kill the calf we have been fattening. We must celebrate with a feast, for this son of mine was dead and has now returned to life. He was lost, but now he is found". So the party began".[4]

What does this parable want to tell us — if we ignore the figure of the jealous brother who makes an appearance later? In my opinion the following: God loves us people regardless of our behaviour, regardless of our merits and our misdeeds. When the son demands his inheritance and wants to go his own way, the father does not become inflamed with such a burning anger that he threatens the son with punishment and annihilation. He is also not moved to begging in order to keep him; he does not remind him that he owes his life and position in the family to his parents. He respects the son's will and gives the requested portion of the inheritance to him. When the son eventually returns due to quite selfish considerations, albeit truly remorseful, the father celebrates a big party and reinstates him into the full rights of a son. This is how I understand the parable: God does not punish, but the person who turns away from Him in order to be free and autonomous punishes himself. Neither does God reward, it is rather the person who turns to God, who rewards himself. But even the terms reward and punishment are out of place in this context because they presuppose a person who punishes or rewards. It is rather a kind of natural law of the kind that who puts his hand into a fire gets burned. Nobody would see a "punishment" in the burn, even if the person who does it considers it self-punishment. It is more the foreseeable consequence of this action.

But the one who puts his life unconditionally into the hand of God will be free of (selfish) love and hatred, of affection and aversion, fear and greed. He knows that his body can be destroyed but not his soul, which is part of the world soul (*atman*), nor his spirit, which is part of the world spirit (*Brahman*) or of the immortal, indestructible existence of God. As soon as he gets independent of God, however, as soon as he himself wants to become law (autonomous), he begins to die spiritually. From now on, he has to take care of himself and has to stand up for himself. By taking more than he really needs, out of greed or fear of future shortage, he takes it away from others who now begin, reacting on that experience, to take for themselves more than they really need. Society starts to split into rich and poor, powerful and powerless, high and low, in one word, into winners and losers. The merciless competition for wealth and power, reputation and pleasure begins. The land of freedom, independence and autonomy, that seemed to be so tempting and enticing, proves to be, as soon as it is entered, a swampy terrain in which you sink in more deeply with every step. The person who emancipates himself from God becomes necessarily an enemy of God and an enemy of men because he now has to care for himself and his next of kin and stand up for himself. He projects this enmity onto God and the people whom he considers his opponents or rivals. The angry, striving, revenging, judging and annihilating God whom we meet in parts of the *First Testament* is consequently a *projection* of man onto God. In other words, he ascribes to God the feelings he nourishes towards God. The Prophets, in turn, used this gloomy image of God in order to force the people back to obedience to Yahweh with its help. That could not go well, but only made things worse. The angrier Yahweh got in the Sermon on the Prophets about the disobedience of Israel, the more disobedient and stubborn the people got. This turned into the vicious circle of reciprocal humiliations and insults that psychotherapists know from countless failed relationships.

> *God is different. He does not react to our good or evil deeds; He does not reward or punish. We reward and punish ourselves, inasmuch as it still makes sense, at all, to apply these categories.*

GOD IS NOT A PERSON AND IS A PERSON

In the *Bible*, God manifests Himself as an absolute ruler who stands above the natural law and the ethical law that He Himself issued on Mount Sinai. He can, therefore, interfere anytime and everywhere powerfully with natural events and with history. Gandhi disagrees with this idea. Even God adheres to His law because He is identical with this law. If He acted against the law, it would be a *self-contradiction*. This is why Gandhi can say: "He and His Law are one. The Law is God. Anything attributed to Him is not a mere attribute. He is the Attribute. He is Truth, Love, Law, and a million things that human ingenuity can name."[5]

For Gandhi, God is identical with His law. But He is even more: "God is not a person. He transcends description. He is the Law-maker, the Law and the Executor. No human being can well arrogate these powers to himself. If he did, he would be looked upon as an unadulterated dictator. This does not befit a man. They become only Him whom we worship as God."[6] God is not a person in the sense that we human beings are persons. He is power, energy, "all-pervading, all-powerful spirit".

On the other hand, it would be wrong to plainly deny God being a person. This sounds like a contradiction and is yet none. God is *both* a person *and* a spirit or power, and He is *neither* the one *nor* the other, as far as we are dealing with terms affiliated to our empirical world. The "magical formula" of *as-well-as* and *neither-nor* refers to the outermost limit of what is accessible to the mind. Gandhi describes this complicated circumstance with simple words, when he says: "Man can express himself only by means of language. But there can be no such medium as language for the Power that is God. Man, however, can describe this Infinite Power only with his imperfect means. If one has grasped this there is nothing left further to ask. Then it would be right to pray to Him in the language of man, for one can comprehend Him somewhat by fitting Him into one's own mould. One ought always to remember, while dwelling on Him, that one is but a drop, the tiniest of creatures of the ocean that is God. One may experience Him by being in Him, but one can never describe Him .... So it is immaterial if some worship God as a Person and some others as Great Power. Both are right, each in his own way. Nobody knows what is intrinsically right and nobody is likely ever to know. The ideal, to be an ideal, must forever remain out of reach. All the other forces are static, while God is the Life Force, immanent and at the same time transcendent".[7]

GOD IS NEITHER MALE NOR FEMALE NOR NEUTER

This statement follows basically from the last one. Regardless of that, the God of the *Bible* bears pointedly masculine features and possesses male qualities. He is inclined to violence, he is angry, jealous, revengeful, judging and destructive, when his commandments are not strictly observed. No wonder that this male God prefers men and those men shaped this God according to their image. Behind this attitude, the opinion stood that women and children, together with the slaves and cattle, belonged to the man's possessions. We herewith get to the root of the discrimination of women in the Abrahamitic religions, in order to hopefully eradicate it once and for all. It is almost unbelievable that women put up with this discrimination over the centuries.

Feminist theology, regardless of whether it is represented by women or men has, therefore, every right to push the idol of the male God off its throne and replace it by a female deity. It has the right to do that not only temporarily but for centuries, at least for as long as the male God reigned in heaven and on earth and ruined the world. In a distant future, however, the knowledge could break ground that God is neither male nor female nor neuter. In my opinion, this knowledge stands behind the following statement of Gandhi: "God is certainly One. He has no second. He is unfathomable, unknowable and unknown to the vast majority of mankind. He is everywhere. He sees without eyes, and hears without ears. He is formless and indivisible. He is uncreated, has no father, mother or child; and yet He allows Himself to be worshipped as father, mother, wife and child. He allows himself even to be worshipped as stock and stone, although

He is none of these things. He is the most elusive. He is the nearest to us if we would but know the fact. But He is farthest from us when we do not want to realize His omnipresence".[8]

GOD IS EXISTENCE, KNOWLEDGE AND BLISS (*SAT, CHIT, ANANDA*)

After it has become clear that God cannot be described appropriately by the terms that originate from our world of experience and thoughts — a fact that can also be denominated as negative theology — we can now, in the knowledge of their inappropriateness, bring our attention to the positive statements about God.

God is *Sat* means, he is existence, he is first and last reality, indestructible, invisible and eternal being, origin of all kinds of being. He is the power that creates, dissolves and recreates everything that exists. As long as we are aware of the fact that each of the three concepts mentioned in the heading is a being beyond the opposition of being and non-being, a knowledge beyond the opposition of knowledge and ignorance, and a bliss beyond the opposition of fortune and misfortune, these terms get a limited statement value: "Where there is Truth, there also is knowledge which is true. Where there is no Truth, there can be no true knowledge. That is why the word *Chit* or knowledge is associated with the name of God. And where there is true knowledge, there is always bliss (*Ananda*). There sorrow has no place. *Ananda* even as Truth is eternal, so is the bliss derived from it. Hence, we know God as *Sat-Chit-Ananda,* One who combines in Himself Truth, Knowledge and Bliss."[9]

GOD IS OMNIPRESENT, OMNISCIENT AND OMNIPOTENT

Omnipresent. If this thought is consequently thought through to the end, it means that God is present in everything, be it animate or inanimate. He is smaller than an atom and at the same time bigger than the Universe or, in Gandhi's pictorial language: "He is *one* and yet many; He is smaller than an atom, and bigger than the Himalayas; He is contained even in a drop of the ocean, and yet not even the seven seas can compass Him".[10]

From the principle of God's omnipresence we can deduce that he is also present, albeit hidden, in the world perceptible by the senses. The world is in a way the visible surface of God's invisible body.

This idea is contradictory to the idea of the *Bible* according to which the world is a creation of God and as such must be considered separately from him. If we take this concept as a basis, it ultimately does not matter, if God, in the process of creation, looks like a craftsman who creates the world so to speak with the labour of His hands, and who forms the man from "dust of the ground", or if He brings them into being through His word. God and His creation are always considered separately. Even in the *New Testament*, this idea is present when, for instance, in the Paternoster it reads: "Our Father in heaven". This idea of a God separated from the world who resides in heaven is called theistic. In the end, it does not matter if God is seen, like in the *Bible*, as a ruler who powerfully interferes with the world affairs, or, like in the era of Enlightenment, as a brilliant designer who created the world like a watchmaker created the clockwork that henceforth runs according to eternal natural laws.

The opposite position to *theism* is *pantheism*, which considers God and the world as one. According to the Dutch philosopher Baruch Spinoza (1632-1677), for example, Nature was just another name for God. Gandhi as a Hindu thinks neither *theistic* nor *pantheistic*. For him, the world rests in God but God is greater than the world. This doctrine is called *pantheistic*. It means that the universe rests in God.

If God is present in nature, albeit hidden, then nature is holy. In Judaism and Christendom, man became ruler over flora and fauna with the following words: "Be fruitful and multiply. Fill the earth and *govern* it. Reign over. the birds in the sky, and all the animals that scurry along the ground."[11] This means desacralisation of nature. It is left to man for his exploitation. The second creation account speaks of a setting up and caring of the Garden of Eden, but this commandment, that aims at a rather non-violent and considerate behaviour towards the extrahuman creation, could not prevail against the first mentioned. The determination of God's omnipresence results, however, not only in God's presence in the saints, but also in the worst criminals and human slaughterers, in a Genghis Khan, Stalin and Hitler. The difference between the saints and the mass murderers can hardly be bigger, in as much as God reveals Himself increasingly in the first while in the latter, he hides increasingly. That also means, however, that even for the latter, during their lifetime, a return to life is possible, albeit highly improbable, because our conduct of life in thinking, speaking and acting develops a positive or negative dynamic that is not easily reversible. Nevertheless, it is true: "No human being is so bad as to be beyond redemption, no human being is so perfect as to warrant his destroying him whom he wrongly considers to be wholly evil".[12]

Omniscient. I do not need to spend time explaining God's omniscience because it means God's omnipresence in time. God is beyond time: "We may copy God, but not He us. We may not divide Time for Him, Time for Him is eternity. For us there is past, present and future. And what is human life of a hundred years but less than a mere speck in the eternity of Time"?[13]

Gandhi felt God's omnipresence and omniscience directly: "There is not a moment when I do not feel the presence of a witness whose eye misses nothing and with whom I strive to keep in tune".[14]

Omnipotent. It is part of God's omnipotence that He can hold it back from us human beings in order to grant us the freedom of decision for or against Him. This idea is alien to the authors of the *Bible*. For them, omnipotence means unlimited power that even exceeds the power of an absolute ruler, and that does not allow any objection or even resistance. As a result, they reach the absurd conclusion that disobedience of man against Yahweh's will must be caused by Yahweh himself. It is consequently not Pharaoh who hardens his heart, and who does not let the people Israel go, but it is Yahweh who hardens his heart in order to manifest his power over him and his people. Now, also the hardening that Yahweh imposes as punishment for the disobedience of the people becomes understandable. He sends the prophet Isaiah with the following message to the people: "Listen carefully, but do not understand. Watch closely, but learn nothing. Harden the hearts of these people. Plug their ears and shut their eyes. That way, they will not see with their eyes, nor hear with their ears, nor understand with their hearts and turn to me for healing".[15] In the following verses, the people are threatened by total annihilation for this hardening, of which they are at least partially innocent. The biblical authors can obviously not resolve the contradiction between the omnipotence of Yahweh and His impotence concerning the disobedience of His chosen people. This impotence and helplessness provokes him to threats of punishment and annihilation against it.

GOD IS ONE, THERE IS NO SECOND

God is, as we learned from Nicholas of Cusa, the coincidence of opposites. From this it does not follow, however, that He is a homogeneous entity. He is rather unity in disparity or, like the Hindus say *Advaita*, non-duality, undividedness. With this term shall be expressed what I elsewhere tried to explain with the magical formula of *As-well-as and Neither-nor*. He is unity as well as duality (plurality) and at the same time neither unity nor duality (plurality). In Gandhi's words: "I talk of God exactly as I believe Him to be. Why should I beguile people into error and work my own perdition? I seek no reward from them. I believe God to be creative as well as non-creative. This too is the result of my acceptance of the doctrine of the manyness of reality. From the platform of the Jains I prove the non-creative aspect of God, and from that of Ramanuja the creative aspect. As a matter of fact, we are all thinking of the Unthinkable, describing the Indescribable, seeking to know the Unknown, and that is why our speech falters, is inadequate and even often contradictory".[16]

Because this is so, it is possible to make contradictory statements about God that all contain a relative truth in themselves. In this context, Gandhi occasionally used the parable of the people who touched elephants while being blindfolded. The one touching the trunk will claim that reality is soft and round. Another one, touching the tusks, will say it is hard and pointed. A third one, touching the elephant's skin, will say, it is rough and chapped. A fourth one, touching the ear, will say, it is smooth and flexible. As soon as the bandages are removed from the test persons' eyes, they recognise that their contradictory statements are in reality no contradictions at all, because they all apply to the reality of the elephant.

GOD IS TRUTH AND LOVE (*SATYA* AND *AHIMSA*)

For Gandhi, truth and love form an inseparable entity. They are like the front and back side of one and the same coin: "*Ahimsa* is my God, and Truth is my God. When I look for *Ahimsa*, Truth says, "Find it out through me". When I look for Truth, *Ahimsa* says, "Find it out through me".[17] "Love and truth are two faces of the same coin and both most difficult to practice and the only things worth living for. A person cannot be true, if he does not love all God's creatures; truth and love are, therefore, the complete sacrifice."[18]

Here we touch the innermost essence of Gandhi's life and teaching. When he uses the words truth (*satya*) and love or non-violence (*ahimsa*), they only correspond partially with the terms we use in the Christian cultural sphere. If the union between truth and love is dissolved, both terms experience a fundamental change in meaning. *Truth without love becomes untruth, and love without truth stops being love in the sense of ahimsa.* It turns, as already seen before, into simple or extended egotism.

The history of the Judaeo-Christian culture is, apart from a few exceptions, the history of betrayal of the truth as understood by Gandhi. In the name of religion, in God's name, human rights were trampled upon, there was humiliation, torturing and killing. This does not only apply to forced conversions, persecution of heretics, burning of witches and religious wars, but also for the secularised forms of violence such as slavery, colonialism, imperialism, fascism, communism as well as the globalised capitalism of our present days, because they are part of the history of the Judaeo-Christian culture. *We are not only responsible for what we do, but also for what we allow to happen.* Christians allowed all that, if they did not even take an active part in it. With this, I do not want to claim that the other world religions have not burdened themselves with their fill of guilt, however, I am afraid that Christendom, the religion of love, as it likes to describe itself, outweighs the others by far, because it is responsible for the fact that the world is now on the brink of self-destruction.

The amount of guilt of Islam in view of wars of conquest, discrimination of women and people of different faith, forced conversion or extermination of "infidels" and apostates, the use of a cruel medieval criminal law (*Sharia*) in the Islamic states as well as an extremely virulent terrorism is also quite considerable, but it is by far surpassed by Christendom.

In short, who uses force and violence in the name of the truth, in the name of God, blasphemes. He does not serve the truth but the untruth. I do not want to be misunderstood. My concern at this point is exclusively the *religious* justification of injustice, force and violence. If something like a sin against the Holy Spirit exists, it consists of committing crimes in the name of God that make God appear like a grim, bloodthirsty and unjust demon in the eyes of the victims. How can, for example, a Palestinian, whose ancestors lived in Palestine for generations, but who was expelled from his homeland in the name of Yahweh, who allegedly gave this country to his chosen people, experience this God in a different way than a God of injustice, violence and humiliation? The same applies, just to give another example, to the countless victims of the "Holy Inquisition", by instigation of which "heretics" were tortured and burned at the stake.

It is all too understandable that they cursed their torturers, the Church and God in the moment of their death. It is not necessary to emphasise that this is no justification of force and violence out of other than religious motives. Gandhi: "Every murder or other injury, no matter for what cause, committed or inflicted on another is a crime against humanity".[19]

When we dealt with the absolute truth claim of the Abrahamtic religions, we saw how devastating the consequences of the separation of truth and love (non-violence) were. The dispute about the truth, the hatred and discord of theologians, denominations and religions eventually brought the religious truth into bad repute, and contributed to the rise of the scientific concept of truth (True is what can be proved through an experiment, in opposition to the religious truth). What I have explained here with reference to the truth applies equally to love (*ahimsa*). Love also changes its character to the opposite as soon as the close relationship to truth is dissolved. It then turns, as we have already seen, into self-love or into an extended egotism of a courting or married couple, a family, group, nation or community with a common ideology. Gandhi says about that: "Without truth there is no love. Without truth it may be affection, as for one's country to the injury of others, or infatuation as of a young man for a girl. Love transcends all animality and is never partial".[20]

Like most Hindus and Buddhists, Gandhi, too, is convinced of the holiness of life — namely all kinds of life. He considers the commandment of *ahimsa*, the non-harming of living beings, the noblest title of glory of Hinduism. In the Judaeo-Christian culture, this teaching finds little attention, although such prominent figures as Francis of Assisi (1181/82-1226) and Albert Schweitzer taught and practised it. Schweitzer said: "Man is only ethical if he considers life as such holy, the life of the plant and the animal as well as human life, and if he dedicates himself helpfully to the life that is in distress".[21]

Schweitzer and Gandhi do, of course, also know that we human beings cannot do without the destruction of plant life, at the least, in order to scrape our living. Cultivation is inevitably connected with the killing of plant and animal life, yes; even a relaxing walk through the forest costs the life of small animals that we unintentionally tread on. In this sense, the principle: Life lives of life, applies. This does not only apply to the relationship of animal life to plant life, it also applies within plant and animal life respectively. Even idyllically looking forests or meadows are venues of a reckless fight for survival, for essential nutrients, water and light, in which the strong will win and the weak will perish.

The result of this fight for existence, lasting already for millions of years, is the miraculous world of plants and animals in its overwhelming beauty, abundance and variety. We human beings alone have the ability and obligation to step out of this natural competition and to follow the law of love and sympathy. Gandhi: "The world is full of *himsa* and nature does appear to be "red in tooth and claw". But if we bear in mind that man is higher than the brute, then is man superior to that *Nature*. If man has a divine mission to fulfil, a mission that becomes him, it is that of *ahimsa*. Standing as he does in the midst of *himsa*, he can retire into the innermost depths of his heart and declare to the world around him that his mission in this world of *himsa* is *ahimsa*, and only to the extent that he practices it does he adorn his kind. Man's nature then is not *himsa*, but *ahimsa*, for he can speak from experience, his innermost conviction, that he is not the body but *atman*, and that he may use the body only with a view to expressing the *atman*, only with a view to self-realization. And from that experience he evolves the ethics of subduing desire, anger, ignorance, malice and other passions, puts forth his best effort to achieve the end and finally attains complete success. Only when his efforts reach that consummation can he be said to have fulfilled himself, to have acted according to his nature. Conquest of one's passions, therefore, is not superhuman, but human, and observance of *ahimsa* is heroism of the highest type, with no room therein for cowardice or weakness".[22]

Although we are, as genetics proved, from the physical point of view closely related to animals, different laws apply in the human world. Schweitzer emphasises the fundamental difference between human and animal world, when he says that in nature, God manifests Himself as enigmatic, but in us human beings He manifests himself as love. There are, in a way, three ascending levels of God's revelation in the world, the inanimate nature, the animate nature and finally man, as long as he follows the eternal law that is God Himself.

If the laws that apply to society are transferred to extrahuman nature, or if the laws of extrahuman nature are transferred to society, only harm can arise from there. The lion who kills the gazelle, the bear that defends his territory, or the deer that outcompetes his rival, do not act badly, they follow their natural instinct of self-preservation and preservation of the species. The ethnologist Konrad Lorenz

(1903-1989) already proved in his book published in 1963: *On Aggression*, that the basic instinct of aggression plays a positive role in extrahuman nature because it serves the preservation of the species. That even applies to man. If it does not degenerate into destructiveness, the instinct of aggression is the root for his constructive and creative abilities, for play and sports.

On the other hand, the transfer of the principle of competition to human society, as done by social Darwinists, racists and capitalists, has a devastating effect on human living together and the relationship of man to extrahuman nature, because it leads to the reckless exploitation of man and nature. It aggravates the social differences and hence lays the ground for violence and war. The principle of competition, the fight for existence that works in such an extremely positive and creative way in nature because it generated the miraculous world of the plant and animal world, has a negative and destructive effect in the human world. Ultimately, it leads on to the complete annihilation of mankind and all higher life on Earth.

It is the privilege but also the obligation of man to realise this fight for existence, this unconditional will for life that pervades the whole of nature, and to exceed it towards a consciousness that recognises itself in everything that lives. *Tat twam asi* (that is you!) is the holy *mantra* through which man recognises the brother in the animal — also in the harmful or dangerous one — and the sister in the plant — also in the poisonous one or in the annoying "weed". No matter how strange such thoughts may seem to us modern people, characterised by Western industrial society with its ruthless exploitation of man and nature, it does in no way prove that they are wrong.

Albert Schweitzer expressed the basic life instinct, that unconditional "will to live", to which we human beings are subject as creatures of nature, too, and that we, however, can transcend by recognising it as such, by the timelessly valid words: "The immediate basic situation of our consciousness, to which we are reverted each time we want to reach an understanding of ourselves and our situation in the world, is: *I am life that wants to live amidst life that wants to live.* When I think about life, I feel obliged to respect any will for life in my environment like my own".[23] As an ethical basic principle he states: "The basic idea of good also consists in demanding to preserve, support and raise life to its highest value; and evil means to destroy and damage life and prevent it from developing".[24]

Friedrich Nietzsche (1844-1900) took the opposite position in his paper "The Antichrist": "*What is good?*" – Everything that increases in man the feeling of power, the will for power, power itself.

What is evil? — Everything that comes out of weakness.

What is happiness? — The feeling that *power is increasing*, that a resistance is being overcome.

Not contentment, but more *power*;

Not peace at all, but war,

Not virtue, but efficiency (virtue in the Renaissance style virtùe, virtue free of morality).

The weak and wayward shall perish: first sentence of *our* human kindness and one shall even help them with it.

What is more harmful than any vice? The compassion with all the wayward and weak – Christendom".[25]

Adolf Hitler (1889-1945), contemporary of Gandhi, thought, spoke and acted out of this spirit. Like Schweitzer and Gandhi, Nietzsche and Hitler also represent extreme human possibilities. Gandhi, however, is no dogmatic who proclaims absolute truths. There are situations in which compassion forces us to release the creature from its suffering. Gandhi himself reports such a case. As a faithful Hindu, he worshipped the cow as holy. He considered killing it a sin because for him, it is the symbol of the nourishing, life-giving nature. But when in the *ashram* a malformed calf was born that was non-viable and suffered indescribably, he had it poisoned in order to release the animal from its suffering. He wrote that he would not have acted differently with his own child.[26] Here we can see for the first time a situation that we will encounter several more times, namely that a situation can seem to be the opposite of what it is. The killing of a suffering non-viable creature is free of violence because it is an act of love, while in this case, failure to act, although apparently non-violent, is in truth violent.

But there are also situations in which one has to weigh up very carefully the right to live between men and animals. When monkeys, which are worshipped, like the cows, as holy in India, were threatening to destroy the harvest of the *ashram* and could not be driven away by any means, Gandhi allowed the killing of a few of them in order to scare them away and save the rest of the harvest.

Conclusion: *Ahimsa* can consequently be described as *comprehensive love, as love to God, to men and to extrahuman nature.* In the end, it is nothing else but the *reflection of God's love in us.*

Such behaviour is natural to the person who lives in community with God. It is not a merit, but just the passing on of God's love to everything that lives, like the moon that does not shine by itself but passes on to the Earth the sunlight that it receives.

THE THREE FILTERS

After having clarified what Gandhi means with truth and love (*satya* and *ahimsa*), I get back again to the three "filters": *truth, love* and *reason*, as far as things are accessible to reason. If we read the *Bible* applying these filters, we get, broadly speaking, the following image: The filters allow approximately one-third of the biblical texts to pass as elements containing revelation, another third proves to be neutral because it hands down historical events, worldly wisdom or literature, and the last third is filtered out as erroneous, immoral and unholy. Gandhi, of course, applies these filters also when reading the holy scriptures of his own religion: "I have no knowledge that the Krishna of the *Mahabharata* ever lived. My Krishna has nothing to do with any historical person. I would refuse to bow my head to the Krishna who would kill because his pride is hurt, or the Krishna whom non-Hindus portray as a dissolute youth. I believe in Krishna of my imagination as a perfect incarnation, spotless in every sense of the word, the inspirer of the *Gita* and the inspirer of the lives of millions of human beings. But if it was proved to me that the *Mahabharata* is history in the same sense that modern historical books are, that every word of the *Mahabharata* is authentic and that the Krishna of the *Mahabharata* actually did some of the acts attributed to him, even at the risk of being banished from the Hindu fold, I should not hesitate to reject that Krishna as God incarnate".[27]

ONCE AGAIN : WHO OR WHAT IS GOD?

Let us return once again to Gandhi's understanding of truth. To the question: Who or what is God?, he replies briefly and succinctly: *God is Truth* (*satya*). The linguistic root of *satya* is *sat*, which means existence, being. The sentence: God is Truth, means consequently also that God is what exists; he is the only real. The world that surrounds us is only real in so far as it is part of the eternal indestructible existence of God.

The concept of *being* is where religion and philosophy meet, because this word, provided that it means God, is in the centre of religion and, provided that it means being or existence, it is in the centre of philosophy, as far as philosophy accepts a metaphysical dimension. "Being", however, does not refer to the being that is perceptible by the senses but the unborn and imperishable, indestructible and eternal reality, that the perishable, temporal reality takes as a basis. From this we conclude: With Gandhi, as well as in Hinduism in general, *religion and philosophy do not exclude each other*, they stand side by side, not against each other.

God and only God is the absolute truth. As soon as the absolute truth enters the world of our perception, however, it becomes relative, it manifests itself in opposites that challenge us to decide: For the good and against the evil, for the truth and against the untruth, for God and against Satan or Mammon. The object of our efforts to find the truth should, however, be the absolute good and true that lies beyond the opposites of good and evil, truth and untruth. In Gandhi's words: "For me, truth is the sovereign principle, which includes numerous other principles. This truth is not only truthfulness in word, but truthfulness in thought also. And not only the relative truth of our conception, but the Absolute Truth, the Eternal Principle, that is God. There are innumerable definitions of God, because His manifestations are innumerable. They overwhelm me with wonder and awe and for a moment stun me. But I worship God as Truth only. I have not yet found Him, but I am seeking after Him. I am prepared to sacrifice the things dearest to me in pursuit of this quest. Even if the sacrifice demanded be my very life. I hope I may be prepared to give it. But as long as I have not realized this Absolute Truth, so long must I hold by the relative truth as I have conceived it. That relative truth must, meanwhile, be my beacon, my shield and buckler. Though this path is strait and narrow and sharp as the razor's edge, for me it has been the quickest and easiest. Even my Himalayan blunders have seemed trifling to me because I have kept strictly to this path. For the path has saved me from coming to grief and I have gone forward according to my light. Often in my progress I have had faint glimpses of the Absolute Truth, God, and daily the conviction is growing upon me that He alone is real and all else is unreal".[28]

REFERENCES

1. Gerhard von Rad: *Theologie des Alten Testaments*, Vol. 1, 217.
2. *Young India*, 28.8.24; CWMG, 29, 48 f.
3. *Young India*, 20.9.1928; CWMG, 43, 11.
4. *Gospel of Luke*, 15:11-32.
5. *Harijan*, 16.2.1934; CWMG, 63, 165.
6. *Harijan*, 24.2.1946; CWMG, 89, 409.
7. *Harijan*, 8.8.1946; CWMG, 91, 427 f.
8. *Young India*, 25.9.1924; CWMG, 29, 188 f.
9. *From Yeravda Mandir*, SWMG, 4, 213
10. *Young India*, 21.1.1926; CWMG, 33, 410.
11. Genesis (I Book of Mose), 1:28, as opposed to the second story of creation *Genesis*, 2:15.
12. *Young India*, 26.3.1931; CWMG, 51, 297.
13. *Harijan*, 17.4.1937; CWMG, 71, 132.
14. *Harijan*, 24.12.1938; CWMG, 74, 313.
15. *Prophet Isaiah*, 6:9 f, see also *Gospel according to St Matthew*, 13:14; *Gospel of John*, 12:39-41; *Acts of the Apostles*, 28:25-27; *Letters to the Romans*, 9:14-18; 11:7-10:25-27.
16. *Young India*, 21.1.1926; CWMG, 33, 410.
17. *Young India*, 4.6.1925; CWMG, 31, 381.
18. "My Dear Child". Letters from M.K. Gandhi to Esther Faering, *Navajivan*, Ahmedabad, 1956, 53 f.
19. *Harijan*, 20.7.1935; CWMG, 67, 263.
20. The Way to God, *Selected Writings from Mahatma Gandhi*, 29.
21. Albert Schweitzer: *Worte des Lebens*, Freiburg, 71.
22. *Young India*, 24.6.1926; CWMG, 35, 359.
23. Albert Schweitzer: *Die Ehrfurcht vor dem Leben*, München, 1982, 111.
24. *Ibid.*
25. Friedrich Nietzsche: *Der Antichrist. Werke*, Bd. 5, Hg. von A. Bäumler, 192.
26. *Gandhi: Freiheit ohne Gewalt*, Köln, 1968, 156.
27. *Young India*, 1.10.1925; CWMG, 33, 32.
28. *Autobiography*, SWMG, 1, xxi.

7
Truth is God

Truth is hard as adamant and tender as a blossom.

—Mahatma Gandhi

The sentence "Truth is God" seems to be, on first sight, the simple reversal of the sentence "God is Truth". But it is not like that for Gandhi: "If it is possible for the human tongue to give the fullest description of God, for myself I have come to the conclusion that God is Truth. But two years ago I went a step further and said Truth is God. You will see the fine distinction between the two statements: God is Truth and Truth is God. And that conclusion I came to after a continuous, relentless search after Truth, which began so many years ago. I found that the nearest approach to Truth is through love. But I found also that love has many meanings, in the English language at least, and human love in the sense of passion becomes a degrading thing also. I found too that love in the sense of *ahimsa* and non-violence has only limited number of votaries in the world. And as I made progress in my search, I made no dispute with 'God is love'. It is very difficult to understand 'God is love' (because of a variety of meanings of love) but I never found a double meaning in connection with Truth and not even atheists have denied the necessity or power of Truth. Not only so. In their passion for discovering Truth, they have not hesitated even to deny the very existence of God — from their own point of view rightly. And it was because of their reasoning that I saw that I was not going to say 'God is Truth', but 'Truth is God' ".[1]

It seems more than doubtful to me, whether Gandhi, by claiming that he found only one meaning of the word truth, solves the problem that all kinds of things, frequently contradicting each other, are regarded as the truth. May be he rather thinks that the high esteem of truth among atheists and agnostics creates a formal basis upon which a consensual clarification of the word truth can be attempted. In this context, he repeatedly mentions the English freethinker and humanistic atheist Charles Bradlaugh (1833-1891), whom he admired and at whose funeral in 1891 he was present while being a law student in London. He writes: "Therefore, I recall the name of Charles Bradlaugh — a great Englishman who lived 50 years ago. He delighted to call himself an atheist. But knowing as I do something of his life, I never considered him an atheist. I would call him a god-fearing man although he would reject the claim and I know his face would redden. I would say: No Mr. Bradlaugh, you are a truth-fearing man, and also a God-fearing man, and I would disarm his criticisms by saying "Truth is God" as I have disarmed criticisms of many a young man".[2]

Gandhi clearly realises that it is not rare that the crimes and human rights violations committed in the name of God are the reason why people become atheists. "Bradlaugh's denial of God was a denial of Him as He was known to Bradlaugh to have been described. His was an eloquent and indignant protest against the then current theology and the terrible contrast between precept and practice."[3]

The same can be said about the atheistic religions of Buddhism and Jainism. In 1927, he writes about Gautama Buddha in his magazine *Young India*: "I have heard it contended times without number and I have read in books also, claiming to express the spirit of Buddhism, that Buddha did not believe in God. In my humble opinion such a belief contradicts the very central fact of Buddha's teaching. In my humble opinion the confusion has arisen over his rejection, and just rejection, of all the base things that passed in his generation under the name of God. He undoubtedly rejected the notion that a being called God was actuated by malice, could repent of his actions, and like the kings of the earth could possibly be open to temptations and bribes and could possibly have favourites.

His whole soul rose in mighty indignation against the belief that a being called God required for His satisfaction the living blood of animals in order that he might be pleased — animals who were his own creation. He, therefore, reinstated God in the right place and dethroned the usurper who for the time being seemed to occupy that White Throne. He emphasised and redeclared the eternal and unalterable existence of the moral government of this universe. He unhesitatingly said that the law was God Himself."[4]

Gandhi considers Gautama Buddha, who, like Gandhi, was Indian and lived among Indians, a great reformer of Hinduism whose objective it was to cleanse Hinduism of all kinds of distortions and overgrowths that had appeared over the centuries. He, therefore, disagrees with the widespread definition of the term *Nirvana*: "*Nirvana* is undoubtedly not utter extinction. So far as I have been able to understand the central fact of Buddha's life, *nirvana* is utter extinction of all that is base in us, all that is vicious in us, all that is corrupt and corruptible in us. *Nirvana* is not like the black, dead peace of the grave, but the living peace, the living happiness of a soul which is conscious of itself, and conscious of having found its own abode in the heart of the Eternal".[5]

I cannot judge if Gandhi's interpretation of Gautama Buddha was correct, or if he, what was not rare in him, processed it creatively. If, with the formula "Truth is God", he includes the followers of atheistic religions and of atheistic Humanism in the circle of truth seekers, it would yet be wrong to conclude from there a general tolerance towards any philosophy whatsoever. He was decidedly opposed to any form of injustice, no matter if it was justified religiously or secularly. A person who inflicts injustice and violence upon other people in the name of God has, in his opinion, no religion, while another person, who denies the existence of God, but who fights for justice and peace, democracy and human rights, is religious.

GOD AND SATAN

There are, as I tried to demonstrate, two types of good, one that is defined by its opposite, evil, and one that is free of all kinds of opposites. Even if the latter is not perceptible by our senses, it exists after all, or more precisely, it alone exists.

The same can be said about the antagonism of God and Satan. There are also two concepts of God here, one that is defined by its opposite, Satan, and one that is free of all kinds of opposites. The first one makes God an idol, the latter comes as close to him as human thinking possibly can. God has no opponent. He alone exists. Only against this background, the following quotations from Gandhi's writings become clear: "Why is there evil in the world, is a difficult question to answer. I can only give what I may call a villager's answer. If there is good there must also be evil, just as where there is light there is also darkness, but it is true only so far as we human mortals are concerned. Before God there is nothing good, nothing evil. We poor villagers may talk of His dispensation in human terms, but our language is not God's".[6]

Gandhi is aware of the difficulty of, on the one hand, admitting the reality of evil and its demonical power in the world, but, on the other hand, of considering it as futile as soon as we approach the sphere in which the opposites coincide. If one asks opposing parties about what is good and what is evil, one usually gets the simple answer: We are good, the others are bad. If one asks the respective other opposing party, one gets the same answer with the one difference that the good are now the evil and *vice versa*. The distinction between good and evil, friends and foes is significant in violently decided conflicts. Religious fundamentalists extend this dichotomy into the metaphysical. They understand world history as a history of salvation, as a fight between the powers of good and evil, God and Satan. In this fight, Satan is defeated by God and destroyed, or he is eternally tormented in hell. Man is forced to decide in favour of God or Satan. If he decides in favour of God, he chooses eternal life, if he decides in favour of Satan, he shares Satan's fate.

Messianic apocalypticists are convinced that apocalypse is imminent. They interpret the present political events in the light of biblical prophecies. According to that, the earthly history is expression of a cosmic war between good and evil, light and darkness, God and Satan. The present world, as they believe, is so hopelessly corrupt that a judgement of God is imminent. They are convinced, as they consider themselves good and orthodox, that they will be spared from the outburst of the eschatological catastrophe as predicted in the *Bible*, as soon as Jesus appears as the eschatological Messiah strutting along on top of the clouds. Their key witness is the Apostle Paul who wrote in the letter to the Thessalonians: "We tell you this directly from the Lord: We who are still living when the Lord returns will not meet him ahead of those who have died. For the Lord himself will come down from heaven with a commanding shout, with the voice of the archangel,* and with the trumpet call of God. First, the Christians who have died will rise from their graves. Then, together with them, we who are still

* Archangels are high ranking angels. In the Bible there is only one archangel metioned – Michael. In Islam the names of the four archangels are Azrael, Israfil, Dschibril, Mikaal.

alive and remain on the earth will be caught up in the clouds to meet the Lord in the air. Then we will be with the Lord forever".[7]

The Revelation of John is also very popular among the Christian apocalyticists because as the last scripture of the *Bible* it opens the view into the future of human history. In the Islamic culture, similar concepts are widespread, with the peculiarity that the Muslims who are killed in the holy war against the infidels are immediately sent to paradise where they will endlessly enjoy sensual pleasures. Suicide assassins are considered by many (not by all!) Muslims also are holy warriors because they sacrifice their life to the propagation of Islam. The term martyr should in my opinion remain reserved to those who sacrifice their life for their conviction but not to people who are ready to die by killing others. The Islamic apocalypticists refer to the *Koran* and the *Hadith* (sayings of the Prophet). Their Messiah carries the name *Mehdi* or *Isa* (Arabic form of Jesus) respectively. For them, Palestine is the venue of the eschatological events, as it is for the Jewish and Christian apocalypticists, only from an opposite point of view.

The Jewish, Christian and Muslim apocalypticists can look back to a long tradition of eschatological prophecies. The Viennese writer and philosopher Günther Anders (1902-1992) points out rightly that primarily peoples threatened by extinction developed apocalyptic concepts of the end time, like for example the people of Israel, or persecuted minorities like the Christians of the first centuries after Christ or the Shiites in Islam: "Expectations of apocalypse do not simply appear in any historical situation and neither in any social group. Every 'eschatological sociology' would show that there were never expectations of apocalypse that were caused by ruling powers. Probably not even those, which would have been handed down intact by ruling powers. One, who rules, insists on one's own continuance and with that on the continuance of the world. Only the one who 'has reached the end' thinks about the end, hopes for the end, and consoles himself with the end. In positive words: Concepts of apocalypse always owe their existence to groups that are condemned to impotence by an almost absolute, or at the least by an extremely absolutistic pressure of a worldly power. Only these need. the idea of the end because with its help they could overcome the degradation that they had to suffer in this world. And this by outbidding the absolute violence that they were subjected to with an even 'more absolute one', that being the violence of the absolute end before which every worldly violence had to vanish".[8]

Günther Anders wonders at the absence of an apocalyptic consciousness in the post-war era. He states a downright "apocalypse blindness" in the fifties, sixties and seventies, even an "apocalypse numbness",[9] because there was, with a few exceptions, no awareness of the atomic threat to human existence, and when there was awareness, it was without consequences. Now-a-days he would not wonder any more. On the contrary, many things suggest that the conscious or inconscious perception of threat to human existence is one of the main causes of the expectations of the end time that are spreading everywhere. As a sensitised Jew due to the Holocaust of the Jews and the atomic bombings of Hiroshima and Nagasaki, Anders recognised very early the epochal significance of the year 1945. Since then, so his matter-of-fact statement, we live in the *end time*, no matter how short or long it may still last. As the knowledge of the making of these weapons cannot be reversed, as the probability of their abolition sinks with every year, as the process of their spreading goes on and as the crises of modern industrial society add up to one mega-crisis rather exponentially, we must expect a massive use of atomic weapons earlier or later that can mean the destruction of all higher forms of life on Earth.

For the atheistic humanist Anders, however, at the end of the days no Messiah will strut along on top of the clouds in order to save those who believe in him. It is rather a blue planet, coated in radioactive clouds, still circling around the Sun. Anders felt like the lone voice in the wilderness. What he did not know, was that after the end of the Cold War, an escape into religious expectations of the end time would begin. Instead of doing all they can do to fight against the atomic danger, many people seek refuge in flight from reality into religious eschatological fantasies. The political influence of the messianic-apocalyptic movements is huge in the Abrahamic religions, and it will go on increasing in all likelihood. According to a survey of TIME/CNN from the year 2002, 59 per cent of the US Americans are convinced of living in the end time. The "Christian right" in the USA has between 50 and 60 million votes at their disposal, and can, therefore, have a decisive effect on the presidential elections. The Presidents Ronald Reagan and George W. Bush were close to these movements as we can gather from Reagan's comments about the Soviet Empire as "empire of evil" and from Bush's comments about Iraq, Iran and North Korea as "axis of evil".

Both Presidents considered and consider themselves as 'reborn

Christians'. The same can be said about the messianic apocalypticists in Israel and in the Jewish Diaspora, which determine the politics of Israel towards Palestinians significantly. And the same is true for the Islamist currents in the countries of Islam, namely Iran. One tends to shrug off such ideas as abnormal delusions of sectarians. Their widespread and their militancy, however, give cause for concern. The political influence of these movements in the Abrahamic religions can hardly be overestimated because they escalate in a reciprocal enemy image like in the Cold War. In the course of intensifying conflicts over resources, markets and transport routes, they can prepare the path for a "war of religions" and trigger doomsday in the form of a self-fulfilling prophecy.

The news that the bloody end time battle in which good will destroy evil, and God will finally destroy Satan or deliver him to eternal damnation will not take place, will not make apocalypticists of all shades abandon their faith. Their arguments will be: "It is in the *Bible*! Do you want to say that the *Bible* lies, that God lies"? Who, from his own experience, knows political delusions like the one of the Nazi's Thousand-Years Empire of the Teutons or the one of the Marxists' classless society as the final result of historio-intrinsic dialectics, knows about the dangerousness of such Utopias. They can definitely lead to a war of cultures, a war of religions that would end with the demise of all higher forms of life on earth. Although both parties in this eschatological battle are convinced that they represent good, they do not realise that evil has long taken possession of them. No matter how noble their declared objectives may be, be it the propagation of freedom, democracy and human rights, of peace and socialism or the erection of the kingdom of God on Earth, they are perverted beyond recognition as soon as they are to be put into practice by force, violence and war.

Result: Apocalyptic messianism is based on the idea of the angry, revenging, punishing, judging and annihilating God, the God who, at the end of days, destroys the bad and evil or sentences them to eternal agony, and who saves the good and rewards them with eternal bliss. In view of such delusions, one is tempted to agree with Sigmund Freud's (1856-1939) diagnosis of religion as a "compulsion neurosis". The same is true for the concept of God in which God appears as the antagonist of Satan. This idea has to be overcome in favour of an image of God that has no opposite.

WAS GANDHI A MYSTIC?

My answer is: Yes, although the word is not found in his texts. At least, he never declared himself a mystic, to my knowledge. It depends also in this case, as so often, on how we define mysticism. The word mysticism comes from the Greek verb *myein* = close, occlude. The mystic occludes himself from the world and its bustle. He closes his eyes, ears, mouth and enters the path inwards. This path, also described as meditation or immersion, opens a new world to him: The experience of unity of all kind of being in the sense of *Advaita* that is described as God, deity, emptiness, *Brahman*, *Atman* or *Nirvana*. Among the few things of Gandhi's personal belongings are the "three wise monkeys" of which one closes his eyes, one his ears and one his mouth. From this point of view, Gandhi was definitely a mystic. He described that immersion into the eternal existence of Truth or God with the wonderful parable of the water drop that falls into the ocean and merges therein.

"Our existence as embodied beings is purely momentary; what are a hundred years in eternity? But if we shatter the chains of egotism, and melt into the ocean of humanity, we share its dignity. To feel that we are something is to set up a barrier between God and ourselves; to cease feeling that we are something is to become one with God. A drop in the ocean partakes of the greatness of its parent, although it is unconscious of it. But it is dried up, as soon as it enters upon an existence independent of the ocean. We do not exaggerate, when we say that life on earth is a mere bubble".[10] "The sum total of all that lives is God. We may not be God but we are of God — even as a little drop of water is of the ocean. Imagine it torn away from the ocean and flung millions of miles away. It becomes helpless torn from its surroundings and cannot feel the might and majesty of the ocean but if someone could point out to it that it is of the ocean, its faith would revive, it would dance with joy and the whole of the might and majesty of the ocean would be reflected in it".[11]

Mysticism becomes problematic when the path inwards turns into a mere reaction to the "path outwards", the addiction to the material world. This is quite frequent in Hinduism with its ideal of *sanyasa*. As much as there is a turn inwards, at the end of which there is the mystical experience of unity with all kinds of existence, there should also be, at the end of this path, a turn and a path outwards, at the end of which the power of Truth, the power of God in the world, becomes effective.

One could also say: At the end of this path, God will be visible and perceptible in the world in the mystic and through the mystic. Both, the path inwards and the path outwards, belong together, according to Gandhi's conviction. They strengthen each other mutually.

KARMA AND REINCARNATION

Being a Hindu, Gandhi grew up with the doctrine of *karma* and reincarnation as naturally as a Christian grows up with the idea of Heaven, in which the redeemed enjoy eternal bliss, and Hell, where the damned are tortured for evermore. The Sanskrit word *karma* literally means doing. It refers to the law of justice according to which good is repaid with good and evil with evil. Through our good and bad thoughts, words and actions, within the narrow frame that disposition and people around us leave to our free will, we form our future fate, and that not only in this world but also in the world of soul and spirit, which we enter, according to Hindus and Buddhists, after our death, in order to eventually reincarnate. Who accumulates positive *karma* will reincarnate in a higher status, which accumulates negative *karma*, will reincarnate in a lower status. That means that our good and evil thoughts, feelings, words and actions tie us to this world. They keep us in the ever-revolving wheel of birth, death and rebirth. This is why in Hinduism and Buddhism, the doctrine of *karma* and reincarnation is not considered a blessing but a curse. Because the ever-revolving wheel of birth, death and rebirth, of ascent due to good and descent due to bad *karma* does not know salvation as such. Man only finds liberation, salvation (*moksha*) through renunciation; renunciation not only of his bad but also of his good *karma*. If he achieves that, he enters God (Hinduism) or *Nirvana* (Buddhism). That is why *Bhagavad Gita* teaches the sacrifice of the "fruits of action", which means of the enjoyment of success.

It is, therefore, our affections and repulsions, our (sensual) love and our hatred, our fear and our greed that are attracted by the material world with, so to speak, magnetic force and once again captivated in a body. According to the teachings of Buddha, all existence is the consequence of a desire. In the moment of death, the body stops existing, the soul, however, that is a part of the world soul, and the spirit, that is a part of the world spirit, continue living and growing until they re-enter a body without the person remembering consciously his past incarnations.

The doctrine of *karma* and reincarnation is considered a characteristic of Eastern religions. It can, however, also be found in natural religions and in the gnostically influenced Christendom, for example in the *Gospel of John*. It describes ultimately nothing else but a principle of revenge extended into the metaphysical. The teaching of *karma* can encourage a bigoted egotism. It can make blind for the suffering and distress of other people because it gives a simple explanation for that: Suffering, distress and humiliation are the result of former failings. If the sufferer puts up with his fate patiently, he accumulates good *karma* and will incarnate in a higher status, a higher caste in his next life. The doctrine of *karma* has consequently a very concrete social and political impact. It makes the loving and helping devotion to the neighbour difficult because his fate is his own fault. It also makes the rebellion against intolerable circumstances difficult because then, bad *karma* would increase. It consequently stabilises an unjust social system.

It was the great reformer of Hinduism, Gautama Buddha, who revolted against this aspect in Hinduism and who questioned the rigid caste system in principle. According to his teachings, the path to salvation is open to every person, as soon as he or she decides to step on the path of renunciation, of non-adherence, that leads to enlightenment (Buddha), to the right life (*dharma*) and to the religious community (*sangha*). Negligence towards the fate of the neighbour is replaced by mindfulness towards him, and sympathy with everything that lives because, according to Buddhist teaching, life is basically suffering and compassion.

Gandhi as a Hindu understood the thought of freeing oneself from *karma* and reincarnation with the *Bhagavad Gita* as abandonment of the "fruits of action" (success). Only when our thinking and feeling, our talking and acting is full of the spirit of Truth (*satya*) and Love (*ahimsa*), meaning being full of the spirit of God, we will be free of the bonds to the world. The process of salvation from the ever-revolving wheel of birth, death and rebirth begins in the moment we invalidate the principle of revenge in good and evil by retaliating evil with good, in order to overcome it this way. That happens by resisting evil non-violently, or by feeling compassion for the suffering of other people while trying to relieve it. "The human body is meant solely for service, never for indulgence. The secret of happy life lies in renunciation. Renunciation is life. Indulgence spells death. Therefore everyone has a right and should desire to live 125 years *while performing service without an eye on result.* Such life must be wholly and solely dedicated to service. Renunciation made for the same of such service is an ineffable joy of which none can deprive one, because that nectar springs from within and sustains life. In this there can be no room for worry or impatience. Without this joy long life is impossible and would not be worthwhile even if possible."[12] "What I want to achieve, — what I have been striving and pining to achieve these thirty years, — is self-realisation, to see God face to face, to attain *moksha.* I live and move and have my being in pursuit of this goal. All that I do by way of speaking and writing, and all my ventures in the political field, are directed to this same end".[13]

REFERENCES

1. *Young India*, 31.12.1931; CWMG, 54, 268.
2. *Ibid.*, 269.
3. *Young India*, 5.3.1925; CWMG, 30, 334.
4. *Young India*, 24.11.1927; CWMG, 40, 370.
5. *Ibid.*, 371.
6. *Harijan*, 7.9.1935; CWMG, 67, 392.
7. *First Letter (of Paul) to the Thessalonikians*, 4:15-17.
8. Günther Anders: *Die atomare Drohung*, München, 1983, 110 f.
9. *Ibid.*, IX.
10. *From Yeravda Mandir,* SWMG 4, 246.
11. *Harijan*, 3.6.1939; CWMG, 75, 216.
12. *Harijan*, 24.2.46; CWMG, 89, 385.
13. *Autobiography;* CWMG, 44, 90.

8
Satyagraha

In the application of satyagraha I discovered in the earliest stages that pursuit of truth did not admit of violence being inflicted on one's opponent, but that he must be weaned from error by patience and sympathy. For what appears to be truth to the one may appear to be error to the other. And patience means self-suffering. So the doctrine came to mean vindication of truth, not by infliction of suffering on the opponent, but one's own self.

—Mahatma Gandhi

This is not the place to go into Gandhi's doctrine and practice of satyagraha in detail. It shall only be mentioned in as far as it is absolutely necessary for the understanding of his religion and the practical consequences that he deduces from there.

Sat > *Satya* > *Satyagraha* is not the only but one of the most important cascades of terms through which Gandhi brings Heaven to Earth so to speak. What does he mean by *satyagraha*? *Satyagraha* literally means: *Holding on to the* truth, in the sense of *power of truth, love or soul*, in contrast to physical strength. And as for Gandhi, truth is synonymous with God, *satyagraha* means at the same time the *power of God* that acts in us and through us. It is the power that enables us to pay back evil with good, hatred with love and violence with non-violence, and thus overcome it:

"It has been my invariable experience that good evokes good, evil–evil; and that, therefore, if the evil does not receive the corresponding response, it ceases to act, dies of want of nutrition. Evil can only live upon itself. Sages of old, knowing this law, instead of returning evil for evil, deliberately returned good for evil and killed it. Evil lives nevertheless, because many have not taken advantage of the discovery, though the law underlying it acts with scientific precision. We are too lazy to work out in terms of the law the problems that face us and, therefore, fancy that we are too weak to act up to it. The fact is, that the moment the truth of the law is realised, nothing is so easy as to return good for evil. It is the one quality that distinguishes man from the brute. It is man's natural law not to retaliate. Though we have the human form, we are not truly human till we have fully realised the truth of the law and acted up to it. The law admits of no escape".[1]

Jesus of Nazareth speaks of exactly this power when he replies to Petrus' question "How many times do I have to forgive my brother when he sins against me? Seven times?" with: "Not seven times but seventy seven times".[2] Seventy seven is a poetical paraphrase for always. Out of our own initiative, we are incapable of that. Each of us can recognise that easily in a self-experiment. It may be acceptable to pay back evil with good once. Lucky is the one who manages twice in a row. But three times is almost impossible, let alone another time. For Gandhi, it is obvious that *satyagraha* is not possible without religion: "He or she must have a living faith in non-violence. This is impossible without a living faith in God. A non-violent man can do nothing save by the power and grace of God. Without it he won't have the courage to die without anger, without fear and without retaliation. Such courage comes from the belief that God sits in the hearts of all and that there should be no fear in the presence of God. The knowledge of the omnipresence of God also means respect for the lives of even those who may be called opponents or goondas".[3]

In other words, *satyagraha* is the ability (not only the desire) to accept violence without *retaliating* with hatred or revenge, but also without *receding,* in order to overcome it this way. The second half of the sentence is important because the underlying idea is that violence, even where it is applied with the intention of defending oneself against a wrongful attack or to overcome unfair social circumstances, misses its objective because it only aggravates the problem that it wants to solve. It proves to be an inept form of conflict solution as long as the objective is a permanent solution of the conflict in the interest of all parties. A *satyagrahi* (non-violent fighter) consequently discards the weapon, if he has one, as useless.

Satyagraha, that cannot be stressed enough, is more than a mere renunciation of the use of violence. It is the use of a *positive, active, regenerating and liberating*, and even a *creative and healing* power. Ultimately it includes a consciously accepted suffering without submitting to the will of the aggressor: "In 1920, I became a rebel.

Since then the conviction has been growing upon me, that things of fundamental importance to the people are not secured by reason alone, but have to be purchased with their suffering. Suffering is the law of human beings; war is the law of the jungle. But suffering is infinitely more powerful than the law of the jungle for converting the opponent and opening his ears, which are otherwise shut, to the voice of reason. Nobody has probably drawn up more petitions or espoused more forlorn causes than I, and I have come to this fundamental conclusion that, if you want something really important to be done, you must not merely satisfy the reason, you must move the heart also. The appeal of reason is more to the head, but the penetration of the heart comes from suffering. It opens up the inner understanding in man. Suffering is the badge of the human race, not the sword".[4]

One can also describe *satyagraha* as an antidote that eliminates the poison of violence that entered our personal and social relationships and that eliminates it, while counter violence only increases it. Gandhi also describes *satyagraha* as *non-violence of the strong* in contrast to *non-violence of the weak.* With *non-violence of the strong*, he means a fundamental or strategic renunciation of violence based on the understanding that violence is an inept form of conflict solution provided that the conflict shall be solved in everyone's interest. With *non-violence of the weak*, he means a pragmatic or tactical renunciation of force, be it because the opponent is vastly superior, because no weapons are available or violent resistance seems inappropriate due to other reasons. This form of resistance is frequently also called passive resistance. In case of massive suppression, this form of resistance is either abandoned or is converted into violent resistance.

Satyagraha or truth force is to Gandhi's belief in a universal method of carrying out conflicts that means it is applicable on all social levels beginning with personal conflicts that each of us experiences, through local, regional, national, international and eventually global conflicts. It must, however, be learned and practised at first on the personal level, in the same way as one does not begin the construction of a house with the roof but with the foundation.

The universal character of non-violence is disputed by many people with the argument that a non-violent resistance is useless against a dictator or even a Hitler, that it is suicidal. Gandhi disagrees firmly with this statement. For him, it is almost a kind of natural law: In order to overcome a given amount of violence, an equal amount of truth force is necessary, just as a given quantity of acid can be neutralised through an equal quantity of lye. Where there is little violence, little non-violence is needed, where there is much violence, much non-violence is needed, and where there is very much violence, also very much non-violence is needed in order to overcome and so to speak eliminate it. That means specifically, many *satyagrahis* must be ready to accept disadvantages and punishment, in some cases even suffering and death, in order to overcome a dictatorship or a totalitarian regime.

As a contemporary of Hitler, Gandhi already had to deal with the critical question if truth force towards a Hitler, for example in the issue of the persecution of Jews, was not doomed to fail *a priori*. He admits: "It is highly probable that . . . . . a Jewish Gandhi in Germany, should one arise, could function for about five minutes and would be promptly taken to the guillotine. But that will not disprove my case or shake my belief in the efficacy of *ahimsa*. I can conceive the necessity of the immolation of hundreds, if not thousands, to appease the hunger of dictators who have no belief in *ahimsa*. Indeed the maxim is that *ahimsa* is the most efficacious in front of the greatest *himsa*. Its quality is really tested only in such cases. Sufferers need not see the result during their lifetime. They must have faith that if their cult survives, the result is a certainty. The method of violence gives no greater guarantee than that of non-violence. It gives infinitely less. For the faith of the votary of *ahimsa* is lacking. The method of violence gives no greater guarantee than that of non-violence. It gives infinitely less".[5]

Non-violent resistance against a dictatorship or a totalitarian regime comes at a price. But nobody should be under the illusion that a violent resistance against them is possible without suffering and victims. On the contrary, they are incomparably much bigger because violent conflicts tend to escalate. Thereafter it is necessary to consider that both belligerent parties tend to sink morally deeper and deeper in the progress of the conflict, while in a non-violent conflict, they rise morally. For Gandhi, non-violence is not only preferable to violence as a means of conflict resolution; it is rather the only suitable means, given that it is about solving the conflict in the interest of all parties.

If non-violent resistance against Hitler would have been successful and at what price, we do not know because there was none, except for small, however promising attempts. What there was, however, is a war against the 'Axis Powers' Germany, Italy and Japan. It cost the lives of at least fifty million people, not to mention the physical and psychological damage, the material damage, the waste of resources and environmental destruction. And what was the result? Even though the Allies did achieve victory against their opponents, but at what price? Apart from the costs already mentioned, the World Wars fostered the military technical development like in a greenhouse; they were jointly responsible for the absurd armament race of the Cold War and prepared the stage for the Third World War, which, being an atomic war will be the final element in the chain of World Wars. Looked at it in this light any attempt to fight war by war ends in complete disaster. Gandhi was right when he accused the Allies of *out hitlering* Hitler, meaning that they outbid Hitler's violence by even greater violence: "If Britain seeks justice, she must appear before the imperial court of God with clean hands. She will not defend liberty and democracy by following totalitarian methods so far as war is concerned. She will not be able to retrace her steps after outhitlering Hitler in war. The last war is a resounding lesson. Her victory, if attained, will be a snare and a delusion. I know mine is a voice in the wilderness. But it will some day ring true. If liberty and democracy are to be truly saved, they will only be by non-violent resistance no less brave, no less glorious, than violent resistance. And it will be infinitely braver and more glorious because it will give life without taking any".[6]

Gandhi's belief in the power of the truth force was unlimited: "Non-violence is the greatest force at the disposal of mankind. It is mightier than the mightiest weapon of destruction devised by the ingenuity of man. Destruction is not the law of the humans. Man lives freely only by his readiness to die, if need be, at the hands of his brother, never by killing him. Every murder or other injury, no matter for what cause, committed or inflicted on another is a crime against humanity".[7]

Nevertheless, that did not negate his realism. It may sound trivial, but without soldiers, weapons, organisation, logistics and money, no war can be fought. The same can be said for the non-violent fight. Without *satyagrahis*, organisation and without money, a non-violent fight is not viable. As in the European states of the twentieth century, there was no non-violent army, not even the knowledge how to create one, there was no alternative to the armed fight. That is, however, as anyone can easily see no argument against non-violence as a method of conflict solution. On the contrary, it is the most powerful argument in favour of beginning as soon as possible with the setup of an organisation and the training of non-violent fighters. European pacifism has restricted itself basically to the no to war and military service. That has little to do with non-violence in the sense of Gandhi, because his concern is the development and application of non-violent actions as a *constructive alternative* to violence as a means of conflict solution. The journey from a pacifist to a *satyagrahi* (non-violent fighter) is, therefore, not shorter than the journey from a soldier to a *satyagrahi*. The non-violent fighter combines the positive characteristics of the pacifist and the soldier and avoids their negative ones.

Gandhi's argument that non-violent action is a universal method of conflict solution does not mean that it is unlimitedly applicable. It has definitely its limits, but they lie quite somewhere else than generally expected. It is, for example, completely inappropriate for acquiring property or power or for conquering foreign markets and countries or for safeguarding natural resources and transportation routes. Who wants to reach these goals, has to make use of direct or indirect violence. On the other hand, violence is the most inappropriate means to fight for or to defend peace, freedom, social justice, democracy and human rights. Such goals can eventually only be reached through non-violent and peaceful means. There is consequently an inseparable correlation between means and purpose, way and goal. They must coincide if the purpose shall be fulfilled, the goal shall be accomplished. We consequently must choose what we really want. *The means to be applied inevitably result from the intended goals.* Everything else is deceit and self-deceit. Nowhere else there is of course as much lying and cheating — even lying and cheating to oneself — as in this field.

A second limitation of the truth force consists in the fact that it requires a long and intensive training that covers and reforms the whole person. We Central Europeans all grew up in a social environment that is more or less saturated with violence and we have internalised the structures of violence of our surroundings. The first and most important task is, therefore, to recognise our share of the structures of violence of this world and to go through a process of purification in order to be released from this violence. Admittedly, people who have become non-violent in this sense are extremely rare. We can learn from Gandhi also in this regard. He understood his *ashram* as a training centre for non-violent fighters and, therefore, called it *Satyagraha-Ashram*. It never included more than a few dozens of people, which is only an extremely small part of the Indian people. If Gandhi had waited until he had an army of well-trained non-violent fighters at his disposal in order to start the fight against the British colonial rule, he would never have got a chance. He was, therefore, forced to compromise and initiate a mass campaign that was formed by a *satyagrahi* leadership and followers who renounced violence only for tactical reasons. The shortcoming of a campaign with such a mixed group of participants is obvious. As there are, in most cases, no suitable successors to be found after the death of non-violent leaders, much of what was achieved under their leadership gets lost. That was the case with Gandhi in South Africa and later in India, and also with Martin Luther King in the USA.

Does that mean that it is better to submit oneself to an aggressor than to offer non-violent resistance? Gandhi was not of this opinion. Violent resistance against injustice and violence is, of course, preferable to a cowardly submission to the aggressor. Gandhi distinguished different steps of development on the way to a non-violent fighter, because obviously, a *satyagrahi* does not fall into one's lap. The lowest level is the cowardly escape or looking the other way while being witness of acts of violence. The first step is the violent resistance against injustice and violence. The second is the non-violent or passive resistance and the third, finally, the non-violent action. "My non-violence does not admit of running away from danger and leaving dear ones unprotected. Between violence and cowardly flight, I can only prefer violence to cowardice. I can no more preach non-violence to a coward than I can tempt a blind man to enjoy healthy scenes. Non-violence is the summit of bravery. And in my own experience, I have had no difficulty in demonstrating to men trained in the school of violence the superiority of non-violence. As a coward, which I was for years, I harboured violence. I began to prize non-violence only when I began to shed cowardice".[8]

Who proceeds from cowardice to non-violent resistance, thus takes a step in the right direction. But he should not stop there. Gandhi says that he himself graduated along these steps. That is why, what not many know, he took part in war several times, although not carrying a weapon but as a paramedic, leader of an Indian ambulance corps or as a promoter of Indian recruits for the British army.

The argument that violence can never be overcome through violence or be kept permanently within bounds through the threat of violence is occasionally contradicted by referring to German history. That is as a matter of fact a strong argument. It says: Although Germany owes its national unity to the war of 1870/71, from which almost inevitably resulted the First and Second World War with their terrible orgies of violence and crimes, post-war Germany evolved into a state that appears to be peaceful both inwardly as well as outwardly. That is unfortunately only half the story. The whole story is that the two most aggressive and expansive powers of the twentieth century, Germany and Japan, proved to be docile students of the Western powers. Instead of conquering foreign countries and subjugating foreign peoples, they took up conquering foreign markets and increasing their wealth by 'peaceful' means. The consequences are basically the same but one does not see them, and, what is more important, they are not disapproved by the "international community", but ignored: It is the heaps of corpses of the famished, the perished of malnourishment and avoidable diseases instead of heaps of corpses of the slain.

It is beyond dispute that the world economy system produces wealth and abundance on the one hand and poverty and shortage on the other hand. That is not changed by the rise of the emerging nations China and India because their astonishing economic growth only refers to relatively small sectors of their national economies. In the end, it is only a transfer of the effects of industrialisation that now do not only affect the countries of the Third World any more, but that also take hold of the old industrial countries in the form of unemployment and relative pauperisation. Germany and Japan now-a-days belong to the pack of wolves with whom they fought fierce battles for world domination in the twentieth century. They have at present been replaced by China and India.

I insist, violence does not solve any conflicts but produces new and worse ones. That this is not obvious is due to their characteristic of quasi passing from one state of matter into another, and, in doing so, of apparently being able to disappear. Just as ice that turns into water, or water that turns into steam apparently disappears, although it continues to exist as an oxygen-hydrogen compound, violence can transform from a solid "state of matter" into a liquid and finally into a gaseous one and *vice versa*. The Norwegian peace researcher Johan Galtung introduced the term *structural* violence for the "solid" state of matter, the term *personal* violence for the "liquid" state, and the term *cultural* violence for the "sublime" one. With structural violence, he means the violence that solidified, so to say, in the property and power relations, with personal violence he means the visible forms of violence in the form of the use of physical violence or use of weapons, with cultural violence he finally means the sublime forms of mental use of violence in the shape of ideologies that justify or glorify violence like racism, fascism, national socialism, communism, fundamentalism, etc. When a country is conquered and a people is subjugated and exploited, personal violence changes into a structural one. If the subjugated people decide to insurrect against the oppressors, the structural violence changes again into a personal one. Likewise, cultural violence can give reasons of justification for personal and structural violence. There is consequently not only an individual *karma* but also a collective one, even *karma* of mankind.

In my opinion, which cannot be found in this form with Gandhi, according to my knowledge, each act of violence, no matter if of aggression or defence, adds new violence to the Himalaya-high mountains of violence that have been accumulated throughout the course of the millenniums by humanity, while each *satyagraha* action takes away a stone, may be even a rock of these mountains. With this, I do not want to argue that it is indifferent if violence is used in aggression or in defence. The violence of defenders against a wrongful attack is of course preferable to the violence of aggressors. I just want to say: Even the violence that is used in defence does not lead out of the labyrinth, in the centre of which it is not the murderous Minotaur who is lying in wait but death of humanity in the shape of the atomic holocaust. *Satyagraha*, non-violence, force of truth, is the Adriane's[9] thread that leads out of the labyrinth of violence, and into a world of peace, of freedom and of social justice.

We must, therefore, become aware of the omnipresence of violence in the world. We have grown indifferent to the everyday and omnipresent violence because we grew up in more or less pronounced relationships of violence. We adapted to it just as deep sea fish have adapted to the enormous water pressure in the deep sea. Our first and most important task is, therefore, to dismantle violence in ourselves, and that can be done through self-purification. Self-purification includes the victory over hatred, greed and fear: "This struggle through non-violence can be otherwise described as a process of purification, the underlying idea being that a nation loses its liberty owing to some of its own weaknesses and we find that immediately we shed our weaknesses, we regain our liberty. No people on earth can be finally subjected without their co-operation voluntary or involuntary. It is involuntary cooperation when for fear of some physical hurt you submit to a tyrant or a despot".[10]

Looking at it objectively, it may even make sense that the principle of revenge, even if it is concerned about moderation according to the principle "an eye for an eye, a tooth for a tooth", leads to duplication of injustice, but not to its attenuation or elimination. In a real conflict situation, this knowledge is certainly forgotten. Mostly, it is not just the principle of giving back as you were given that is ruling then, but rather do hatred, rage and revengefulness demand a duplication or triplication of revenge. One cannot wonder enough that the vast majority of people have been following the principle of revenge for millenniums, although it has proved to be completely unsuitable as a permanently satisfactory solution of conflicts for all people involved. This is why the world is like it is. For those however, who stepped over the threshold of understanding of the effect of non-violence, Gandhi's "five simple axioms of *ahimsa*" become natural truths:

"1. Non-violence implies as complete self-purification as is humanly possible;
2. Man for man the strength of non-violence is in exact proportion to the ability, not the will, of the non-violent person to inflict violence;
3. Non-violence is without exception superior to violence, i.e., the power at the disposal of a non-violent person is always greater than he would have if he was violent;
4. There is no such thing as defeat in non-violence. The end of violence is surest defeat;
5. The ultimate end of non-violence is surest victory – if such a term may be used of non-violence. In reality where there is no sense of defeat, there is no sense of victory".[11]

Satyagraha is not the final level in the cascade of terms *Sat>Satya>Satyagraha*, yet other levels fall into line in the shape of the *constructive programme* and the *non-violent methods of action*, that pour into numerous deeper lying water basins respectively. The constructive programme depends on the conditions of the country for which it was developed. Gandhi mentions as the three most important aspects of the constructive programme that he worked out for India: firstly the manual spinning and weaving as a constructive addition to the boycott of British textile products; secondly abolition of untouchability, which he considered an eyesore of Hinduism; and thirdly the reconciliation of the religious communities of the Indian subcontinent, namely of Hindus and Moslems. For him, each of these objectives had its value in itself, at the same time their realisation was also an important contribution to gaining independence. The underlying idea was that the English utilised the numerous divisions and enmities within the Indian society in order to build up and maintain their dominance according to the precept: "Divide and Rule". Overcoming these divisions and enmities would, therefore create the precondition for a successful fight against the British colonial government. Gandhi considered the constructive programme almost as a concretion of God in this world. In 1941, he extended the constructive programme to an Eighteen Points Programme, to which belonged, among others, the promotion of basic education, of village industries, of education in health and hygiene, equal rights for women as well as the fight against tobacco, alcohol and drug addiction.

The *non-violent action* as the second pillar of *satyagraha* splits up again into legal and illegal forms of actions. Among the legal ones are, in states with democratic constitutions, meetings, marches, silent vigils, petitions, strikes, boycotts, etc. Among the illegal ones are civil disobedience and the methods of non-violent confrontation. Who wants to learn more about the planning and execution of actions and campaigns, may be referred to the extensive literature about this subject.

Like a man needs both legs to advance, a non-violent activist also needs both, the constructive programme and the non-violent action, in order to advance towards the intended goal. In Germany, the constructive programme would obviously be different from the one in India. It would, however, also concentrate on the basic principles of simplicity, self-restriction, sustainability and environmental compatibility.

Gandhi's fight against the British colonial government in India became famous worldwide. But it only covers a fraction of his activities in this field. The fight against racial discrimination and economic exploitation of the Indian minority in South Africa was no less important to him, and he dedicated twenty years of his life to it. After his return to India in 1917, he undertook his first non-violent campaign against the English landowners in Champaran in the then province of Bihar who were ruining the farmers by overcharging for leases. A year later, he mediated in a textile workers strike in Ahmedabad in favour of the workers. The abolition of untouchability was even more important to him than the liberation of India from the yoke of colonialism. In this field, he was at least partially successful, contrary to his attempts for the unity of the religious communities, especially the Hindus and Moslems. The consequences were massacres and expulsions at the time of division of the country into India and Pakistan in 1947.

Conclusion: *Satyagraha*, truth force, brings Heaven to Earth. It is the source which could turn the desert of our social relations into a fruitful oasis, into a Garden of Eden, provided we knew how to exploit it. *Satyagraha* means the ability to repay evil with good, in order to overcome it. It concretely means: Suffering for the truth. This suffering includes a freeing, even redeeming power that has an effect on the one who causes the suffering, as well as the one who has to endure it.

At the end, I would like to let Gandhi speak again who, in the following quotation, summarises everything that I have explained in this paragraph: "The world rests upon the bedrock of *satya* or truth. *Asatya* meaning untruth also means non-existent, and *satya* or truth also means that which is. If untruth does not so much as exist, its victory is out of the question. And truth being that which can never be destroyed. This is the doctrine of *satyagraha* in nutshell".[12]

REFERENCES

1. *Young India*, 15.5.1924; CWMG, 27, 414 f.
2. Mt 18:21 f.
3. *Harijan*, 18.6.1938; CWMG, 73, 244.
4. *Young India*, 5.11.1931; CWMG, 54, 48.
5. *Harijan*, 27.5.1939; CWMG, 75, 415 f.
6. *Harijan*, 29.9.1940; CWMG, 79, 257.
7. *Harijan*, 20.7.1935; CWMG, 67, 263.
8. *Ibid.*, 164.
9. Greek mythology tells the story of a king named Minos on the island of Crete in the Mediterranean Sea to whom the Greeks were under tribute. Every nine years, he demanded from them to provide seven virgins and seven young men whom he threw as a fodder to Minotaure, a cross between man and bull that he held captive in a labyrinth. With the help of Ariadne, the daughter of Minos, Theseus killed Minotaure and saved the virgins and young men.
10. The Nation's Voice, *Navajivan*, Ahmedabad, 1958, 110.
11. *Harijan*, 12.10.1935; CWMG 68, 57.
12. *Satyagraha in South Africa*, Ch. XV; CWMG 34, 235.

9
Sarvodaya

Visualise the face of the poorest and weakest man that you have ever seen in your life and ask yourself if the step you are about to take is in any way useful to him.

—Mahatma Gandhi

Apart from the *satyagraha* cascade, there are further cascades for Gandhi in the field of economy, society and culture (education, life reform, natural therapy, etc.). As a matter of fact, there is almost no area of life on which he did not comment from the perspective of Truth, which is God. From the before mentioned I will cover, because of its outstanding significance, in the following only the economic concept, which he named *Sarvodaya* (welfare for all).

The cascade, in this case, is Sat > Satya > Sarvodaya, at which Sarvodaya, similar to *satyagraha*, is divided into a large number of concretions. Among these is primarily the abolition of the opposites of capital and labour, rich and poor, city and countryside, mental and physical work, as well as criticism of industrialism, preference of local products (*swadeshi*), economical use of resources, environmental protection, and sustainability, among others.

Gandhi calls his economic concept deliberately "welfare for all" to distinguish it from Jeremy Bentham's (1748-1832) and John Stuart Mills' (1806-1873) utilitarian concept of the "The greatest happiness of the greatest number". It is the poorest of the poor whose fate must be improved at first and most of all: "Talk to them of modern progress. Insult them by taking the name of God before them in vain. They will call you and me fiends if we talk about god to them. They know, if they know any God at all, a God of terror, vengeance, a pitiless tyrant".[1]

Gandhi is convinced that with an equitable distribution of goods of the world, there is enough for all. God provides enough in order to satisfy the basic needs of all people, but not enough to satisfy the greed of even one single man. Who takes more for himself than he really needs for life, namely for the satisfaction of his basic needs, which are: nourishment, clothes, dwelling, education and health care, takes it away from other people. He becomes guilty of theft. Viewed in this light, as inhabitants of industrialised countries, we are all thieves. This statement reminds us of the famous sentence of the French socialist and anarchist Pierre Proudhon (1809-1865): "Property is theft". Not all property, Gandhi would say, but that property, which is not necessary for the fulfilment of our basic needs: "God never creates more than what is strictly needed for the moment, with the result that if any one appropriates more than he really needs, he reduces his neighbour to destitution. The starvation of people in several parts of the world is due to many of us seizing very much more than they need. We may utilise the gifts of nature just as we choose, but in her books the debits are always equal to the credits. There is no balance in either column".[2]

Gandhi himself tried to realise this principle in his life as far as possible. His appearance, so extremely strange, even bizarre to European eyes, arose from the wish to live as simply as possible in order to let others live. Every man who is fit for work is obliged to work, meaning physical work: "May not men earn their bread by intellectual labour? No. The needs of the body must be supplied by the body. "Render unto Caesar that which is Caesar's' perhaps applies here well. Mere mental, that is, intellectual labour is for the soul and is its own satisfaction. It should never demand payment. In the ideal State, doctors, lawyers and the like will work solely for the benefit of society, not for self. Obedience to the law of bread labour will bring about a silent revolution in the structure of society. Man's triumph will consist in substituting the struggle for existence by the struggle for mutual service. The law of the brute will be replaced by the law of man".[3]

Gandhi adopted the doctrine of bread labour from Tolstoy (1828-1910) and John Ruskin, and he turned it into a basic rule of the *ashram*. He himself used to spin for four hours every day, except when he was sick or travelling. That did not stop him from producing his huge intellectual oeuvre that includes a hundred thick tomes.

Work is, however, not only an obligation, it is also a right of a man who is fit for work because only work gives man the right of satisfaction of his basic needs. The Ganges of rights emanates, according to him, from the Himalaya of obligations. Based on such considerations, he arrived at a radical criticism of *industrialism*. Under this term, he subsumes Western capitalism and Eastern communism. As a consequence of industrialism, he understood: firstly an ever-growing unemployment with its devastating political, social, emotional and mental consequences; and secondly, the intensification of social discrepancies within national societies and in world society. According to information by the news magazine *Der Spiegel*, people in the wealthiest countries of the world earned, fifty years ago, fifty times as much as those in the poorest countries; now-a-days they earn one hundred and thirty times as much.[4]

One only has to take a look at the machine hall of a fully automated factory and one knows where jobs have gone. The thesis that the redundant manpower migrates into other economic sectors has long been refuted because rationalisation is also entering the service sector, destroying huge amounts of jobs. The consequence: massive unemployment, relative and finally absolute pauperisation of the people affected. But even the owners themselves are not happy because abundance as well as shortage sickens people physically, psychologically and mentally in the long term. In the world, there is a silent world war raging that most people are not aware of at all. Fifteen million people famish or die of avoidable diseases every year. That is one and a half times as many casualties as the Second World War claimed per year.

Gandhi's concept of *sarvodaya* aims at the adjustment of the social discrepancies. He, therefore, directed his attention to raising the standard of living of the oppressed and exploited classes that formed the majority of the Indian population and still do. Gandhi was laughed at as a hopeless social romantic, reactionary, utopian, even as a technophobe and Luddite who wanted to put the wheel of history into reverse because of his campaign for the spinning wheel, which seemed to match perfectly, in Western eyes, his extremely bizarre appearance. If we think about them longer, however, his deliberations prove quite reasonable and worth considering. The economic expansion only of the emerging nations China and India should open the eyes of all thinking people that the Earth does neither possess enough raw materials nor is the biosphere resilient enough in order to satisfy the desires of the more than a billion people in each of these countries.

At the beginning of the nineteenth century, India still possessed a highly developed textile industry on a non-industrial basis that gave work and income to countless peasants, spinners, weavers, dyers, toolmakers, artists and merchants. This industry was destroyed by the English through the exportation of British manufactured goods within a few decades. The newly unemployed textile workers either perished or moved to the already overstaffed agricultural sector. Gandhi realised that that was one of the main causes of the impoverishment of the Indian rural population. Gandhi wanted to reverse this disastrous development, not by setting up a modern Indian textile industry, because it did not help the rural population if a brown coloured capitalist replaced the white one, but by reviving the non-industrial textile production in the whole country for the purpose of self-supply. By the sale of their surplus production on local markets, the peasants could even gain a small extra income. Instead of (industrial) *mass production*, he wanted *production by the masses*.

The reactivation of the Indian textile production on a non-industrial basis was only one part of his programme for the revival of village handicraft, because for him, India did not consist of the few big cities that sucked the life out of the country but of the seven hundred thousand villages scattered nationwide. It was their pauperised inhabitants that needed help, not by alms but by giving them work and income. He was not against technical improvements that *made* work *easier* for the people. He was only opposed to machines that *replaced* manpower with the consequence of massive unemployment. He rejected the allegation of Luddism: "What I object to is the *craze* for machinery, not machinery as such. The craze is for what they call labour-saving machinery. Men go on 'saving labour' till thousands are without work and thrown on the open streets to die of starvation. I want to save time and labour, not for a fraction of mankind, but for all. I want the concentration of wealth, not in the hands of a few, but in the hands of all. Today machinery merely helps a few to ride on the backs of millions. The impetus behind it all is not the philanthropy to save labour, but greed. It is against this constitution of things that I am fighting with all my might".[5]

The question if such a policy, if put into practice, would not only bring us back into the Middle Ages but may be even into the Stone Age, is valid. I do not see that danger. A lot of modern technology may remain. How much is hard to say. One should may be approach this question pragmatically. The *policy of adjustment* is first priority. Once adjustment has been essentially achieved, one will see what is left of modern technology and industry.

A further aspect of Gandhi's concept of Sarvodaya is the principle of *swadeshi*. With that, the preference of local products is meant. Instead of buying products from all over the world, that is offered in the world market we should buy products from our nearest surroundings, even if they should be of slightly inferior quality and a little more expensive, because this way, we ensure jobs in our neighbourhood and avoid long-distance commerce that wastes resources and destroys man and environment. The economist E.F. Schumacher (1911-1977) denounced rightly the absurdity that truckloads of biscuits are transported from *A* to *B* while biscuits of another company are transported from *B* to *A* with minimal differences of price and quality.

Gandhi conjured his compatriots and especially the leaders of the Indian National Congress not to join the dance of the nations around the golden calf of industrialism. The attempt of industrialising India following Western or Eastern patterns could only lead to ruin: "Industrialism is, I am afraid, going to be a curse for mankind. Exploitation of one nation by another cannot go on for all time. Industrialism depends entirely on your capacity to exploit, on foreign markets being open to you, and on the absence of competitors. It is because these factors are getting less and less every day for England, that its number of unemployed is mounting up daily. The Indian boycott was but a mosquito bite. And if that is the state of England, a vast country like India cannot expect to benefit by industrialisation. In fact, India, when it begins to exploit other nations — as it must if it becomes industrialised — will be a curse for other nations, a menace to the world".[6]

That is even truer for India's big neighbour China. Both, as newcomers on the world market, must challenge the world dominating nations in the same way that Germany and Japan had to do in the first half of the twentieth century, in order to be able to continue their process of industrialisation. The consequences are known and they are foreseeable also in the case of China and India, considering that the main parties in this conflict are atomic powers.

If India had adopted Gandhi's concept of *sarvodaya* instead of following Nehru's ideas of socialism, we would possibly have today, after the collapse of Soviet Communism, a functioning and fascinating alternative to globalised capitalism. It would doubtlessly have required an extensive isolation of India against the world market. It is obvious that the imperial powers would not have accepted it. They would probably have tried to force it open, in the same way as they did with Japan and China in the nineteenth century. Then, the hour of "Civilian Defence" would have come.

In the seventies and eighties of the last century there were already very sophisticated and far reaching proposals for such an alternative economy. They did not enjoy a lasting success. On the contrary, what was developed in those days sounds today like a fairy tale of old times. Gandhi's hope that Europe, that had initiated the process of worldwide industrialisation, would come to its wits, turned out to be an illusion: "What may be hoped for is that Europe, on account of her fine and scientific intellect, will realise the obvious and retrace her steps, and from the demoralising industrialism she will find a way out. It will not necessarily be a return to the old absolute simplicity. But it will have to be a reorganisation in which village life will predominate, and in which brute and material force will be subordinated to the spiritual force".[7]

It does not appear that the rat race of humanity into the abyss of self-destruction could still be stopped. If at all, a turn of one hundred and eighty degrees in the sense of Gandhi's concept of *satyagraha* and *sarvodaya* would be necessary. But it is not in sight. On the contrary, the ambition of trying to equal the example of the rich and mighty industrial Western nations is stronger than ever in the world. That does by no means invalidate the turnaround of individuals and communities. Even if we cannot stop fate any more, nothing of what happens out of the spirit of truth is in vain because it carries the sense and value in itself.

Even though the preoccupation with Gandhi's alternative economic concept may seem academic now-a-days, it is worth sparing a few thoughts about it. The first step would be an analysis of the world situation that consequently renounces illusionary expectations of salvation *à la Bible*, *Koran*, Hegel, Marx, Lenin or Mao. Secondly, it would be necessary to set new priorities. Globalised capitalism with its aggravation of social discrepancies ought to be replaced by the objective to reconcile the difference between rich and poor, powerful and powerless, high and low in society and between the societies. As a third step, this objective ought to be put into practice by individuals and groups, organisations and nations. Each step taken to reconcile social discrepancies, even the smallest one, is not lost. If it is true that from the point of view of eternity, all evil that happens in the world is lost because it does not exist, and that all good that happens does not get lost because it alone exists, than every effort in this field is worth doing. Gandhi adjusted his life to this principle. This is why he calls himself with reason a non-violent socialist: "I have claimed that I was a socialist long before those I know in India had avowed their creed. But my socialism was natural too me and not adopted from any books. It came out of my unshakable belief in non-violence. No man could be actively non-violent and not rise against social injustice, no matter where it occurred. Unfortunately Western socialists have, so far as I know, believed in the necessity of violence for enforcing socialistic doctrines. I have always held that social justice, even unto the least and the lowliest, is impossible of attainment by force. I have further believed that it is possible by proper training of the lowliest by non-violent means to secure redress of the wrongs suffered by them. That means is non-violent non-co-operation".[8]

The number of those who dismiss Gandhi's concept of *sarvodaya* with a weary smile as utopian or with an upset "nonsense" is certainly not small. One of the favourite counter-arguments is: If one puts his concept into practice, the world economy would collapse after only a few days. I doubt that behind this argument there is more than the attempt of ridiculing a serious concept. Such a concept can, of course, not be realised overnight. How could it be different with a development that moved, for more than two hundred years, only into one direction: more wealth for few and more poverty for many. Even if "humanity" — what sounds almost bizarrely utopian — could agree on establishing a new economic-political priority, namely reconciling the difference between rich and poor, it would take several centuries until a situation would be reached in which social discrepancies would be reasonably adjusted on the basis of a soft, adapted and mid-level technology — given that we had so much time. It is understandable that there are countless contemporaries who discard the concept because they want to have more than to be more, to use Erich Fromm's (1900-1980) words. They should, however, not delude themselves about the consequences of their greed.

Conclusion: Within the framework of this book, I cannot provide more than a brief outline of Gandhi's concept of *sarvodaya*. I am also aware of the fact that it goes directly against the intellectual mainstream. They assume that the technical-industrial 'progress' is irreversible, but it turns out to be more and more a progress into catastrophe. There is no proof that Gandhi's concept is wrong. On the contrary, if the analysis of the world economic system as a system of structural violence should be correct, as exposed in the previous chapter, it proves to be one, may be even the only constructive alternative to capitalism. Opposite to Marx's vision of a classless society, it has no great sex-appeal — especially for intellectuals — because it is based on physical work of all who are fit for work and a simple lifestyle. Physical work, however, is not only the foundation of our bodily, emotional and mental health; it is also the foundation for the right of satisfaction of our basic needs. Despite its relatively modest standard of living, it would be a society with a high culture, because peace and freedom, social justice and a life in harmony with Nature would widely be realised in it. Beyond that, the concept has the advantage of being realisable. A simple consideration is enough to prove that if we want to guarantee only the standard of living of an average German to the world population, the biosphere of the Earth would be ruined after only a few years. *It is, therefore, up to us to become socialists in the sense of Gandhi.*

THE TREE OF LIFE AS A SYMBOL OF THE KINGDOM OF GOD

We can also comprehend the totality of Gandhi's reform concepts in the symbol of the Tree of Life. *Sat*, which means the imperishable and indestructible being, the basic concept of religion and philosophy, forms the common root of this tree of two trunks. *Satya*, the religious truth or God, is one of the two trunks, the philosophical truth or existence is the other one. The five monastic vows *(truth, non-violence, chastity, non-possession and non-stealing)* are the main branches that in turn ramify into the side branches *Satyagraha, Sarvodaya, abolition of untouchability, reform of the caste system, harmony of religious communities, gender equality and development of villages through handicraft, basic education, hygiene, natural therapies, etc.* This Tree of Life with its mighty trunks, its strong branches and its protruding crown is at the same time a symbol for the kingdom of God, *Rama Raj* or *Khudai Raj*, whom we will re-encounter with Jesus. It is a symbol for the regained paradise: "Life is a perpetual triumph over the grave. If there is a fundamental distinction between man and beast, it is the former's progressive recognition of the law and its application in practice to his own personal life. All the saints of the world, ancient and modern, were each according to his light and capacity a living illustration of that Supreme Law of our Being. That the brute in us seems so often to gain an easy triumph is true enough. — That, however, does not disprove the law. It shows the difficulty of practice. How should it be otherwise with a law, which is as high as truth itself? When the practice of the law becomes universal, God will reign on earth as He does in Heaven. I need not be reminded that earth and heaven are in us. We know the earth, we are strangers to the Heaven within us".[9]

Only the one who visualises Gandhi's vision of the kingdom of God, that is based on truth and takes a concrete shape in *satyagraha* and *sarvodaya*, can fully understand the distance between this "concrete utopia" and the world in which we live.

REFERENCES

1. *Young India*, 15.9.1927; CWMG, 40, 17.
2. Ashram Observances in Action, *Navajivan*, Ahmedabad, 1955, 62.
3. *Young India*, 13.11.1924; CWMG, 29, 265 f.
4. *Der Spiegel*, 26/2006, 70.
5. *Young India*, 13.11.1924; CWMG, 29, 265 f.
6. *Young India*, 11.12.31; SWMG, 6, 377 f
7. *Young India*, 6.8.1925; CWMG, 32, 256.
8. *Harijan*, 20.4.1940; CWMG, 6, 235.
9. *Harijan*, 26.9.36; CWMG, 69, 400.

Part II

JESUS OF NAZARETH

10
Historical-Critical Theology

Christian traditions must be explained from their inner truth and all written traditions can give it no truth if it does not have one.
—Gotthold Ephraim Lessing

INTRODUCTORY REMARK TO THE METHOD

For Gandhi, Jesus was, as we have seen, one of the great teachers of mankind, even if he did not recognise him as the only begotten son of God in the sense of the dogma. He regarded the *Sermon on the Mount*, that he took very seriously, as one of the most important religious texts of all times and considered it almost equivalent to the *Bhagavad Gita*, to which he maintained an intimate relationship like to his beloved mother. While dedicating my time to Jesus and Gandhi, these two great figures of religious history, their close congeniality got my attention, irrespective of the enormous distance in time, space and cultural circle that separates them. They are, in a way, "brothers in spirit" and would have got along without many words if they had met personally.

The historical-critical *Bible* research realised that, despite the gospels, we know only very little about Jesus of Nazareth, the man of flesh and blood, who lived and acted in Palestine at the beginning of the Christian Era. That is because neither Jesus in contrast to Paul left any written documents, nor did the men and women who were on the move with him through Galilee and to Jerusalem kept any records. What we know about Jesus is exclusively based on oral tradition and that is, as is generally known, not very reliable. One more thing has to be added. The small community that accompanied Jesus experienced, a few days after his death on the cross, his "resurrection" or "raising from the dead" that they announced to the world as the message of salvation. This propagation superimposed and changed the tradition of the historical Jesus so much that his image was almost completely concealed by the image of the resurrected Jesus Christ.

In contrast to Jesus, we are in a far more fortunate position with Gandhi. Gandhi left behind countless written documents. They fill a hundred burly tomes. Beyond that, there is an abundance of written documents of assistants and journalists so that we are very well informed about his life and working. After all, we have to take into consideration that Jesus, according to the opinion of historical-critical theologians, was active in public only for one to two, at the most three years. What we know about his life was, so to say, just a short flash in history, like a meteor that runs a short tracer across the night sky and then disappears. Gandhi's case is completely different. He died at the age of 79 and his whole life is at our disposal in an immeasurable abundance of testimonies and personal accounts. His life, therefore, runs a long tracer across the night sky of human history.

The close affinity between their lives and teaching literally calls for a *reciprocal illumination* through comparison. I am well aware of the danger of such a proceeding, namely of finding similarities where there are none. Nevertheless, I think that the project makes sense. Only the results can prove eventually whether it turns out to be fruitful. What is meant by historical-critical theology? In short, it is the analysis of biblical texts and their transmission history with the methods of modern science. It evaluates extra-biblical sources, analyses the biblical texts from different points of view, detects contradictions within and between them, examines their credibility and sorts them according to time and place of origin in order to determine dependencies. Because of this research, we know far more about the historical Jesus now-a-days than all generations in between him and us, yes we know even more than his contemporaries, except for the small group of his followers. How can such a "miracle" be explained?

Jesus' speeches and the reports about his actions were initially passed on orally, mostly in small narrations (periscopes) that were only collected and written down many years later. When they were passed on, they were, in parts, considerably altered and complemented by miracles and all kinds of legends that were widely spread in antiquity. There were also put words in Jesus' mouth that the historical Jesus with certainty did not say. The historical-critical method provides a procedure of subtraction that allows eliminating those words and actions that were ascribed to Jesus after his death. What remains, can be considered authentic though controversial in individual cases.

Modern technology allows uncovering subjacent layers of a painting in order to get information about its origination process that way. The historical-critical theology proceeds similarly. It attempts to reconstruct the original image from the text material of the *Second Testament* by methodically eliminating subsequent "over-paintings" of Jesus' image. By doing so, however, it becomes evident that the image is only partially reconstructable. Many things are missing completely, others survived only fragmentarily or vaguely.

The scriptures collected in the *New Testament* originated for the most part in the second half of the first century. Place and time of their origin must be deduced from evidence. Their authors are mostly unknown. The same applies to the gospels. Only Paul emerges clearly as missionary of the Gentils and author of the authentic Pauline epistles. The Pauline epistles form the oldest text stock of the *New Testament*. Their time of origin is believed to have been 49-58 A.D. Thus roughly twenty years lie between Jesus' death and the first epistles by Paul. There is unfortunately little information about Jesus' life and teaching in the Pauline epistles. They are followed by the first gospel, the Gospel according to "Mark". Time of origin of this initially anonymous gospel is supposed to be the years after the conquest of Jerusalem and the destruction of the temple, place of origin is Syria. It means that within forty years of Jesus' death, the over-painting of the image of Jesus was well advanced. Similarly, the original of the anonymous *Gospel of Matthew*, a Jewish Christian was also written in the eighties/nineties of the first century AD. It too is supposed to have originated in the Syrian region. Whether the medical doctor Luke, a companion of Paul was the author of the gospel of the same name, is also negated today by historical-critical research. Its time of origin was presumably between 85 and 90 A.D. It was probably written by a Gentile Christian for Gentile Christians. The place of origin is unknown. For the Gospel according to John, 100-110 A.D. is assumed to be the time of origin and Syria or Asia Minor, more precisely Ephesus, to be the place of origin. This makes it the most recent of the four gospels. It is considerably different from the three other gospels in content and structure. These are called Synoptics because of the many similarities they show, and because of their similar 'perspective'.

In historical-critical research, the two-sources-theory gained general acceptance. It is supposed that the authors of the *Gospels of Matthew* and *Luke* took their material primarily from two sources:

the gospel of Mark and of a lost collection of sayings of Jesus, called source of sayings or shortly Q.[1] Besides the text of the *Gospel of Mark* and the source of sayings, the later evangelists offer so-called unique material. These are metaphors, narrations and sayings of Jesus that are found with only one of the evangelists, respectively.

The Acts of Luke, like the Gospel with the same name, originated probably in the years 85 to 90. The remaining epistolary literature and the Book of Revelation are dated to the last decade of the first century.

A GLIMPSE INTO THE LIFE-OF-JESUS RESEARCH

The question about the historical Jesus is a product of the era of Enlightenment. Until then, the gospels were considered reliable reports about Jesus' life, death and resurrection. Significant for this mindset is a comment by Martin Luther (1483-1546) regarding the contradictions and discrepancies that can be found everywhere in the scriptures of the *Second Testament*: "The gospels keep no order regarding Jesus' miracles and actions, it is not important anyway. If an argument about the Holy Scripture arises, and one cannot compare it, then it is better to let it go".[2]

The history of the life-of-Jesus research begins in the year 1778 in a spectacular way. In that year, Lessing published a paper entitled: "About the purpose of Jesus and his disciples: Another fragment by the anonymous from Wolfenbüttel", a text from the legacy of the orientalist Hermann Samuel Reimarus (1694-1768) from Hamburg who died ten years before. It is the last of seven fragments that Lessing published in the years 1774-1778. Reimarus took the view that Jesus of Nazareth was completely different from the one described in the gospels. According to Reimarus, Jesus wanted to bring the Jewish people together as a political-religious leader and lead a rebellion against the Roman occupation force, but he failed and was executed by the Romans as a rebel. He himself acknowledged defeat on the cross with the words: "My God, my God, why have you abandoned me!"![3] His disciples did not want to accept this terrible end of the movement, and did not feel like returning to their former businesses. They, therefore, took Jesus' dead body, buried it furtively and made up the legend about his physical resurrection. As with reason they feared sharing Jesus' fate, they converted the zealot Jesus who had planned the violent insurrection against the Romans into the peaceful preacher of the mount whom we know from the gospels. According to Reimarus, Christianity was, therefore, based on lie and deceit, and remained faithful to this beginning in the further course of its history.

Reimarus' theory is considered as refuted among theologians. But it is the beginning of an immeasurable sequence of texts that have the purpose to discover the *historical Jesus*, namely the living human being, in order to set him against or aside the *Jesus Christ* of the ecclesiastical doctrine, who had been turned into a stiff dogma. Albert Schweitzer displayed a summary of this literature in his monumental work "History of the Life-of-Jesus Research", published in 1913 in an extended edition. Therein, he acknowledges the achievement of the life-of-Jesus researchers with the words: "The investigation of Jesus' life was the school of truthfulness for theology. The world had never before seen and will never again see such a painful and sacrificial struggle for truth like the one by the life-of-Jesus research of the last 100 years".[4] It was also Schweitzer who clearly recognised the failure of the life-of-Jesus research of the nineteenth century. The puzzle pieces provided by the texts of the *New Testament* cannot be put together to a consistent image of the historical Jesus. The attempt of assembling them to an exhaustive image through psychology and imagination only led to the fact that the depictions of Jesus revealed more about their authors and their time than about the historical Jesus. The *New Testament* scholar Joachim Jeremias (1900-1979) from Göttingen wrote: "The rationalists describe Jesus as a moralist, the idealists as the epitome of humanity, the aesthetes praise him as a brilliant artist of speech, the socialists as a friend of the poor and a social reformer, and the countless pseudo-scientists turn him into the protagonist of a novel. These lives of Jesus are all images of wishful thinking".[5]

It is tragic that eventually even Schweitzer succumbed to the temptation of designing a life of Jesus from the existing material. He thought that Jesus tried to enforce the beginning of God's rule by shouldering the walk of suffering to the cross out of disappointment about the non-appearance of the eschatological Messiah and Son of Man expected by him and his contemporaries. He called this theory "consequent eschatology",[6] that explained Jesus' life and teaching from the point of view of Jesus, the early Christian community's and Paul's expectation of the last days. It is now-a-days considered obsolete.

The theological research was continued no less dramatically after Schweitzer. The important theologian Rudolf Bultmann (1884-1976) considered Jesus a Jewish prophet and rabbi,* the liberation theologians in Latin America declared him the liberator from poverty, oppression and exploitation, the theologian and psychologist Hanna Wolf calls him the "first anima-integrated man of world history", not to mention the more recent novel-like Jesus-biographies. Every author and every time produced and produce a sort of image of Jesus in which they find themselves. Hanna Wolf also calls Jesus the "greatest projection screen of world history. He had to be everything at all times".[7]

Initially, the conservative theologians who adhered to the Christ dogma defended themselves with the term of a "positive theology" against the attacks of the life-of-Jesus researchers. It was only towards the end of the nineteenth century that they proceeded to counterattack with the book by Martin Kähler (1835-1912) published in 1892 with the programmatic title: "The So-called Historical Jesus and the Historic, Biblical Christ". Joachim Jeremias (1900-1973) summarises the content of Kähler's book as follows: "One has to assimilate the title of this text very carefully if one wants to understand Kähler's concern. Kähler makes a difference, on the one hand, between "Jesus" and "Christ", on the other hand between "historical" and "historic". By "Jesus", he understands the man from Nazareth, how he had been and was described by the life-of-Jesus research, by "Christ" he means the saviour promulgated by the church. With "historical" he refers to the mere facts of the past, with "historic", what remains significant. And he now opposes the so-called "historical Jesus", as the life-of-Jesus research had attempted to reconstruct him, and the historic, biblical Christ, as announced by the apostles. His theory is: "Only the biblical Christ is comprehensible to us, and he alone remains significant for faith. Only in the way the gospels describe him to us, and not how the presumably scientific reconstructions present him, he 'evokes the irrefutable impression of the most complete reality'. Initially however, Kähler's call went unheard; it was not before our days that it had a full impact, when Rudolf Bultmann adopted it".[8] Under Bultmann's significant influence, critical theology crosses over "completely and openly turning its coat", like Jeremias expressed it, to the enemy camp after 150 years of life-of-Jesus research: "It says

---

* Honorary title for a jewish Tora scholar.

no to its whole history; it admits that Kähler is right and declares the efforts regarding the historical Jesus an insoluble and fruitless enterprise; it withdraws into the storm-free fortress of Kerygma, the proclamation of Christ."[9]

Bultmann declares that the historical Jesus, insofar as he can be reconstructed at all from the sources, is ultimately meaningless for the Christian faith. For him, the theology of the Second Testament only begins at Easter, with the proclamation of the resurrected one as the Messiah and Saviour of the world by the early Christian community in Jerusalem. The first sentence of his "Theology of the New Testament" consequently reads: "Jesus' message is one of the preconditions of the theology of the New Testament but it is not a part of it". Jeremias comments this sentence by stating that this is as if the history of Buddhism began only after Buddha's death or the history of Islam only after Mohammed's death. As Bultmann speaks about preconditions, there must obviously be others as well: "The events around Easter experienced by the disciples, the Messiah belief of Judaism and the myth of the Gentile environment that provided the clothing with which Jesus of Nazareth was dressed".[10] To put it plainly: The historical Jesus and his message are eventually insignificant for faith. With that, the pendulum of the theological disputes about the historical Jesus has reached its utmost counter-position. Bultmann, in a way, takes the position of Paul who was not interested in the "Christ according to the flesh" because the latter only stood in the way of his proclamation of the "Christ according to the spirit".

What began as demythologisation with Bultmann, therefore, ends in a new "scientific" mythology. The biblical myth of the incarnated God, the way he appears namely with Paul and John, becomes an object of scientific-theological consideration in his *Theology of the New Testament*. That has nothing, absolutely nothing, to do any more with the historical Jesus who wandered through Palestine with his small community, and with his message of the present beginning of God's rule.

Such an extreme position evoked a counter movement already among the disciples and critics of Bultmann. The *historical Jesus* of the life-of-Jesus research and the *Jesus Christ* of the credos, that was from then on the magical formula that also Joachim Jeremias embraced, belong inseparably together. Who abandons the historical Jesus places himself in danger of falling victim to *Docetism*, a gnostic "false doctrine" that regarded Jesus Christ as God who had taken a human shape only in pretence. Who, however, abandons the Christ of faith puts himself at risk of succumbing to *Ebionitism*, also an ancient "false doctrine" that regarded Jesus Christ merely as a human being filled with God's spirit. Jeremias summarises his theological position in the sentence: "The good news of Jesus and the testimony of faith of the early church belong insolubly together".[11]

Nevertheless, there are questions remaining: Does the magical formula that unites in the name "Jesus Christ" the *Jesus* of the historical-critical research and the *Christ* of faith, or rather forces them to unite, not prove, in the end, to be a formula compromise that only pretends to unite what is incompatible after all? Is the "struggling for truth" (Albert Schweitzer) that fascinated whole generations of theologians, really only a mock fight? Can we still speak the Apostles'Credo today, which reads: "I believe. in Jesus Christ, His (i.e., God's) only Son, our Lord. He was conceived by the power of the Holy Spirit and born of the Virgin Mary. He suffered under Pontius Pilate, was crucified, died, and was buried. He descended to the dead. On the third day he rose again. He ascended into heaven and is seated at the right hand of the Father. He will come again to judge the living and the dead".

What does that mean in a world in which the ancient and medieval conception of the world belongs irretrievably to the past, in which no enlightened person would believe in the virgin birth or the physical resurrection or the ascension of Jesus? What do we think when we speak such sentences? And further, how shall the unity of God and man in Jesus Christ be understood even though the one excludes the other? God is infinite, omnipresent, omniscient, almighty and immortal; the human being Jesus, however, finite, mortal and anything but omnipresent, omniscient and almighty. How is that supposed to fit together? Does the confession to this contradiction require sacrificing our reasoning mind on the altar of faith (*sacrificium intellectus*) ?

The questions that the Christian faith addresses to the life-of-Jesus research are certainly no less precarious. What do we really know about the historical Jesus, and is this knowledge, if we had it, really relevant? Does the knowledge about the historical Jesus help us in situations in which we are faced with violence, oppression, cruelty, misery, suffering and death? Is the knowledge about the historical Jesus really enough to enable people to do charity or even to love their enemy? In short, is the allegation of faithful Christians that modern science ends inevitably in faithlessness not justified, as much as the reproach of enlightened humanists that the Christian faith ends inevitably in intolerance and gloomy superstition? I nevertheless think that there is a solution to this apparently insoluble problem. There is a way of overcoming the abysmal gap between the *historical Jesus* and the *Christ of faith*. We already know the one who can show us this way: It is Mahatma Gandhi.

REFERENCES

1. Translator's note: Q for Quelle, the German word for source.
2. Cited by Albert Schweitzer: *Geschichte der Leben-Jesu-Forschung*, Tübingen, 1926, 13.
3. Mt., 27, 46.
4. Albert Schweitzer: *Geschichte der Leben-Jesu-Forschung*, Tübingen, 1926, 5.
5. Joachim Jeremias: *Das Problem des historischen Jesus*, Stuttgart, 1961, 8.
6. Eschatology is the study of the last things. This salvation history thinking covers two ranges of topics: The question of the individual's fate after death, and the question of the future of history as a whole.
7. *Jesus der Mann*, Stuttgart, 1979, 70.
8. Joachim Jeremias: *Das Problem des historischen Jesus*, Stuttgart, 1961, 9.
9. *Ibid.*
10. *Ibid.*, 11.
11. *Ibid.*, 22.

11
Tendencies

We can hardly understand any more with which long labour pains the historical view of Jesus' life was born.

—Albert Schweitzer

The historical-critical research recognised a multitude of influences to which the oral tradition of Jesus' life and teaching was subject. Without it, the texts of the New Testament cannot really be understood in the form in which they are available today. I can only admire the diligence and detective work with which the researchers analysed the biblical texts. To describe their results would fill a big book. I, therefore, have to restrict myself to name the most important influencing factors and to explain them through examples. These are:

1. Visualization tendency,
2. Superposition tendency,
3. Fulfillment tendency,
4. Adaptation tendency,
5. Intensification tendency,
6. Weakening tendency,
7. Harmonizing tendency.

VISUALISATION TENDENCY

We are quite well informed about the religious life of the early Christian communities through the Acts of the Apostles and Paul. The resurrected Jesus was celebrated in the early Christian communities ecstatically, his presence, even his bodily existence was experienced immediately and overwhelmingly. Community members experienced themselves as replete with Christ's spirit; they entered a trance, shouted with joy, delivered prophetic speeches or uttered unintelligible words and sentences. Paul describes these phenomena that he calls charisms ("gifts of the Holy Spirit") in the first Epistle to the Corinthians: "Let love be your highest goal! But you should also desire the special abilities the Spirit gives – especially the ability to prophecy. For if you have the ability to speak in tongues you will be talking only to God, since people won't be able to understand you. You will be speaking by the power of the Spirit, but it will all be mysterious. But one who prophecies strengthens others, encourages them, and comforts them. A person who speaks in tongues is strengthened personally, but one who speaks a word of prophecy strengthens the entire church. I wish you could all speak in tongues, but even more I wish you could all prophecy. For prophecy is greater than speaking in tongues, unless someone interprets what you are saying so that the whole church will be strengthened".[1]

When in the Acts, the Outpouring of the Holy Spirit over the gathered community is described, what is obviously meant is speaking in tongues publicly. The gathering crowd thought that those people must be drunk. In a certain way they indeed were. They were drunken by Jesus' spirit, by the Holy Spirit. The statement that the pilgrims who were in Jerusalem heard the Jesus people talking in their own language is a posterior legendary interpretation of the report about the incident. It might be possible that, on this occasion, Peter delivered his first speech to the crowd that was standing around. Its content, however, was probably totally fabricated by Luke.[2]

The early Christians had no scruples of putting words of the "resurrected" Jesus, whose living presence they had experienced, in the historical Jesus' mouth. In this way, a whole series of "false" Jesus words emerged, but one could not accuse the authors of deliberately lying or manipulating. Three examples may illustrate that: Firstly, the announcement of the destruction of the temple[3] in the gospels is not considered Jesuanic by researchers because the temple was only destroyed in the year 70 A.D. by the Romans. This saying of Jesus is rather evidence for the fact that the Gospel according to Mark can only have been written after 70. Secondly, Jesus' thanks to the Father in Matthew 11:25-27 implies a relationship between God Father and God Son that from the theological-historical point of view can only be expected much later. Therefore, this saying is a community creation that was put in Jesus' mouth aposteriori. The same applies, thirdly, to the well-known I-am-words of the Gospel of John. Jesus did never speak such words for all that we know today.

Conclusion: Although Jesus had died on the Cross on the "preparation day" before the Paschal festival, he continued to live as the resurrected one in the early Christian community of Jerusalem and the early Christian communities.

SUPERPOSITION TENDENCY

An important, may be the most important result of the historical-critical research consists in the understanding that the form in which Jesus' image appears in the scriptures of the *New Testament* was shaped by the belief in the resurrected Jesus Christ. Because, in the faith of the community, the resurrected one had become equal to God, he appears now in his earthly existence, about which the gospels want to inform us, as the Son of God, equipped with supernatural powers. He appears as:

1. Lord of nature (natural wonder),
2. Lord over illness (miracle of healing),
3. Lord over demons (exorcism),
4. Lord over Satan (legend of temptation),
5. Lord over death (resurrection of the dead),
6. Lord over sin (forgiveness of sins),
7. Lord of time (announcement of suffering, knowledge of the future about the apocalypse),
8. Lord of thoughts (he could read other people's minds), and
9. Lord over the powers of this world (such as at Matthew 26:53 and John 19:11).

Therefore, we have to say farewell to many things that the gospels tell about Jesus. He did not walk on the water. He did not stop the storm. He did not feed five thousand or four thousand people. He did not raise Lazarus, whose body was already reeking, from the dead. He did not heal any cripples. He did not forgive any sins. He did not know what was expecting him in Jerusalem and did, therefore, not announce his suffering three times to his disciples. He could not read other people's minds and had no power over the mighty of this world who sentenced him to torture and death. Many things, however, support the idea that he was a healer. That applies especially to psychosomatic ailments that were no less widespread in his time than today. His message must have had a liberating, encouraging and comforting effect on many of his listeners. If the Gospel of Matthew reports that he taught like somebody with a (divine) authority and not like the scribes, it sounds credible.

If we deduct the tales of miracles and demonstrations of divine power, the gospels shrink quite considerably in terms of their historical content. The same applies to the legends that surround Jesus' birth, his childhood and youth, as well as his "raising from the dead" or "resurrection" and the empty tomb. That means that we have to say farewell to many texts that we are fond of, like the Lukan nativity story. It turns out to be a legend. Even as a legend, it has, I do not deny it, its own warmness, power and "truth". It is not an accident that myth tells that the almighty God took the shape of a helpless child, and on top of that not of a royal child but a child of poor people who sought refuge in a stable on their journey.

The story of the calling of the disciples also bears clear legendary characteristics. It creates the impression that Jesus plays the role of God who demands unconditional obedience, in view of whose commanding call the filial duty towards parents and even the reverence towards the deceased father cease.

FULFILMENT TENDENCY (SCRIPTURAL PROOF)

If Jesus was the Messiah (Christ) from the house of David as promised in the scriptures of the *Old Testament* — and the early Christians had no doubt about that —, then everything that was said about the Messiah in the scriptures had to be applicable to Jesus. As there was only incomplete knowledge about his life at the time of origin of the gospels, the gaps were filled with divinations of the prophets. I am giving three examples:

First Example: We do not know Jesus' exact place of birth. It is probably Nazareth. At the prophet Micah, however, it reads: "But you, O Bethlehem Ephrathah, are only a small village among all the people of Judah. Yet a ruler of Israel will come from you".[4] With this prophecy, Micah thinks of a messianic ruler who is supposed to come from Bethlehem, David's home town, where Samuel allegedly anointed him king secretly, at Yahweh's behest. If Jesus was the Messiah of Israel, he must have been born in Bethlehem.

Second Example: As the evangelist Matthew did not know any details about Jesus' and his disciples' entry in Jerusalem, he filled the gap with the description of the entry of the messianic king in Jerusalem that he found in the works of the prophet Zechariah. The evangelist himself establishes the connection to the prophecy of the *First Testament*. If Jesus was the Messiah, he must have entered Jerusalem as described at Zechariah. For the readers of the Gospel of Matthew, a parallel between Zechariah 9:9-10 and Matthew 21:1-11 becomes proof of Jesus' messiahship.

Third Example: The Servant Songs of Second Isaiah can downright be considered the key texts for the interpretation of Jesus' fate. The early Christendom recognised the servant as Yahweh's chosen one, who, in place of Israel, even in place of all people, suffered persecution, torture and death in order to reconcile God. The first Servant Song reads: "Look at my servant, whom I strengthen. He is my chosen one, who pleases me. I have put my Spirit upon him. He will bring justice to the nations. He will not shout or raise his voice in public. He will not crush the weakest reed or put out a flickering candle. He will bring justice to all who have been wronged. He will not falter or lose heart until justice prevails throughout the earth. Even distant lands beyond the sea will wait for his instruction".[5]

No wonder that in the texts of the *New Testament*, allusions to and quotations from the Servant Songs can be found everywhere. The first song is quoted by Matthew and Luke; the second one in the Acts of the Apostles and by Paul. The third one by Matthew and the fourth one by Paul, John, Matthew, Luke, the Acts, the Epistle to the Hebrews, the *Book of Revelation* and the first *Epistle of Peter*. The following text from the fourth song reads, as a matter of fact, as a prophecy of Jesus' expiatory sacrifice for the sins of the humans: "Yet it was our weaknesses he carried; it was our sorrows that weighed him down. And we thought his troubles were a punishment from God, a punishment for his own sins! But he was pierced for our rebellion, crushed for our sins. He was beaten so we could be whole. He was whipped so we could be healed. All of us, like sheep, have strayed away. We have left God's paths to follow our own. Yet the LORD laid on him the sins of us all. He was oppressed and treated harshly, yet he never said a word. He was led like a lamb to the slaughter. And as a sheep is silent before the shearers, he did not open his mouth. Unjustly condemned, he was led away. No one cared that he died without descendants, that his life was cut short in midstream. But he was struck down for the rebellion of my people. He had done no wrong and had never deceived anyone. But he was buried like a criminal; he was put in a rich man's grave. But it was the LORD's good plan to crush him and cause him grief. Yet when his life is made an offering for sin, he will have many descendants. He will enjoy a long life, and the LORD's good plan will prosper in his hands".[6]

For the down-to-earth point of view of the historical-critical scientist, the circular character of this "scriptural proof" is obvious. The text from the *First Testament* provides the interpretative pattern for Jesus' fate. For who read it later, the striking similarity of the texts was seen as a "scriptural proof", although the prophecy from the *First Testament* did not refer to Jesus at all. It is also completely unlikely that he referred it to himself.

ADAPTATION TENDENCY

No doubt, Jesus was a Jew and grew up in an environment that was characterised by Judaism. As Galilee, the land on Lake Kinneret, was inhabited by a mixture of Jewish people and Gentils after the conquest of the Northern Empire by the Assyrians in the year 722 B.C. and the abduction of big parts of its native population, the young Jesus very soon learned about pagan religions and practices. To what extent they influenced his doctrine of a universal religion, cannot be said with certainty, it is nevertheless probable. We will later come back to his doctrine. At this point, we are only interested in its adaptation to the environment in which it spread. That happened in two directions: Towards an integration into orthodox Judaism, on the one hand, and towards an adaptation to the religious concepts of Hellenism, a cultural mixture of oriental, Greek and Roman elements that characterised the Eastern part of the Mediterranean since Alexander's campaigns of conquest (356-323 B.C.).

In the Acts of the Apostles, Lucas depicts a conflict between the "Hebrews" and the "Hellenists", which had allegedly originated from the neglect of the widows of Hellenists in their "daily maintenance".[7] According to Luke, it was solved by the election of seven deacons, who should forthwith attend to this task. Luke, who tends to harmonising the euphemism anyway, relates at most only half the truth of this matter. This conflict dealt with the first internal dispute of the community about the propagation of the resurrected Jesus. The "Hebrews" were predominantly Aramaic speaking, law-abiding Jews of the Jesus community, who were reinforced, as Luke notes, by a "great number of priests,[8] who had obediently adopted the faith.

The "Hellenists", on the other hand, were Greek speaking Diaspora Jews, who had grown up in the religious world of Hellenism with its divine myths and mystery cults, and who had — for whatever reasons — returned to Jerusalem.

The Hebrew, pious, law-abiding Jews, were seeking to get the "runaway" Jesus back into Judaism, basically in the way his family had wanted to get him back home thinking that he was "out of his mind".[9] For them it was clear: Jesus had only been sent to the lost sheep of Israel, his message was exclusively meant for the people of Israel, which he intended to gather and lead back to obedience towards Yahweh. The appointment of the twelve disciples and their exalted position as the judges of the twelve houses of Israel can probably be attributed to them, too.[10] The most extreme expression of this tendency is, in my eyes, described in the story of granting the request of a heathen woman. The Syrian Phoenician comes to Jesus, falls at his feet, and asks him to heal her daughter who is obsessed by an "impure spirit". Jesus holds her off with the words: "Let the children eat their fill first, for it is not right to take the bread away from the children and throw it to the dogs".[11] The humble persistence of the woman overwhelms him, so that he finally grants her request and heals her daughter. In the story, heathens are called dogs, a highly contemptuous expression not unusual for pious Jews in the times of Jesus, whereas the Jews are called children (of God). I regard the story as a "creation by the community" from the "Hebrew" faction of the early community of Jerusalem. Even the "remote healing" itself is an indicator that this is a legend. I cannot believe that the historical Jesus who preached the good news of the borderless love of God to man in particular towards the poor and suppressed, the humiliated and despised, should have diffentiated between the "chosen people" and the "heathens". The Gospels report consistently that Jesus did not only preach in synagogues, but preferably in the open. In Galilee, which was to a great extent inhabited by heathens, that also meant that heathens would gather to listen to him. There is no mention with even a single word that Jesus or his disciples had held them off. And twice he also presented Samaritans who were despised by orthodox Jews as role models to his fellow believers.[12] I do not have any doubt that Jesus broke the fetters of the chosen belief and advanced to a universal religion. Thus he discarded the Hebrewization of faith in God. Let us now attend to the Hellenisation tendency.

The "Hellenists" around Stephen, the first martyr of Christendom, were not just deacons, as we have already heard, but appeared as evangelists who "translated" the message of the resurrected Jesus into the religious language of Hellenism. For them, Jesus became the saviour, Redeemer and Son of God, the way he appears with Paul and John later on. The influence of the antique myths of the dying and resurrecting God on the teaching of Christ (Christology) is indisputable. The Greek Heracles, the Babylonian Tammuz, the Syrian Adonis, the Phrygian Attis, the Egyptian Osiris, the Thracian Dionysos and others provide the pattern of interpretation for the myth of the death and resurrection of Jesus. Karlheinz Deschner writes about the Babylonian god Bel Marduk, whose fate features many parallels to the biblical Jesus: "There are certain obvious similarities between the Christian icon and the equally resurrecting Bel-Marduk. The Babylonian deity, that was eventually the most revered, was regarded as the creator of the world, the god of wisdom, medicine and incantation, the saviour sent by the father, the resurrecter of the dead, lord of all lords and king of kings, and as the good shepherd. Just like the Christ of the *Bible*, Bel-Marduk was captured, interrogated, sentenced to death, flagellated and executed together with a criminal, while another criminal was released".[13]

Of no less importance was the influence of the Hellenist mystery cults on the development of baptism and communion. The farewell supper of Jesus with his disciples was reshaped into the Holy Supper, where God is, so to say, eaten, that means incorporated by the adepts, who thus are blessed with participating in His immortality.

After all, the widespread religious-philosophical teaching of Gnosis in the Hellenist world had profoundly shaped the proclamation of the message of the resurrected Christ. Gnosis (ancient Greek: knowledge, finding) depicts the philosophical collection of religious truths. It is an ambiguous and diverse phenomenon that can only be grazed in the course of this study. Gnosis developed around the same time as Christianity. Its origins, however, date back in time as far as the era of Zarathustra (approx. 600 B.C.). It was him who already differentiated between an 'evil' creator of the world Ahriman and a 'good' god Ahura Mazda. Later on, gnostic thinkers absorbed Jewish, Christian, Egyptian, Greek and other traditions. As is the case of apocalypticism, Gnosis originated from circles that were excluded from shaping public life, who subsequently protested against this world and who sought their salvation in an escapist belief. This is the reason for their world-negating character. Characteristic for Gnosis is a radically dualistic world view based on the opposites of good god and evil world creator (Demiurg), spirit and matter or spirit and flesh, light and darkness, life and death: "According to gnostic mythology there was a mixing of light and darkness (spirit and matter) as a result of the wrongdoing of a light creature or the attack of the powers of darkness against the world of light. . . . . leading to the creation of the world and of humans, whose bodily shells contain light particles. It is the objective of the powers of light to recollect the dispersed light that is caught in matter and to lead it back to the world of light. This corresponds to the teaching of salvation, according to which the "spark of light" in man has to be liberated from its enslavement by the powers of darkness and the bodily prison. This happens from the outside through man's awakening by a liberating being . . . . . so that the spirit endowed human. achieves the insight into his true divine existence, which is his salvation from ignorance and his liberation from the powers of darkness."[14] Gnostic influence is obvious in many parts of the New Testament, namely with Paul and the evangelist John. Typically gnostic with Paul are the opposites of spirit and flesh, light and darkness as well as the conversion of the prophet and rabbi Jesus of Nazareth into a pre-existing saviour who incarnated in Jesus, suffered the death at the cross in order to save all believing in him from the empire of Satan and of Beliar, the "God of this era".[15]

In the Gospel of John the influence of Gnosis becomes even more prominent, such as, e.g., in the light and darkneess metaphors of the prologue, in the pre-existing Jesus (logos), who is sent by God into the world in order to redeem those who believe in him as the way, the truth and the life.[16] It is unnecessary to pile up further quotations. Everyone can find them on her or his own.

Conclusion: Within the first centuries of our era, early Christianity changed into a syncretistic religion that incorporated elements from different religions and cults of antiquity, thus reshaping it thoroughly. The adaptation of the specifically Jewish expectation of a Messiah to the religious world of Hellenism was an essential precondition for the swift spread of the new doctrine in the Roman Empire. To its Jewish origin, the young Christendom owes the claim of power it raised for the Messiah Jesus Christ, and the "sharp intolerance" towards the competing religions, it started to persecute and exterminate cruelly once it had risen to be state religion. This "night side" of the young religion was hardly less involved in its unstoppable spread in the Roman Empire than its "day side" in the form of the readiness of some Christians to suffer persecution and martyrdom.

INTENSIFICATION TENDENCY

For oral tradition there applies the rule that the events reported tend to get dramatised and intensified in the course of time. A typical example for this tendency is the depiction of the end of the disciple and "traitor" Judas Iscariot. Paul does not know anything at all about him. With Mark, we only find the short note that he had gone to the high priests and offered to turn Jesus in. "When they heard that, they rejoiced and promised to give him money for that."[17] We do not hear anything about his death. With Matthew, he regrets his deed and hangs himself. John claims that he, being the cashier of the Jesus community, misappropriated funds.[18] Finally, in the Acts of the Apostles, the story of his end is dramatically embellished. Peter tells the disciples:

"With the pay for his misdeed he bought a piece of land. Then, however, he plunged forward to the ground, his body burst, and all intestines fell out".[19]

The intensification tendency plays also a significant role in the resurrection of Jesus. The oldest resurrection document of the *New Testament* is found in Paul's Epistle to the Corinthians. There, the resurrection is still clearly recognisable as a vision of Peter, the disciples and Paul. Even the Gospel of Mark that came up some 20 years later only knows the empty grave.[20]

The other evangelists provide more or less elaborate resurrection reports. In order to counter critical enquiries, the embodiment of Jesus is increasingly highlighted, not without getting entangled in contradictions. On the one hand, the resurrected one is a spiritual being that can pass through closed doors,[21] whereas, on the other hand, he is incarnate for so real that the doubting Thomas lays his fingers into the stigma of nails and his hand into the wound on his side[22] and the resurrected is even eating and drinking with the disciples.[23] With Matthew, the women embrace the feet of the resurrected, whereas with John, Jesus fends off the embrace of Mary Magdalene with the words: "Do not hold me, for I have not yet risen to the Father."[24] Anyhow, the discovery of the empty grave, of which Paul does not know anything, yet, requires the bodily resurrection of

Jesus as a precondition. The most consequential manifestation of the intensification tendency for Christendom was the proclamation of the historical Jesus to be the Messiah and his successive augmentation to become God-man and pre-existing Son of God, which found its conclusion in the Christ dogma of Chalcedony (451 A.D.) An intensification tendency hardly less significant was the switching back of Jesus' status as the son of God to an earlier time. First of all, Jesus is quasi adopted by God through his awakening, later the adoption is predated to the transfiguration scene on a high mountain, then again to the baptism by John, furthermore to the virgin conception as depicted by Matthew and Luke, and finally, in a last stage with Paul and John, Jesus becomes Logos who was with God from the beginning (pre-existence).[25]

THE WEAKENING TENDENCY

In the Gospels, we often come across Jesus as an ethical rigorist. We only need to think of the hard, seemingly even unfulfillable demands of the Sermon on the Mount or the instructions for the missionary journey of the disciples,[26] the authenticity of which must, however, be questioned. No wonder then that a tendency developed quite soon to soften these "commandments". It would, however, turn out to be fully implemented only in the third and fourth century, when Emperor Constantine (288-337) offered the Christians the alliance of throne and altar.

Rigorous in a similar way as the "commandments" of the *Sermon on the Mount* was Jesus' famous aphorism: "Rather goes a camel through the eye of a needle than a rich man to the kingdom of God". Then, to the frightened question of the disciples, who could be saved at all then, he answers: "For men, this is impossible, but not for God, because for God everything is possible".[27] This remark can be understood as a word of consolation for the rich, and it has actually been understood as such. It can be understood as the consideration of divine kindness that exceeds all human measures. But it can also be a hint, that the answer to the question: "Who is a rich man?" decides whether the hard judgement of Jesus applies to him. A rich man who uses his wealth for the benefit of society, and who leads himself a simple, may be even spartan life with his family, does not, in my opinion, fall under Jesus' verdict. Gandhi has described this kind of rich man as a trustee of the wealth that he is entrusted with. Whether Jesus has thought of this kind of rich man, is, admittedly, uncertain.

THE HARMONISING TENDENCY

As we have seen, the conflict between the 'Hebrews' and 'Hellenists' already emerged during the time of the early community of Jerusalem. Luke, the author of the Acts of the Apostles, defuses this conflict by trivialising it as a quarrel about the daily maintenance of the widows of the "Hellenists".

Evangelist Matthew proceeds in a very similar way. According to him, Jesus says at the beginning of the *Sermon on the Mount*: "Do not think that I came to abolish the law and the prophets. I have not come to abolish but to fulfil. Amen, this is what I tell you: Until heaven and Earth disappear, not even the smallest letter of the law shall go before everything has taken place. Who abolishes even one of the smallest commandments and teaches the people accordingly, will be the smallest in the kingdom of heaven, but who keeps them and teaches them to be kept, will be great in the kingdom of heaven.[28] Among the most important components of the Mosaic laws are circumcision, the observance of Sabbath, the prohibition of images and the purity regulations that were, however, partially called into question by Jesus. Matthew harmonises the sharp conflict between Paul and the orthodox faction of the early community of Jerusalem around the brother of the Lord, Jacob, by simply placing their teachings beside each other, irrespective of contradictions this may evoke.

The tendencies I describe, which often alter life and teaching of the historical Jesus beyond recognition, can be summarized under the heading of *mythologisation tendency*. The term mythologisation was coined by Rudolf Bultmann, who deduced from this observation the demand to "demythologise" the texts of the *New Testament*. In order to save its timeless content, one would need to recognise the contemporary coaching of the message of Jesus and translate it into the language of a modern view of the world. A demythologisation carried out systematically results in the loss of numerous ideas and beliefs that have grown dear to us Christians. But it does not matter. We must not cling on desperately to beliefs that have become untenable and escape into an idyllic world of myths and legends. The *Second Testament*, even the whole *Bible* has to go through the aqua fortis of scientific biblical criticism, even at the risk that nothing remains of it at the end. If, however, something does remain, then it will be much less vulnerable to criticism and possibly turn out to be more valuable than all that we have regarded as indispensable components of Christianity until then.

Nothing valuable in the *Bible* shall be abandoned, but all that is worthless or even damaging. The discussion about what belongs to the first and what to the latter category will continue to keep future generations of theologians and laymen busy. This is good, since there is no advance in understanding without a productive dispute. Far more important than the advance in understanding is, however, the advance in belief, which can only be achieved when the truth realised is implemented in our life.

REFERENCES

1. *First Letter to the Corinthians*, 14:1-5.
2. *Acts of the Apostle*, 2:1-13.
3. Gospel According to St Mark, 13:1 f.
4. Prophet Micah, 5:1.
5. Prophet Isaiah, 42:1-4.
6. Prophet Isaiah, 53:4-10.
7. *Acts of the Apostles*, 6:1-7.
8. *Acts of the Apostles*, 6:7.
9. *Gospel according to St Mark*, 3:21.
10. *Gospel according to St Matthew*, 19:28.
11. *Gospel according to St Mark*, 7:24-30.
12. *Gospel of Luke*, 10:25-37.
13. Karlheinz Deschner: *Abermals krähte der Hahn*, Reinbek, 1972, 99.
14. Wörterbuch des Christentums, Stichwort: Gnosis, Gnostizismus.
15. *Second Letter of the Corinthians*, 4:3-6.
16. Gospel of John, 14:6.
17. *Gospel according to St Mark*, 14:10.43.
18. Gospel of John, 12:6.
19. Acts of the Apostles, 1:18.
20. Gospel According to St mark, 16:9-20 is a supplement added in the second century.
21. Gospel of John, 20:19.
22. *Ibid.*, 20:25-29.
23. Gospel of Luke, 24:41-43; Acts of the Apostles, 1:4.
24. Gospel of John, 20:17.
25. *Ibid.*, 1:1.
26. *Gospel according to St Mark*, 6:6-13.
27. *Gospel according to St. Matthew*, 19:24 f.
28. *Ibid.*, 5:17-19.

12
The Life of Jesus

The Church lives off the fact that the results of the scientific life-Jesus-research are not known to it.

—*Hans Conzelmann*

The result of the historical-critical theology, in what concerns Jesus' biography, can at first glance only be disappointing for Christians who are familiar with the Gospels. There is no stable with ox and donkey, no star from Bethlehem, no three Wise Men, etc. For Jesus, too, the same down-to-earth statement of Gandhi rather applies: "All the world teachers, you should know began with a zero!"[1] About the life of Jesus we know very little, despite the reports of the Gospels. Scientists now-a-days agree that the author of the Gospel according to Mark, on which depend the Gospels of Matthew and Luke when it comes to the external order of events, only collected the words and stories of Jesus that were spread in young Christian communities and put them into a fictitious timeframe. The eminent biblical scholar Martin Dibelius (1883-1947) remarked that the first Christian reports contained no biographical material that rightly deserved to be called that. Nevertheless, some information can be found in the Gospels, especially among the synoptic, that can possibly be traced back to the historical Jesus, even if controversial in certain cases. They have, so to say, survived as 'Jesuanic primary rocks' among the overlying transmission layers. Let us try to compile the few things that we know with some certainty.

Neither Jesus' day of birth nor his day of death is known, not even his birth and death years. Some of the assumptions lie far apart. His birth data stated range, however, from 7 to 0 "before Christ". Some researchers opt for the year 4 before Christ as the most probable year of birth. As, according to Luke, Jesus started acting publicly "around the age of thirty".[2] this date would fall into the years 26 and

27 after Christ, provided that the hypothesis of the year of birth in 4 B.C. and Luke's information of the age of Jesus at the beginning of his public appearance were correct. The period of his public work is specified differently by the evangelists. According to the Synoptics, it is one to two years, according to the historically least reliable John, it is at least three years. Thus Jesus' death would fall into the years 28-29 A.D. Most historical-critical theologians, however, date Jesus' death to the years 30-33 A.D.

We learn almost nothing about childhood and youth of Jesus. He was probably born in Nazareth, as already mentioned. His mother's name obviously was Maria, his father's Joseph.[3] It is improbable that he was a descendant of King David because this idea is only based on the Messiah claim that the early Christian communities raised. Jesus had numerous siblings. The names of his brothers — Jacob, Joses, Judas and Simon — were handed down by Mark, the names of his sisters are unknown. The 'Brother of the Lord' Jacob would play an important role after Jesus' death in the early Christian community of Jerusalem.

Jesus, therefore, grew up in a family with many children. He was probably the first born. As is the custom in families with many children, the young Jesus was probably called early for the supervision and care of his younger siblings. In all probability, he also came to know abject poverty. That could be an explanation for his devotion to the weak and helpless.

About the father, we only know that he was a carpenter and builder. Builder sounds more sophisticated than it was. The houses in the villages of Palestine were mostly made of one only room roofed with reeds, hey and twigs. In that room, the whole family lived. Joseph was, therefore, rather a handyman specialised in the construction of simple houses and all kinds of repair work. Jesus probably learned the crafts from him in his early adolescence. As he is not mentioned any more in the Gospels later on, we can presume that he died young. It seems that Jesus loved him very much. The fact that he addressed God in later years with the filial Abba (Dad), suggests that he recovered in him the characteristics of his biological father. But with this, we already move on to the unsteady ground of speculation. The death of the beloved father could have created a grave crisis for the young Jesus which he overcame by replacing the loving father by the loving God Father with whom he maintained an intimate relationship.

Joachim Gnilka thinks that Jesus lived with his family until he met John the Baptist. I think this is unlikely. After the death of his father, it seems that at least an estrangement, if not a break-up, happened between him and his family. It is rather probable that he went wandering while earning his living as a carpenter. The tale of Jesus' tour with his disciples through the Jewish-pagan North of Palestine, to Tyre and Sidon, may possibly be a recollection of the time before his public appearance, because he might have told the disciples about it. It is, however, also thinkable that the way of propagation of the gospel was dated back into the life of Jesus after his death. It remains a secret where he spent his years of wandering and learning apart from that, if he established contact with Essenes, Pharisees scribes and zealots. From the freshness, liveliness and vividness of his language, we can meanwhile conclude that he learned among ordinary people. It is uncertain if he was literate after all; what we know is that he left no written documents. He was also not a scholar type. His charisma showed best in free speech and personal encounter.

The encounter with John the Baptist takes centre stage in Jesus' biography because it indicates the beginning of his presence in public. How important it was for him can easily be seen from the fact that the Baptist is mentioned 26 times in the Gospels and 6 times in the Acts. It is certain that Jesus was baptised by John in the waters of Jordan. This fact gave some problems to the Christians of the early days because, according to their opinion, Jesus was the immaculate and, therefore, sinless sacrificial lamb that appeased Yahweh's wrath over the sinning humanity and who sacrificed his life as ransom for many.[4] The baptism by John, however, presupposed a confession of sins and consequently the sinfulness of the person to be baptised. Quite possibly the legendarily filigreed story of the heaven splitting apart, of the Holy Spirit descending on him like a dove and a voice from Heaven saying: "You are my dearly loved Son, and you bring me great joy",[5] was made up in order to smoothen this contradiction. May be it can also be interpreted as an adoption ritual according to Psalm 2, 7 ("you are my son. Today I have become your Father".) That does not exclude that Jesus had an experience of calling in connection with his baptism, and that he spoke about it later to his disciples. It is unrecorded if Jesus spent some time with the Baptist. It is, however, likely because the messages of the Baptist and Jesus have a number of significant similarities without hiding the crucial differences. We will look into them in detail later.

After his stay with the Baptist, Jesus started acting in public. He started preaching in synagogues and in the open and gathered a circle of men and women around him who accompanied him as a small community. As far as we know, this circle was formed by simple people: fishermen, craftsmen, peasants, may be also day labourers and homeless people, and not forgetting, some well-off widows who financed the subsistence of the small community.

Mark reports that his family set out to look for him after they knew about his public appearances, "in order to bring him back by force because they said: "He is out of his mind".[6] Much speaks for the authenticity of this tradition because it is uncommon to say something like that about the Son of God. Mark goes on telling that Jesus reacted in a distant and dismissive way to the wish of his relatives to speak to him: "Who is my mother, and who are my brothers"? Then he looked at those around him and said, "Look, these are my mother and brothers. Anyone who does God's will is my brother and sister and mother"[7]. Here we see an important feature of Jesus' teaching that we will elaborate on later. Jesus deliberately replaces the family in which he was born into by the family of those who fulfil God's will. Nevertheless, this does not imply a break with his family because Jesus apparently returned to his home village and preached in the local synagogue. The reaction of the villagers, as reported by Mark, is significant: "Where did he get all this wisdom and the power to perform such miracles? Isn't he just a carpenter, the son of Mary and the brother of Jacob, Joseph, Judas, and Simon? And his sisters live right here among us".[8] Then Jesus told his disciples: "A prophet is honoured everywhere except in his own hometown and among his relatives and his own family".[9]

After Jesus' death, his mother and brothers joined the early Christian community of Jerusalem. Together with Peter and John, Jacob belonged to the three "columns" of the early community that Paul mentioned in the letter to the Galatians.[10] In later years, he even seemed to have replaced Peter as a leader of the community.

Jesus' sermon about the Kingdom of God apparently had a healing and liberating effect on his listeners. This applies especially to psychosomatic illnesses, which were in those days probably no less common than today. This is why it is not surprising to learn that he soon had the reputation of a miracle worker, exorcist and healer. People came in flocks to his sermons. They brought possessed people and invalids to him in hopes that he would heal them; this is why he was often surrounded by a huge crowd. In spite of that, his legacy in the fertile landscape at the North and West bank of the Lake of Genneseret was divided. On the one hand, people came in flocks in order to hear and see him and become witnesses of his miracles. On the other hand, his call for a return to God attracted little attention. The enthusiasm remained on the surface. This is the reason for the berating words about Bethsaida, Chorazin and Capernaum.[11]

When sending the twelve disciples, it is possibly an antedating of the missionary work of the post-Easter community into Jesus' lifetime. We know from Paul's Epistles that there were itinerant preachers who worked as missionaries in the way Mark described it. On the other hand, the terrifying, almost repulsive hardness of the instructions is definitely Jesuanic. If it was not him who already sent them on the missionary trip, he at least prepared them for it. He himself led the unsteady life of an itinerant preacher "who had no place to lay down his head".[12]

It is uncertain if Jesus was already in conflict with the rulers in Galilee because of his work. The fate of the Baptist implies that men who attracted the masses became suspicious of being rebels, the more so if they did not cut down on criticising the rulers.

The question why Jesus moved to Jerusalem with his small community for the Paschal festival cannot be answered with certainty. It was probably because he was interested in promulgating his message in the centre of religious Judaism. It is completely unlikely that he knew or even suspected which fate was expecting him there. It is more probable that he and his community went to Jerusalem with high expectations where they were received enthusiastically by the pilgrims who were gathered in Jerusalem because his reputation as a miracle worker, healer and prophet was by then widespread. For Jesus and his movement applies what Walter Nigg wrote about Francis of Assisi (1181/82-1226) and the Franciscans: "The initial period of the Franciscans was filled with an unequalled enthusiasm that roared through Italy like a Whitsun storm. An infectious buoyancy and purity of intention was characteristic of this era in a way that one can always only see at the very first beginning of a movement. Its power and magic one cannot imagine big enough. A very peculiar splendour hangs above this time of origin".[13]

What happened in Jerusalem in detail remains unclear despite the relatively extensive reports of the gospels. Apparently, Jesus was deeply disappointed and by the religious mass business in and around the temple. He considered the cult of sacrificial offerings as a mere religious profiteering where the temple priesthood, traders, cattle dealers, publicans and others made money. The rich were supposed to donate a bull, the wealthy a wether and the poor two doves for sacrifice, not to speak about monetary sacrifices and temple taxes. Jesus apparently criticised the externalised sacrificial cult in the temple and the hustle and bustle of the pilgrim festivals severely. There was probably also a prophetic symbolic action that we know as "temple cleansing".[14] The historical core is likely to have been that Jesus asked the merchants and money changers to leave the front court of the temple. In doing so, he possible knocked over a few "tables of the money changers and stalls of the dove dealers". It was probably no more that a localised incident because otherwise the temple guards would have interfered and arrested the "trouble maker". Because of the *intensification tendency,* the event is dramatised in the Gospel of John: Jesus now made a whip from some ropes and chased them all (!) out of the Temple. He drove out the sheep and cattle scattered the money changers' coins over the floor.[15] It should be noted, however, that through his sermon and the symbolic action he antagonised not only the temple priesthood but also all those who made a living from religion. The decision of putting him away by denouncing him to the Romans as a rebel was taken in the High Council,[16] possibly even in a smaller circle to which the most influential members of the council belonged, apart from the high priest.

Jesus may have guessed what kind of dark clouds were brewing above his head. In any case, he celebrated a never-to-be-forgotten last supper with his disciples that stuck in their memory. He probably blessed bread and wine and passed them to his disciples as usual. It is possible that there was a traitor with the name of Judas among his disciples. We know nothing about his motives. Jesus would doubtlessly also have been arrested without his involvement. The arrest was made by temple guards who were armed with swords and sticks. It is quite unlikely that Roman auxiliary troops were also involved as reported by John. Because of the *intensification tendency*, it must have been entire legions arresting Jesus and still flinching at the sight of him and falling to the ground.[17] The disciples fled head over heels except for Peter who followed the henchmen up to the front court of the high priest's palace. The denial of Jesus by Peter probably has a historical core because such a deeply shameful, even guilty behaviour cannot have been made up. Jesus' interrogation in front of the High Council could quite well have been an interrogation in front of a few hurriedly summoned members of the Sanhedrin. We do not know of what Jesus was accused. The only certainty is that Jesus was found guilty. In the opinion of most historical-critical theologians, there was no *confession of being the Messiah* by Jesus in front of the Sanhedrin. "Very early next morning", as we learn from Mark, "the high priests, elders and scribes, which was the whole Sanhedrin, adopted a resolution about Jesus: They got him tied up and taken away, and delivered him to Pilate".[18]

Pilate, known for his ruthlessness and cruelty, made short work of Jesus. He sentenced him as a rebel against Roman rule, though it should be noted that due to a misunderstanding, Jesus' message of the present beginning of the Kingdom of God might indeed have appeared to him as a capital crime. The zealots also wanted to establish the Kingdom of God in Palestine, though after a violent insurrection against Roman foreign rule. But that happened only forty years later in the Jewish War (66-70 A.D.). We will never be able to clarify definitely which role the inscription on the cross 'King of the Jews' played (if it ever existed). It is possible that the opponents of Jesus denounced him to Pilate stating that he claimed to be 'King of the Jews' (Messiah).

After the proclamation of sentence, Jesus was scourged and ridiculed by the hangman's assistants. He was then led out of the city to the place of execution Golgotha. The episode with Simon of Cyrene who was forced by the soldiers to carry the cross or at least the crossbar could be historical. Among the historical-critical scientists, there is now-a-days almost no doubt about the crucification and death of Jesus on the cross, though even his death on the cross was questioned in novelistic designed lives of Jesus. As the disciples had fled, only the women remained as eyewitnesses. They saw the horrific events from a distance. Jesus' words on the cross are mostly taken from the psalms and attributed to him afterwards. That does not exclude that Jesus prayed on the cross. With some certainty, the cry that initiated his dying has been handed down. It is possible that Jesus died asking for forgiveness for his tormentors. But it is also possible that he died in despair. Whether two other delinquents were crucified with him is uncertain, as well as the story of pardoning Barabbas. It is also possible that quite a crowd of the residents of Jerusalem, whom Jesus had made his enemies, requested his death at the court case, but it was definitely not the whole people.

Jesus' dead body was doubtlessly taken down from the cross the same Friday evening and buried because otherwise the Sabbath would have been desecrated. There was in any case a regulation in the *First Testament* that requested to bury those who had been executed at the stake the same day because elsewhere the land would be contaminated. The stories about the funeral by Joseph of Arimathea and Nicodemus and the finding of the empty tomb are more or less legendary.

Theologians produced a lot of printed paper in order to reconstruct the exact sequence of events in Jerusalem. In my opinion, this is futile because they were already lying so far back in time in the moment when they were set out in writing that the exact course of events could not be traced back any more. This is why there is a multitude of inaccurate and contradictory information to be found in the gospels. I am also not sure if the efforts made in this regard belong to the good fruits that mattered so much to Jesus. In the end, the exact reconstruction of the events in Jerusalem that led to the crucifixion of Jesus is not so important. It is completely sufficient to understand that, on the first hand, Jesus was sentenced to death by the Roman prefect Pontius Pilate after a trial, and crucified the very same day, and, secondly, that the high priest and at least a part of the Sanhedrin participated in Jesus arrest and extradition to the Romans.

REFERENCES

1. *Harijan* 28.1.1939.
2. *Gospel of Luke*, 3:23.
3. *Gospel according to St Mark*, 6:1-6.
4. *Ibid.*, 10:45.
5. *Ibid.*, 10:11.
6. *Ibid.*, 3:20
7. *Ibid.*, 3:33-35.
8. *Ibid.*, 6:3
9. *Ibid.*, 6:5
10. *Letter of Paul to the Galatians*, 1:19; 2, 9.
11. *Gospel according to St Matthew*, 11:20-24.
12. *Gospel according to St Matthew*, 8:20.
13. Walter Nigg: *Große Heilige*, Zürich, 71.
14. *Gospel according to St. Mark*, 11:15-19.
15. *Gospel of John*, 2:13-22.
16. The High Council or Great Sanhedrin was the highest religious governing committee of the Jews, which also acted as an important political

intermediary between the Romans and the people. It consisted of Sadducees, scribes, Pharisees and elders and was headed by the High Priest. It had 72 members; 27 were sufficient to pass resolutions.

17. *Gospel of John*, 18:6.
18. *Gospel according to St Mark*, 15:1.

13
The Message of Jesus about God's Rule

The time promised by God has come at last! The Kingdom of God is near! Repent of your sins and believe in the Good News!
—Jesus of Nazareth

The result of the historical-critical research regarding the biography of Jesus is poor. This is mainly because early Christendom was dominated by the expectation of Jesus' return as Messiah and Son of Man. It reckoned daily with the outbreak of an apocalyptic catastrophe in which Yahweh would destroy the irretrievably corrupt old world and replace it by a new one. Such ideas were widespread at the time of Jesus because they were standing in the tradition of the prophecy of the *First Testament*. Thus far as the return of Jesus as Messiah and Son of Man was delayed or failed to materialise respectively, the interest for the life and teaching of Jesus arose. In the course of this, his doctrine was in the foreground right from the beginning, because its strict observance decided about who would be saved in the Last Judgement and who would be condemned to eternal agony.

What we know now-a-days about the historical Jesus and his doctrine goes basically back to the tradition of the synoptics. From the tenth chapter, we know how manifold myths and legends as well as community prophecy and theology interfered with this tradition. It is nevertheless worth trying to reconstruct the doctrine of Jesus from the existing text material, even if we probably never reach absolute certainty about what Jesus was teaching.

The church critic Karlheinz Deschner resumes the doctrine of Jesus in a few sentences as follows: "Apart from the proclamation of the imminent Kingdom of God, centre stage of Jesus' sermon was obviously taken by the commandment of love, love to God and the neighbour, also to the enemy. He seems to have been dominated by a tendency to extreme radicalism: fight against cult and exhibition of piety, against the self-righteous and judging, against oppression of the weak, exploitation of the poor, against violence, retaliation and murder. These were probably the basic traits of his message".[1] By this scale, he measures the church history from ancient times to the present and reaches a devastating verdict.

JESUS AND JOHN THE BAPTIST

The meeting with the Baptist was for Jesus, as already mentioned, of vital significance. From him, he apparently received important stimuli for his doctrine. John is described as an ascetic in the gospels. He wore a garment of camel hair, a leather belt around his hips and lived on locusts and wild honey. He appeared as a prophet announcing the imminent judgement of Yahweh on the world. He called the people for a return to God and for penitence and baptised the penitent in the waters of Jordan to cleanse them from their sins. He was convinced that the Last Judgement of Yahweh, where the just were baptised with the holy ghost, the sinners, however, were thrown into purgatory, was imminent so that it would be possible to maintain ritual purity through a law-abiding life and, therefore, appear pure in front of Yahweh's seat of judgement. The people who asked him what to do were requested by him to share their possession with the poor He did not request from the tax collectors and soldiers to abandon their ignoble jobs inasmuch as we can believe the Gospel according to Luke. He only requested from the first not to ask for more than what had been established and the latter not to abuse or blackmail anybody and to be content with their pay.[2] It is unlikely that Pharisees and Sadducees came to him in order to be baptised. He supposedly exclaimed: "You brood of snakes! Who warned you to flee God's coming wrath? Prove by the way you live that you have repented of your sins and turned to God. Don't just say to each other, "We're safe, for we are descendants of Abraham". That means nothing, for I tell you, God can create children of Abraham from these very stones. Even now the axe of God's judgment is poised, ready to sever the roots of the trees. Yes, every tree that does not produce good fruit will be chopped down and thrown into the fire".[3] The historical background of this *Bible* passage is probably that John was hard on the rich and mighty as well as on the temple priesthood who all collaborated with the Roman occupiers.

In the Synoptic Gospels, the Baptist appears as precursor of Jesus. They report in unison that Jesus was baptised by John. That needs to be explained because Jesus was not in need of baptism because in view of the early Christians he was sinless. According to Matthew, John did not want to let Jesus be baptised by him. He says to him: "I am the one who needs to be baptised by you, so why are you coming to me"? and gets the answer: "It should be done, for we must carry out all that God requires".[4] The Synoptics report that after Jesus' baptism the heavens opened and the Spirit of God descended like a dove upon him and a voice from heaven said: "This is my dearly beloved Son, who brings me great joy".[5] Yet, Jesus' baptism appeared to be too improper for John the Evangelist, after all. With him, the scene is completely elevated into the mythical. The Baptist sees Jesus approaching and says to the bystanders: "Look ! The Lamb of God who takes away the sin of the world!" ![6] In reality, the meeting between Jesus and the Baptist was probably quite different. Jesus is completely unknown when he came to be baptised by John whose reputation is widespread in the whole of Israel. It is quite possible that in doing so he had an inaugural vision, but the bystanders certainly did not realise any of that.

We do not know how long Jesus was with the Baptist. Many things, however, indicate that he joined the disciples of John and spent some time with him. But they soon went separate ways. Jesus began appearing in public and gathering his own community. Some of John's disciples apparently changed sides, yet it seems that a kind of competition arose between the disciples of John and the disciples of Jesus, though the reliability of these informations is doubtful.

John and Jesus did not only take different paths in physical terms but also in their preaching. Instead of the *threatening message* of the imminent final judgement of the angry, judging, punishing and annihilating God, that is the centre of John's preaching, with Jesus, the *glad tidings* of the loving, merciful and kind God who turns his attention to all people, especially the poor and those without rights, the despised and humiliated, comes to the fore. However, for Gandhi as well as for Jesus, his God is a loving but not a lovely God. He is also terrifying because he imposes the hardest tests to those who love him most. Even Jesus would not be spared from this experience.

GOD'S RULE OR MESSIAH'S RULE ?

In the opinion of the majority of the historical-critical theologians,

Jesus' preaching focuses on the *Kingship of God.*[7] But what does he mean with this term? As he explains it nowhere, we must assume that it was known to his audience. The term God's rule is ambiguous because it makes us spontaneously think about a relationship of dominance of the kind that exists between slaveholder and slave, master and servant, bourgeois and proletarian, boss and subordinate. That is not meant here. It is, on the contrary, the abolition of all power relationships of men over men as well as over the extra-human nature as we met it in Gandhi's "slavery" in his relationship to God. It may sound paradox, but in this rule, the most extreme freedom and the most extreme lack of freedom concur. While the revocation of dominance between men usually results in threats of penalties and, in the case of a refusal to submit, in painful penalties aimed at restoring the power relationship, such threats of penalties and sanctions are missing completely in the relation between man and God. Insofar, the myth of the Fall of Man in the *Bible*, in which Yahweh punishes Eve and Adam severely, needs correction; likewise the constant threats of priests and prophets of Yahweh's burning wrath against the disobedient and stubborn people. God gives us human beings the freedom of choice to opt for or against him and thus distinguishes us from the rest of creation that does not know this kind of freedom. Who turns to God and complies with the great law that he is himself, does so of his own free will. Who turns away from God in order to go his own way and shapes his life himself, does this in full freedom, too. If he chooses the latter, as Adam and Eve did, God is not angry, he does not threaten with punishment and annihilation in order to re-establish his rule. He remains the same he always was and will always be. People who choose the path into freedom from God's rule "punish" themselves, insofar as this word can be used reasonably in this context, because the path into freedom will soon lead to dependence on people, nature and their own passions. Even more, by dissolving the connection to God, who is eternal life, they choose with it death, and not only the first one, the biological death to which all biological life is subject, but also the second one, the spiritual death. They fall into the nothing.

Therefore, the term God's rule was quite familiar to devout Israelites. There are, nevertheless, two tradition lines in the *Bible* that we must differentiate: *God's rule* and *Messiah's rule*. Both refer to the history of Israel; God's rule refers to the premonarchic era and Messiah's rule to the monarchic era.

MESSIAH'S RULE

In the eighth chapter of the Book of Samuel, there is the crossroads where both tradition lines separate. The people come to the judge Samuel and ask him to appoint a king who shall rule over them as is the custom among other peoples. Samuel prays, therefore, to the Lord and the Lord replies: "Do everything they say to you, for it is me they are rejecting, not you. They don't want me to be their king any longer . . . . . Do as they ask, but solemnly warn them about the way a king will reign over them".[8] Samuel gives a vivid description of the rights of a king who will rule over them: "The king will draft your sons and assign them to his chariots and his charioteers, making them run before his chariots. Some will be generals and captains in his army, some will be forced to plough in his fields and harvest his crops, and some will make his weapons and chariot equipment. The king will take your daughters from you and force them to cook and bake and make perfumes for him. He will take away the best of your fields and vineyards and olive groves and give them to his own officials. He will take a tenth of your grain and your grape harvest and distribute it among his officers and attendants. He will take your male and female slaves and demand the finest of your cattle and donkeys for his own use. He will demand a tenth of your flocks, and you will be his slave. When that day comes, you will beg for relief from this king you are demanding, but then the LORD will not help you".[9]

But the people did not listen to Samuel's warnings. They wanted to be like other peoples. They wanted to have a king who administered justice and who stood in front of them and conducted war. Samuel fulfilled the people's request and anointed Saul King. It followed the period of prosperity under Saul, David and Salomon during which Israel supposedly became a middle-sized power prevailing against the surrounding major powers Assyria-Babylon, Persia and Egypt.

After Salomon's death, in 931 B.C., the Davidic Kingdom was divided into a Northern and a Southern Kingdom. The Northern Kingdom declined and later perished. It was conquered by the Assyrians in the year 722 B.C. The Southern Kingdom lost its independence after the conquest by the Babylonians in the year 586 B.C. The upper class of the Southern Kingdom was sent into exile to Babylonia. At the latest after the return of the banned from Babylonian exile in the year 538 B.C., the desire for restoration dawned in the people, even more the wish to surpass the Davidic Kingdom by the powerful intervention of Yahweh and his anointed one from the tribe of David. In this context, Nathan's prophecy plays an important role, the key phrases of which read: "I (Yahweh) will establish your (David's) descendants as kings forever; they will sit on your throne from now until eternity".[10] This prophecy proved to be wrong as so many, because David's throne did not last eternally. But as so often, the very disproval of a prophecy releases the belief in its future fulfilment. The people believed that Yahweh and his anointed one would bring home the sons of Israel who were dispersed among the peoples, that they would reunite the separated Kingdoms and let them shine in new splendour.

While in the beginning, the expectation of the Messianic Kingdom was still oriented completely to the here and now, it acquired later on more and more phantastic traits under the influence of apocalyptic ideas from Babylonia, Persia and Egypt. The prophets proclaimed that the old world, because it was irredeemably corrupt, would be destroyed by Yahweh in a terrible natural disaster and it would be replaced by a new one in which the Messiah would rule eternally as eschatological ruler over the peoples: "I saw someone like a son of man coming with the clouds of heaven. He approached the ancient one and was led into his presence. He was given authority, honour, and sovereignty over all the nations of the world, so that people of every race and nation and language would obey him. His rule is eternal, it will never end. His Kingdom will never be destroyed.[11] These words of the Prophet Daniel from the second century B.C. should become the interpretive pattern for the return of Jesus, risen from the dead as eschatological Messiah and Son of Man.

There is no doubt that the early Christian community in Jerusalem saw Jesus by all means in this religio-nationalistic tradition which was extremely virulent particularly in times of national humiliation through Roman rule over Palestine. Rudolf Bultmann writes in his book about Jesus: "In any case, the Jewish people at the time of Jesus were moved most strongly by Messianic hopes".[12] In Luke's tale about Emmaus, the two disciples report to Jesus, risen from the dead, whom they do not recognise: "He (Jesus) was a prophet who did powerful miracles, and he was a mighty teacher in the eyes of God and all the people. But our leading priests and other religious leaders handed him over to be condemned to death, and they crucified him. We had hoped he was the Messiah who had come *to rescue Israel*".[13] And in the Acts of the Apostles, the disciples ask the resurrected one: "Lord, has the time come for you to free *Israel* and restore our *Kingdom*"? and he replied, "The Father alone has the authority to set those dates and times, and they are not for you to know".[14]

In John's Book of Revelation, the Jewish-Christian tradition line of the apocalyptic ruler, anointed by Yahweh, reaches a peak. In it doomsday, which already played an important role in the apocalyptic speeches of the biblical Christ of the synoptic Gospels, is painted in the most screaming colours. At the end of this violence and torture orgy, Satan is heavily chained for a thousand years and thrown into an abyss. The Christian martyrs, however, are raised from the dead and live for a thousand years under Christ's rule in the Messianic Kingdom.[15]

The image that the *Bible* draws of the Messiah would be imcomplete if we saw in him only the despot to whom Yahweh speaks in the second psalm: "You are my son. Today I have become your Father. Only ask, and I will give you the nations as your inheritance, the whole earth as your possession. You will break them with an iron rod and smash them like clay pots".[16] He is also presented as the King of Peace in the *Bible*, for example in Isaiah[17] and Zechariah.[18] But the peace of the Messianic Kingdom is nevertheless a peace created by war and violence. Even in Isaiah and Zechariah, extremely bellicose voices alternate with peaceful ones in rapid succession when referring to the Messiah.

GOD'S RULE

The tradition of God's rule can be traced back, as already mentioned, to the premonarchic era when Yahweh was still King of Israel. It was the time in which the league of the twelve tribes of the Israelites tried to put in place a socially just society under the rule of Yahweh, certainly with all its imperfections and weaknesses but also with a series of institutional measures that were supposed to avoid or at least reduce a division of the society between rich and poor, mighty and powerless, high and low. We know about them through the 25th chapter of the Book of Leviticus and, intensified, through the 15 th chapter of the Book Deuteronomy. The protection of the weak, meaning widows and orphans, strangers and poor, was the responsibility of the judges of Israel, which was time and again demanded by the prophets later on in the monarchic era. *Social justice was understood as the foundation of social peace.* At least to some extent, one can also find in the prophets' writings the demand not to rely on arms, chariots and horses, but on Yahweh's protection against external enemies. Again and again, the prophets oppose, on behalf of Yahweh, idolatry as well as the abuse of power by kings and priests, and for that they accept persecution, suffering and death. In chapters 60 to 66 of the third Book of Isaiah, the message of the Kingdom of God of the *First Testament* reaches its peak. The judgement on the irredeemably corrupt world and the splendour of the New Jerusalem are pictured in sharp contrast.

Apocalypticism like *Messianism* was an influential intellectual movement in the centuries before and after Christ was born. It also penetrated deeply into the preaching of the biblical Christ, such as in the eschatological speeches of Jesus in the synoptic gospels, as well as in the preaching of the early Christian communities and of Paul, already earlier on. Till today it is a "long runner" among the fundamentalists of the Abrahamic religions. The revelation of John plays an important role in this context. It brings the two traditions lines of the Kingdom of Messiah and the Kingdom of God together by placing them one after the other. The Kingdom of the thousand years in which the Messiah rules over the Christian martyrs comes first. It is followed by the final victory over Satan and death, followed by the judgement on all the dead. The Kingdom of God in the shape of the New Jerusalem forms the glorious culmination of the script.

In times of crisis, the apocalyptic expectation of the Kingdom of Messiah and God became virulent again and again, as for example around 1000 A.D., during the time of the great plague in the 14th century or at the time of reformation in the 16th century. In a secularised form, we find the vision of the Kingdom of God in the *classless society* with Marx (1818-1883) and the Marxists as well as in the *society free of domination163* with Bakunin (1814-1876) and the anarchists. We find it furthermore with Gandhi as *Ram Raj*, *Khudai Raj* or *Panchayati Raj*, which means a social order basically based on *rural self-government*. Gandhi, however, differs from the Marxists and anarchists in one basic aspect: he discards violence, lying, cheating, and the like in the fight for realisation of God's rule on Earth.

There is no doubt that the *biblical Christ* stands completely and utterly in the apocalyptic and Messianic tradition of the *First Testament*. This does not prove that the same applies for the *historical Jesus*. In my opinion, he was radically and uncomprisingly opposed to Messianism. This concept contradicts a prevailing conception in theology and church. It, therefore, requires a thorough justification.

REFERENCES

1. Karlheinz Deschner: *Abermals krähte der Hahn*, Reinbek 1972, 135.
2. *Gospel of Luke*, 3:10-13.
3. *Gospel according to St Matthew*, 3:7-10.
4. *Ibid.*, 3:13-15.
5. *Ibid.*, 3:17.
6. *Gospel of John*, 1:29.
7. In contrast, Joseph Ratzinger/Benedict XVI, in his book about Jesus under reference to Evangelist John, claims that Jesus' self-revelation as the Son of God was the core of his message.
8. *First Book of Samuel*, 8:7-9.
9. *Ibid.*, 8:11-18.
10. *Second Book of Samuel*, 6:16.
11. *Prophet Daniel*, 7:13 f.
12. Rudolf Bultmann: *Jesus*, Tübingen 1961, 21.
13. *Gospel of Luke*, 24:19-21.
14. *Acts of the Apostles*, 1:6.
15. *Ibid.*, 20:1-6.
16. *Psalms*, 2:7-9.
17. *Prophet Isaiah*, 9:1-6; 11:1-16; 61:1-11.
18. *Prophet Zakaria*, 9:9.

14
What did Jesus Teach about God's Rule?

> *"Kingdom of God" — and not any more "Christ" — must become the central concept of ecclesiastical theology.*
>
> — *Claus Petersen*

When, where and how would it begin? Where does it have its place, in this world or in the next world, in the present or in the future? Did it already germinate to take shape in Jesus and his small community, or is it yet to come and were just anticipated symbolically in Jesus' miracles. Will it come subsequent to a cosmic catastrophe through which God will destroy the irredeemably corrupt world and replace it by a "new heaven and a new earth"?[1] For each of these possible interpretations, evidence can be found in the texts of the *Second Testament*. We have the same situation again that we had while discussing the historical Jesus: From the text material of the Second Testament, we cannot get a clear, consistent image that is without contradiction. Theologians presented different interpretations in the course of time. But which is the right one? We cannot say with certainty. May be it has not yet been found. In the end, each person has to decide him or herself which one he or she considers correct. We should, however, withstand the temptation of considering one of them as the *only* right one. William Wrede (1859-1906), a contemporary of Albert Schweitzer, already brought the attention to this risk when he wrote: "Every researcher acts in a way that he conserves of the words handed down what can be integrated into his construction of facts and his perception of historical possibility; everything else, however, he will reject".[2]

Within the limits of this study, I cannot analyse in detail the different and partially contradictory interpretations of Jesus' message of the Kingdom of God. I have to restrict myself to explaining why Jesus, in my opinion, was no apocalypticist in the sense that he was expecting the imminent doomsday.

THE HOLISTIC INTERPRETATION OF JESUS' MESSAGE ABOUT GOD'S KINGDOM

There are many reasons for the thesis that Jesus was expecting God's rule not as a consequence of a powerful intervention of God into history any time soon, but that he was already experiencing it as reality present inside him and his small community. Here, only the most important shall be mentioned:

To the question of the Pharisees, when the Kingdom of God would be coming, Jesus replies unmistakably with the words: "The Kingdom of God can't be detected by visible signs. You won't be able to say, "Here it is" ! or "It's over there!' For the Kingdom of God is already among you".[3] He considers the disciples blessed because they become eye witnesses of the beginning of God's rule: "Blessed are the eyes that see what you have seen. I tell you, many prophets and kings longed to see what you see, but they didn't see it. And they longed to hear what you hear, but they didn't hear it".[4] "I tell you the truth, of all who have ever lived, none is greater than John the Baptist. Yet even the least person in the Kingdom of Heaven (meaning the Kingdom of God) is greater than he is!" ![5] For Jesus, the Baptist is obviously the one who will announce the beginning of God's rule in the near future, probably even the Elijah who, according to popular belief, will return before the beginning of God's rule in order to prepare the people for it. He considers himself and his small community as those in whom it has taken its germinating shape and will from that moment on grow like the "mustard tree".[6] That is why he draws the limit of eras between the old and the new aeon between the Baptist and himself. The words show one more time his radical turning away from the eschatological expectations of the Baptist because the Kingdom of God will not break ground in the near future with the throes of a natural disaster. It will not be completed through catastrophe and judgment either. It is rather *present* and anyone who changes his ways will have a share.

The key to the understanding of Jesus' good news of the *present* beginning of God's rule could be the already mentioned word of Jesus, insofar as it really goes back to the historical Jesus: "I saw Satan fall from heaven like lightning"![7] With this sentence, Jesus comments the report of the astonished disciples about the miracles that they did in the course of the proclamation of the beginning of God's rule. It remains open, however, if Jesus' words belong into this historically dubious context. Jesus himself exorcises the demons with "God's finger" because God overpowered and chained Satan as the highest master of the demons so that now, the house of the powerful (meaning the world under Satan's rule) can be looted.[8]

Among the strongest arguments in favour of the thesis of the present beginning of God's rule in Jesus' community and his *powerful propagation in this world* is the double parable of the mustard seed and the sour dough, because it does not show any *apocalyptic time break*: "The Kingdom of Heaven is like a mustard seed planted in a field. It is the smallest of all seeds, but it becomes the largest of garden plants; it grows into a tree, and birds come and make nests in its branches . . . . . The Kingdom of Heaven is like the yeast a woman used in making bread. Even though she put only a little yeast in three measures of flour, it permeated every part of the dough".[9] "Besides, who would patch old clothing with new cloth? For the new patch would shrink and rip away from the old cloth, leaving an even bigger tear than before. And no one puts new wine into old wineskins. For the old skins would burst from the pressure, spilling the wine and ruining the skins. New wine is stored in new wineskins so that both are preserved".[10] The last mentioned words of Jesus stand isolated and are, as such, difficult to understand. They make sense, however, when we relate them to the Kingdom of God. The Kingdom of God is the radically new; it enforces, in order not to perish, the *renewal of the individual and the society*. Only this way, the new spirit, the new cloth, the new wine can be saved from decay.

When the disciples asked Jesus, who was the greatest in heaven, he called a child, put it in the midst of them and said: "I tell you the truth, unless you turn from your sins and become like little children, you will never get into the Kingdom of Heaven. So anyone who becomes as humble as this little child is the greatest in the Kingdom of Heaven".[11] For Jesus, the children were citizens in the Kingdom of God because he considered them innocent and sinless. The purpose of turning back is, therefore, to become like children. That means that we should take thankfully everything that we really need from God's hand and that we should not want more for fear of future shortage, which obviously does not mean that we should stop working. Jesus' wonderfully poetical speech about the flowers on the field and the birds under the sky has to be understood like this.[12] For Jesus, children also become models for the adults because they are in a relationship of love and dependency with their parents, provided of course, they have loving and caring parents who have the well-being of their children in their mind and not of their own. Children take what they need for life quite naturally from the hands of their parents and reflect the love that they get. I suppose that Jesus thought about the successful relationship with his own father which he transformed into a relationship to God-father after the death of his father. One cannot imagine a greater contrast than the one between Jesus' attitude towards children and the doctrine of the original sin by Augustine (354-430) who considers children sinners, because they are conceived and born "in sin", who can only be saved by the sacrament of baptism administered by the Church. It remains unbelievable how one individual could imprint his sexual neurosis on a whole cultural circle.

If it is true that Jesus declared children to be citizens of the Kingdom of God and considered them as models for the adults instead of considering adults as models for children as it is common practice, then it is not understandable why they should perish in the eschatological catastrophe. Especially for them, Jesus' words apply: The last will be the first and the first the last. In short, *the apocalyptic texts in the Bible must be assigned to the angry, bigoted, judging, punishing and annihilating God.* The question is, however, how this image of God can be brought in line with Jesus' idea of a loving, kind, merciful father-mother-God of the kind that we encounter in the story of the prodigal son.

By accumulating words of Jesus that support the thesis of the *present* beginning of God's rule, I see the danger of overshadowing the words that contradict it, or even omitting them. It is, therefore, absolutely essential to deal precisely with them. Concerning the great eschatological speech of Jesus that can be found in all synoptic, the historical-critical theologians agree that it cannot be ascribed to the historical Jesus. The same applies for the speech about the Last Judgment handed down by Matthew.[13]

The words that summarise Jesus' good news in the Gospel according to Mark, however, seem to be related to the future: "The time promised by God has come at last! The Kingdom of God is near! Repent of your sins and believe the Good News"![14] The sentence: "The time *has come* at last" does, however, not point to the future at all, but to the present. Hence, the words allow, by all means, the interpretation: *It is beginning now; it already exists as a seed and will develop anytime soon.* The following words of Jesus seem, however, to be definitely relating to the future in view of the Kingdom of God: "I tell you the truth, some standing here right now will not die before they see the Kingdom of God".[15] If we take the words of the mustard seed and the sour dough as a basis instead, nothing speaks against the interpretation that exactly this powerful growing of the "mustard tree" that Jesus is still expecting in his generation, is meant.

In the end, the plea of the paternoster "May your Kingdom come soon"[16] remains. Although it doubtlessly suggests a futuristic interpretation, it does not make it absolutely necessary. The parable of the mustard seed emphasises the nondescript beginning of the Kingdom of God in the shape of Jesus' community and predicts a brilliant future for it, which will not become reality through God's direct intervention in history in the form of the apocalypse but through the work of Jesus and his growing community which is inspired by God. It is, therefore, natural to ask for the coming of the Kingdom of God *in the sense of its further propagation*. The plea: "May your will be done on earth, as it is in heaven" means basically the same, because God's rule can also be defined by stating that in it, God's will be done. The work of Jesus and his community came at least quite close to this.

Conclusion: The historical Jesus turns *radically* away from the contemporary messianic-apocalyptic movement to which the Baptist also belonged. *Jesus contradicts firmly the devaluation of this world, which is presumably doomed because of its corruptness.* The Kingdom of God is not *of* this world, like all the other kingdoms, but it is *in* this world. The apocalypse would consequently amount to the *destruction of the developing Kingdom of God.*

That implies necessarily: Jesus was *no apocalyptic* in the sense that he was expecting the imminent doom of the world. But why then did early Christendom make him an apocalyptic? In my opinion, that is related to the catastrophe of Good Friday. Due to it, the enthusiastic expectation that he and his followers were filled with was literally crucified. The "mustard seed" was apparently crushed by Satan before it could grow and develop. If the Kingdom of God was still to come, not due to the work of *people inspired by God* but through the *powerful intervention of God in history* creating a tribunal for the world that had come under the spell of Satan. With Jesus' "raising" from the dead, God would announce his powerful intervention. With Jesus' resurrection, the resurrection of the dead would begin. He would be the first resurrected, who would be followed shortly by all others, some for eternal bliss, others for eternal damnation.

I have called my interpretation of Jesus' message of the Kingdom of God a *comprehensive* one because it is *in this world as well as out of this world;, it is past as well as present and future.* It does also not deny the evil in this world that can only be overcome by the power of voluntarily accepted suffering, i.e., *satyagraha*.

Let us summarize what differentiates Jesus' message of the present beginning of God's rule from the apocalyptic ideas of his contemporaries:

1. Jesus' God is not an angry, judging, punishing and annihilating God; He was a God of justice and peace, of love and life. Apocalypticism must, therefore, be assigned to the angry, judging, punishing and annihilating God of the *First Testament*.
2. The imminent turn of eras through God's powerful intervention in history, as expected by Jesus' contemporaries, is antedated by him to the present, even to the past, namely as the borderline between the eras of John the Baptist, on the one hand, whose message is rooted completely in the mindscape of the *First Testament*, and Jesus and his small community, on the other hand, in whom the Kingdom of God was gradually taking shape.
3. Jesus was convinced that God had overcome and bound Satan. This is why there was no obstacle any more for him in the propagation of God's rule in this world. His "healing miracles" were for him the visible signs for the final victory of God over Satan. In Jesus' view of the world there is no room for the prospect of a doomsday as punishment for the sinful world and its subsequent recreation by God's almighty will.
4. Hence, we have to put aside all apocalyptic doomsday prophecies including all threats of eternal punishment in Hell through Jesus in the *Second Testament* as not Jesuanic. They constitute a relapse into the mindscape of the *First Testament*.

WAS JESUS IN HIS RIGHT MIND ?

Even if Jesus, as it is my opinion, was no apocalypticist, we have to question if he was not completely *blind to reality*. How could he believe in the unstoppable growth of God's rule in this world in view of the overwhelming power of evil, palpably incarnated in his days in the cruel rule of the Romans? Did his belief not break to pieces at last on the cross? Did he not have to recognise and acknowledge the entire power of evil and taste the bitterness of death? As a matter of fact, we cannot say with certainty that he did not die in despair, we cannot say with certainty whether he did not pass this hardest of all tests, after all. It is actually thinkable that Jesus believed in God's intervention for his salvation to the bitter end, because God could not allow the "mustard seed" of the Kingdom of God to be trampled on by Satan. That could be a plausible explanation for the words on the cross if they are historical: "My God, my God, why have you abandoned me" ?[17]

The comparison with Gandhi could also prove to be fruitful in this respect. Both, Jesus and Gandhi, were obviously convinced of the irresistible power of non-violence over violence, of truth over untruth, of love over hatred and of God over "Satan". Gandhi said: "Non-violence is the greatest force at the disposal of mankind. It is mightier than the mightiest weapon of destruction devised by the ingenuity of man. Destruction is not the law of the humans. Man lives freely only by his readiness to die, if need be, at the hands of his brother, never by killing him. Every murder or other injury, no matter for what cause, committed or inflicted one another is a crime against humanity".[18] "Non-violence is an active principle of the highest order. It is soul force or the power of the godhead within us. Imperfect man cannot grasp the whole of that Essence — he would not be able to bear its full blaze — but even an infinitesimal fraction of it, when it becomes active within us, can work wonders. The sun in the heavens fills the whole universe with its life-giving warmth. But if one went too near it, it would consume him to ashes. Even so is it with the Godhead. We become godlike to the extent we realise non-violence; but we can never become wholly God".[19]

Even considering the overwhelming destructive force of the atomic bomb, he adheres to the belief in the power of non-violence. On February 10th, 1946, he wrote in his magazine Harijan: "There have been cataclysmic changes in the world. Do I still adhere to my faith in truth and non-violence? Has not the atom bomb exploded that faith? Not only has it not done so, but it has clearly demonstrated to me that the twins constitute the mightiest force in the world. Before it the bomb is of no effect. The two opposing forces are wholly different in kind, the one moral and spiritual, the other physical and material. The one is infinitely superior to the other which by its very nature has an end. The force of the spirit is ever progressive and endless. Its full expression makes it unconquerable in the world. In saying this, I know that I have said nothing new. I merely bear witness to the fact. What is more, that force resides in everybody, man, woman and child, irrespective of the colour of the skin. Only in many it lies dormant, but it is capable of being awakened by judicious training. It is further to be observed that without the recognition of this truth and due effort to realise it, there is no escape from self-destruction. The remedy lies in every individual training himself for self-expression in every walk of life, irrespective of response by the neighbours".[20]

Where does this belief come from? It comes from the conviction that untruth, considered under the perspective of eternity, does not exist and can, therefore, not win. I recall Gandhi's statement that we can also call his Creed: "The world rests upon the bedrock of *satya* or truth. *Asatya* meaning untruth also means non-existent, and *satya* or truth also means that which is. If untruth does not so much as exist, its victory is out of the question. And truth being that which is can never be destroyed. This is the doctrine of *satyagraha* in a nutshell".[21]

In the cultural context of Judaism, this understanding could definitely take the shape of a vision as expressed in Jesus' words: "I saw Satan fall down from Heaven like a lightning". What to think of this belief at the sight of the daily triumph of evil in the world, what in view of a development that brings us day by day closer to the abyss of an atomic, ecological, economical and spiritual self-destruction, an abyss from which we are only separated by a few steps? For the world as a whole, there is, in my opinion, no hope any more, unless we make wish the father and imagination the mother of the thought. It is, however, also true that wherever evil is repaid with good, and in this manner overcome, God's rule begins to germinate into reality. Insofar, Jesus' and Gandhi's belief in the power of truth and non-violence are by no means outdated.

It is possibly with Jesus as well as with Gandhi an inevitable delusion. They both lived to such a high degree within the truth that their vision of the reality of this world was blurred. Thus, Gandhi believed that India was, because of its thirty years long and finally successful non-violent and partially peaceful fight for independence, like no other country enabled to show the path into the land of freedom, justice and peace to the world. The division of the subcontinent into

India and Pakistan, the associated bloody conflicts and the renunciation of the Congress politicians from the principles of truth and non-violence taught him better. Even though he never lost faith in the unlimited power of truth and non-violence, he acknowledged that he had been wrong. The last years of his life were overshadowed by what he called the "agony of his soul". Jesus may have felt quite similar. His dream of the unstoppable propagation of the Kingdom of God was shattered when faced with the brutal violence that he fell victim to. He nevertheless overcame this violence through his suffering and defeated death though he suffered it.

JESUS' JUDGEMENT SERMON

Does that mean that with the historical Jesus there is no judgment sermon? Not at all. In the same way that Jesus *updated* the expectation of the Kingdom of God of early Judaism, he also *updated* its expectation of judgment. Judgment does not stand any more at the end of the day but begins with refusing to turn back. The judgment that Jesus announces, frequently with hard words for the rich, the powerful and the pious hypocrites, consists of the *exclusion from the Kingdom of God*. It is, however, not God and much less Jesus who excludes them but the unrepentant exclude themselves by refusing to repent. They annul the relationship to the truth, which is God, and for this reason for the faithful, not only the source of the mortal but also of the eternal life. At the end of their lives, they die not only the *biological*, the first death, which is the fate of all of us, but they also suffer the *spiritual*, the second death. They fall into nothingness. The hectic voracity for life and sensual pleasure that we find everywhere in our society, could very well have its origin in the conscious or unconscious knowledge about this circumstance. As long as we live, the denial of repentance is still revisable; repentance can still be carried out. That is, in my opinion, the meaning of the parable of the infertile fig tree[22] and the story about the dissimilar sons[23].

Should this interpretation be correct, the doctrine of *eternal punishment* that is closely related to the proclamation of judgment of the biblical Christ has become obsolete? I cannot believe that Jesus, who promulgated the good news of the present beginning of God's rule, the good news of God's inexhaustible love towards men and, as we may add, towards extra-human nature, is supposed to have threatened with eternal punishment. In my view, this doctrine is the incarnation of sadism, inseparably related to the judging, sentencing and punishing God whom we encountered in some parts of the *First Testament*. Even more, it still exceeds the gloomy image of this God by far. After all, Yahweh punished the sinner by annihilating only him, at most by punishing his descendants up to the third and fourth generation, but not with eternal damnation. From the historical point of view, this doctrine had, like Augustine's doctrine of the original sin, devastating consequences, because the menace of eternal agony of the sinners is pending like a heavy black cloud over Christendom. It spreads fear and terror and ties the faithful to the salvation-giving church. If we do not want to presume that Jesus was mentally schizophrenic, we have to make our choice between the Jesus who promulgated the message of love of God and humanity, and the Christ who threatened eternal punishment in hell.

The seriousness of the decision situation, in which Jesus as the preacher of God's rule places us, must not be downplayed. After all, this is dealing with all or nothing, salvation or perdition. It does not only refer to the future but in equal measure to the present. Christians expect salvation in the *other* world, the Kingdom of Heaven; Jews expect it in the *future* world, the Kingdom of the Messiah. For Jesus however, it begins in *this world* even if it reaches beyond this world. This world is potentially the Kingdom of God just as it is at present, a replica of hell. It, therefore, depends on us human beings if we turn it into heaven or hell. I agree with the Buddhist *Thich Nhat Hanh* when he explains: Whoever is angry with his brother, whoever does evil, does not go to hell, he *is* in hell.[24] Likewise we can say: Who does good, does not go to heaven, he *is* in heaven. The border between this world and the other world, between time and eternity, present and future has been abolished. "To practice non-violence in mundane matters is to know its true value. It is to bring heaven upon earth. There is no such thing as the other world. All worlds are one. There is no 'here' and no 'there'".[25] This interpretation, in my opinion, also gives us an understanding of Jesus' words: "Everyone who has given up house or wife or brothers or parents or children for the sake of the Kingdom of God, will be repaid many times over in this life and will have eternal life in the world to come".[26]

One could object: The second death will be in the end the most terrible of all punishments, virtually a "metaphysical execution". Even if a man chooses a life that bears this consequence, God in his inexhaustible mercy ought to save him eventually from himself. I cannot see it like that. The consequence would be: No matter what we do, if Hitler or Jesus, Stalin or Gandhi, we eventually all end up in one and the same "heaven" where culprits and victims meet. Such a thought seems absurd to me. One can possibly even say that for people who live in hell — and those who do evil do, after all, live in hell — the second death constitutes salvation after having realised what damage they have done. If we, however, take the idea of *Karma* as the starting point, there is even for a Hitler or a Stalin a possibility of rising to the highest heights of proximity to God from the deepest depths of abjectness through countless incarnations.

FOR WHOM DID JESUS TAKE HIMSELF ?

Jesus asks his disciples on the way to the villages close to Caesarea Philippi: "Who do people say I am?" "Well," they replied, "some say John the Baptist, some say Elijah, and others say you are one of the other prophets." Then he asked them, "But who do you say I am" ? Peter replied, "You are the Messiah". But Jesus warned them not to tell anyone about him.[27] Luke adopts the passage from Mark without any profound changes. Matthew, however, goes several steps beyond that. Here, Jesus answers to the confession of Peter: "You are the Messiah, the Son of the living God", with the words: "You are blessed, Simon son of John, because my Father in Heaven has revealed this to you. You did not learn this from any human being".[28] We have here another example of the *intensification tendency*. What Mark treats like a secret, supposedly only known by Jesus himself, the demons and the disciples, and what is not revealed until the hearing in the High Council in Jerusalem,[29] is evident in Matthew and Luke right from the beginning. They did not refrain any more from presenting Jesus as the Messiah and attributing this awareness to him. A temporary peak of this development is reached with the Evangelist John. For him, Jesus' life story is a story of self-revelation as Messiah and Son of God.

The question of who Jesus himself thinks he is, meaning the question about his self-conception or, as one used to say in the past, about his *self-awareness*, has kept theologians busy at all times. No wonder that the answers, like elsewhere, differ greatly or even contradict each other. Two books came out almost simultaneously in 1901 which were contradictory to each other. One book by William Wrede entitled *The Messianic Secret in the Gospels* and the other by

Albert Schweitzer's *The Secret of Messianity and Suffering: An Outline of Jesus' Life*. In his work, Wrede tries to prove that the historical Jesus did not consider himself as the Messiah but that everything related to Jesus' messianity was rather added to Jesus' life in the Gospel, according to Mark by the Christians of the first generation. The resurrection was, according to Schweitzer in The Quest of the Historical Jesus; for Wrede the messianic event in Jesus' life was real. Mark's presentation eventually emerged from the urge of moulding Jesus' earthly life messianically.[30]

Wrede's opinion gained acceptance among researchers in contrast to the one of Schweitzer who attributed to Jesus the knowledge about his (future) messianity. Peter's messianic confession seems to contradict this fundamentally. Meanwhile, the *Bible* passage allows a completely different interpretation, if we include the lines that follow it: Then Jesus began to tell them that the Son of Man must suffer many terrible things and be rejected by the elders, the leading priests, and the teachers of religious law. He would be killed, but three days later he would rise from the dead. As he talked about this openly with his disciples, Peter took him aside and began to reprimand him for saying such things. Jesus turned around and looked at his disciples, then reprimanded Peter. "Get away from me, Satan" ! he said. "You are seeing things merely from a human point of view, not from God's".[31] Why these hard words now that Peter was the disciple who was closest to Jesus and who had recognised him as the Messiah recently. Now he sees Satan in him, who approaches him as the tempter. Why this harsh rejection while Peter's "reproaches" were apparently motivated by his worries about the beloved leader of the group? If Jesus, as it is my opinion, did not have any previous knowledge about what was expecting him in Jerusalem, the reason given by Mark ceases to exist. This suggests the assumption that Jesus' harsh reaction in reality referred to Peter's messianic confession. Did Peter put pressure on Jesus to let himself be proclaimed Messiah and to restore the "Kingdom for Israel" as the leader of the messianic-apocalyptic movement of his times ? Did Jesus possibly reject this request as a *satanic temptation* ?

Furthermore, we know today or believe to know that Jesus did not claim for himself any of the majestic titles that Christianity attributes to him. He would probably have rejected them with no less harsh words if they had been offered to him, as he rejected Peter's messianic confession according to my opinion. That applies to the title Son of David, Son of Man according to the meaning of Daniel 7:13 and especially for the title Son of God in the sense of the Christ dogma. It is also true for the titles of High Priest, Lord and Saviour. It is possible that he considered himself a prophet. If he permitted being called master (Rabbi) is uncertain. Apart from that, I agree with Claus Petersen that the historical Jesus did not make use of any privileges: "Kingdom of God means, among other things, fundamental equality in the sense of equality of all people, and it goes completely against this principle to place somebody, even Jesus himself, above all others, to allow and build up hierarchies".[32]

The somewhat shocking conclusion that we can draw from this analysis is: The title *Christ*, the Greek version of the Jewish majestic title of Messiah, that became his last name in the course of time, was attributed to Jesus *against his will*. The historical Jesus was not called Jesus Christ but *Jesus of Nazareth*. If he nevertheless holds the title Christ with good reason, remains unaffected by that because that is a *question of faith*.

The thesis that Jesus did not attribute any majestic titles to himself can be corroborated by a number of quotes from Jesus. As such, Jesus decidedly rejected any kind of homage. He reprimands the rich man who *falls down on his knees* before him with the words: "*Good* Teacher, what must I do to inherit eternal life" ? by telling him "Why do you call me good? Only God is truly good".[33] Luke passed down a story, in which a woman in view of Jesus' mother exclaims: "God bless your mother — the womb from which you came, and the breasts that nursed you" ! Jesus replied coolly, "But even more blessed are all who hear the word of God and put it into practice".[34] Jesus' rejection of social distinctions becomes even more obvious in the story about the rank dispute of the disciples in Mark 9:33-37, even if its elaboration was probably a community formation. Jesus' words contained herein that form its historical core, were probably: Whoever (in the Kingdom of God) wants to be first must take last place and be the servant of everyone else. In my opinion, what Jesus wants to make clear here is: In the kingdoms of this world, there are social differences between rich and poor, mighty and powerless, high and low, educated and uneducated people. It shall not be like that in the Kingdom of God. There, equality and coequality prevail because the strong serves the weak, the healthy the sick and knowing the ignorant. Jesus uses similar arguments in the instruction about ruling and serving that follows shortly afterwards. Here, it is also about a rank dispute of the disciples, this time about the places of honour in the Kingdom of God: "You know that the rulers in this world lord it over their people, and officials flaunt their authority over those under them. But among you it will be different. Whoever wants to be a leader among you must be your servant, and whoever wants to be first among you must be the slave of everyone else".[35] The Kingdom of God, therefore, distinguishes itself from the kingdoms of this world by the principle of serving instead of ruling.

If Jesus, however, went as far as Gandhi, who refused to accept any kind of leadership role in respect to his fellow campaigners, must remain unavowed: "There is nothing like Gandhism. I have no followers. I am my own follower. No, no, even I have not succeeded in being my true follower, have I? Do I put my own thoughts into practice? How then can others be my followers? I would like others keeping me company and walking the same way. But how can I know who would walk ahead and who would fall behind? You are all my fellow-students and co-workers, fellow-servants and fellow-researchers. Forget the idea of being followers. Nobody is leading and nobody is following. Nobody is a leader and nobody is a follower. We are all going together in one line. I have said this quite often but I am repeating it in order to remind you".[36]

This statement could certainly be misunderstood. It applies exclusively to the circle of the *satyagrahis*. From the Indian National Congress, Gandhi occasionally requested almost dictatorial powers. If he were to assume the leadership of the independence campaign as an "expert for non-violent action", he demanded his instructions to be strictly followed. He was, therefore, not without good reason called a "Congress dictator".

Even if the historical Jesus did not regard himself as the Messiah, probably even rejected this title with sharp words, the question whether he, nevertheless, was or became the Messiah, remains untouched. This much is certain: Peter, and with him the original Christian community of Jerusalem, recognised and acknowledged the Messiah in the resurrected. This is a *statement of faith* independent of what Jesus thought about himself. As statements of faith, the majestic titles attributed to Jesus are allegedly untouchable to criticism. They are neither provable nor refutable. The difficulty however remains: Where do statements of faith begin and where do they end? Are Jesus' walking on the water or the feeding of the five thousand statements of faith? Are the Marian dogmas and the dogma of the ex-cathedra infallibility of the Pope included? Do the dogma of the Trinity and the dogma of Christ belong to them? These questions will still keep us busy.

The result of our investigation up to now about Jesus' teaching is modest. We know now, or rather think we know what Jesus' message was focused on: *The good news of the present beginning of God's rule.* We also believe that we know what he did not teach: That he was the Messiah, the future son of man or even God's son in the sense of the dogma of Christ. He did also not teach about the imminent Last Judgement of God on an irredeemably corrupt world and definitely not about eternal suffering in hell for sinners. We now want to turn our attention to the things he did teach.

REFERENCES

1. *Prophet Isaiah*, 65:17; 66:22; Apoc 21:1.
2. Cited by Albert Schweitzer: *Geschichte der Leben-Jesu-Forschung*, Tübingen, 1926, 371.
3. *Gospel of Luke*, 17:20 f.
4. *Ibid.*, 10:23 f.
5. Mt. 11:11.
6. Jesus obviously had little knowledge of nature since he thought that a mustard seed was able to grow into a giant tree.
7. *Gospel of Luke*, 10:18.
8. *Ibid.*, 11:14-23.
9. *Gospel according to Matthew*, 13:31-33.
10. *Ibid.*, 9:16-17.
11. *Ibid.*, 18:3.
12. *Ibid.*, 6:25-34.
13. *Ibid.*, 25:31-46.
14. *Gospel according to St Mark*, 1:15.
15. *Gospel according to St. Mark*, Mk. 9:1.
16. *Gospel according to St. Matthew*, 6:10.
17. *Gospel according to St. Mark*, 15:34. These words are identical with Psalms, 22:2.
18. *Harijan.*, 12.7.1935; CWMG, 67, 263.
19. *Harijan.*, 12.11.1938; CWMG, 74, 130.
20. *Harijan.*, 10.2.46; CWMG, 89, 345.
21. *Satyagraha in South Africa*, Ch. XV; CWMG 34, 235.
22. *Gospel of Luke*, 13:6-9.
23. *Gospel according to St Matthew*, 21:28-32.
24. *Lebendiger Buddha, Lebendiger Christus*, 1996, 98.

25. *Harijan*, 26.7.1942; CWMG, 83, 124.
26. *Gospel of Luke,* 18:29 f
27. *Gospel according to St. Mark*, 8:27-30.
28. *Gospel according to St. Matthew,* 16:17.
29. *Gospel according to St. Mark*, 14:61 f.
30. Albert Schweitzer: *Geschichte der Leben-Jesu-Forschung,* Tübingen 1926, 378.
31. *Gospel according to St. Mark*, 8:31-33.
32. *Die Botschaft Jesu vom Reich Gottes*, Stuttgart 2005, 50.
33. *Gospel according to St Mark*, 10:17 f.
34. *Gospel of Luke,* 11:27 f.
35. *Gospel according to St. Mark*, 9:34 f.
36. *Speech at Gandhi Seva Sangh*-III, CWMG 77, 378.

15
Jesus' Ethics: The Sermon on the Mount

You shall therefore be perfect like your heavenly father also is.
—Jesus of Nazareth

Ethics gives an answer to the question: What shall we do, what shall we refrain from? There are numerous statements about ethics to be found in the gospels, but especially in the speech composition of Matthew that is known under the name of "Sermon on the Mount".[1] In the Gospel according to Luke, there is a kind of short version of the Sermon on the Mount called "Sermon on the Plain".[2]

The Sermon on the Mount has given rise to many interpretations. Here, I will only mention a few of the most important: The first one originates from Matthew himself. The name Sermon on the Mount is a quote from Matthew 5:1 and is considered an allusion to Mount Sinai where Moses received the Tablets of the Law with the Ten Commandments. Jesus could thus have been conceived by Matthew as a kind of second Moses.

In the Catholic theology, an interpretation is quite common which understands the Sermon on the Mount as the second step of a two-steps-ethics. The Ten Commandments are regarded as ethical norm for laymen, the Sermon on the Mount, on the contrary, as a norm for priests, monks, nuns and saints, who dedicate their life entirely to the service to God and men.

The Second Testament scholar Gerhard Lohfink, in his book *At Whom is the Sermon on the Mount Directed*? About the credibility of the Christian,[3] holds the thesis that the recipient of the Sermon on the Mount is the people of God, in the first place God's chosen people of Israel, and then, as Israel refused to accept God's call, the "people of God" of Christians. It could consequently not constitute a compulsory ethics for a nation or for humanity.

The Reformer Martin Luther, in the context of his doctrine of justification, reads it as a radical intensification of the Ten Commandments in order to take away from man the wrong pride for works that could make him look justified before God, so that he, conscious of his bondage to the power of sin, would only seek refuge in the grace of God as imparted by Jesus Christ (*sola gratia, sola fide*).

Albert Schweitzer interpreted the Sermon on the Mount in the context of his consistent eschatology as "interim ethics". According to him, as it invalidates all "normal" human behaviour, it applies only to the short time between his earthly preaching and his return as the heavenly Messiah and Son of Man. Because the return failed to materialise, it has for the most part become obsolete.

Francis of Assisi, however, took it literally and adjusted his life unconditionally to it. Rightfully, he is considered the "symbol of Christ" of the Middle Ages.

Which of these interpretations comes closest to what the historical Jesus was teaching? I think it is the one of Francis of Assisi. With the Sermon on the Mount, one cannot govern the world, the former German Imperial Chancellor Bismarck (1815-1898) is alleged to have said. He is right, with the Sermon on the Mount, one cannot govern the empires of this world, because it is the *constitution* of the Kingdom of God, which is radically different from the empires of this world. The Sermon on the Mount applies wherever individuals, communities and peoples engage in implementing in their life and through their life the Kingdom of God, the present beginning of which was announced by Jesus.

Through the linguistic guise in which he put Jesus' words, Matthew fostered the fatal misunderstanding that the Sermon on the Mount should be read as *God's demand* on man. If it is understood this way, the total failure of man in view of such a demand is certainly inevitable. In my opinion, however, it is not supposed to be understood as a demand but as a *promise*. What is unaccomplishable as a demand can easily be accomplished if done as a *devotion to God*, who is the truth. It becomes, so to speak, the second nature of man. This is why Jesus can say: "Come to me, all of you who are weary and carry heavy burdens, and I will give you rest. Take my yoke upon you. Let me teach you, because I am humble and gentle at heart, and you will find rest for your souls. For my yoke is easy to bear, and the burden I give you is light".[4] The historical Jesus did probably not refer to *his* yoke but to the *yoke of the Kingship of God.*

There is a master key to the understanding of the Sermon on the Mount. It is the *inexhaustible love of God* to men, and not only to men but to the whole Universe in which he is also present, in as far as we believe in his omnipresence. The love that we human beings devote to God, our fellow human beings and the extra-human creature is eventually nothing else but the *reflection* of this love of God. Metaphorically speaking: Where people follow the law of truth and love, they turn into a fountain that transforms the desert of our social relationships into a blooming Garden of Eden. It is thus no merit at all, if people pass on God's love like a well the trough of which runs over.

Peter's question gives us a clear hint for the understanding of the Sermon on the Mount: "How often should I forgive someone who sins against me? Seven times" ? "No, not seven times", Jesus replies, "but seventy seven times" ![5] Seventy seven times is a poetical paraphrase for always. You shall always forgive your human brother, not only your biological brother, your tribal kinsman or a member of your people. The same applies equally for the human sister, of course. That obviously exceeds the abilities of each man who intents to do that on his own initiative. Everyone can easily try that out on his own. To forgive once when treated unjustly is difficult enough, twice in a row even more difficult, three times almost impossible. When Peter says: Is seven times enough? he already demands the impossible. We cannot constantly overdraw our "psycho-account" without falling ill. It imperiously asks for compensation, just like the bank. But who devotes himself like Jesus or Gandhi unconditionally to the truth that is God, experiences the miracle that his psycho-account is not only balanced but so overfull that he cannot do anything else but passing on the abundance.

It is also there, where the enormous spiritual power emerges that emanates from such people. Jesus was always surrounded by crowds of people, as we know, likewise Gandhi, who felt bothered beyond measure by "giving *darshan*". And Brother Masseo besieges Francis of Assisi with the question: "Why you, why you" ? And to Francis' unexpected question in return, he replies: "I ask why the whole world runs after you, why everybody wants to see you, listen to you and obey you. You are no beautiful man; you are not very erudite, you are not noble. What is it that the whole world runs after you?"[6] This spiritual power that Gautama Buddha and Socrates too had at their disposal, explains itself from the ability of retaliating evil with good. Let us remember Gandhi's statement:

"It has been my invariable experience that good evokes good, evil – evil; and that, therefore, if the evil does not receive the corresponding response, it ceases to act, dies of want of nutrition. Evil can only live upon itself. Sages of old, knowing this law, instead of returning evil for evil, deliberately returned good for evil and killed it. Evil lives nevertheless, because many have not taken advantage of the discovery, though the law underlying it acts with scientific precision. We are too lazy to work out in terms of the law the problems that face us and, therefore, fancy that we are too weak to act up to it. The fact is, that the moment the truth of the law is realised, nothing is so easy as to return good for evil. It is the one quality that distinguishes man from the brute. It is man's natural law not to retaliate. Though we have the human form, we are not truly human till we have fully realised the truth of the law and acted up to it. The law admits of no escape".[7]

This power unfortunately also exists in the negative as a demonic power that appeals to the lower instincts of man often under the pretext of high and highest ideals. People who possess it are dangerous enough, but their actions only turn disastrous when they succeed in getting into the command centre of a state machinery, where each of their orders will find willing executors.

While in the First Testament, love of neighbour primarily turns towards family members, members of one's own tribe, own people or own religious community,[8] for Jesus, the neighbour is in every person we meet and who needs help. That becomes clear in the parable of the good Samaritan, a story that, even if not by Jesus, was created entirely in the spirit of Jesus: "Who is my neighbour" ?, is the question asked by an expert in religious law at the end of a dialogue that had started with the question: "Teacher, what should I do to inherit eternal life" ? Jesus replies, "What does the law of Moses say? How do you read it?" He gets the answer: *"You must love the LORD your God with all your heart, all your soul, all your strength and all your mind. And, 'Love your neighbour as yourself' "*. Jesus praises him with the words that were supposed to motivate the man to let words be followed by deeds: "Right! Do this and you will live" ! It is only now that the man asks Jesus, "And who is my neighbour"?[9] Jesus does not reply with a definition but, in order to impart the truth, he tells a story in an oriental manner, that becomes unforgettably branded in one's mind: Your neighbour is the person you meet, even more though the person who is in need and wants help: "A Jewish man was travelling from Jerusalem down to Jericho, and he was attacked by bandits. They stripped him of his clothes, beat him up, and left him half dead beside the road. By chance a priest came along. But when he saw the man lying there, he crossed to the other side of the road and passed him by. A Temple assistant walked over and looked at him lying there, but he also passed by on the other side. Then a despised Samaritan came along, and when he saw the man, he felt compassion for him. Going over to him, the Samaritan soothed his wounds with olive oil and wine and bandaged them. Then he put the man on his own donkey and took him to an inn, where he took care of him. The next day he handed the innkeeper two silver coins, telling him, "Take care of this man. If his bill runs higher than this, I'll pay you the next time I'm here".

After these preliminary remarks that are indispensable for the correct understanding of the Sermon on the Mount, now a few selected passages:

THE BLESSINGS

In order to understand them rightly, one has to know that they apply to those who tread the path of turning back and of repentance, the path into the Kingdom of God. We may absolutely imagine that figuratively as a big marching column formed by a people or mankind as a whole, a marching column at the forefront of which the super-rich, super-powerful and super-famous are marching. They are followed by the rich and mighty and so on, up to the most miserable and most despised. When the call for turning back is sounded, it becomes a matter of fact that among those who turn back, the first will be the last on the path into the Kingdom of God, and the last will be the first, because the rich and mighty must at first forego their wealth, power and prestige before they can enter the Kingdom of God. What they have in common is the imposition of turning back.

In the German ecumenical *Bible* translation that I use, the blessing reads: Those who are poor before God are blessed because to them is the kingdom of heaven. Poor before God probably refers to those who own the spirit of poverty, which means those who lead a simple life so that others can live. In my opinion, that conforms better to what Jesus meant than the unconditional blessing of the poor at Luke.[10] Who is grinding poor, who literally owns nothing except an unrestrained greed for money, wealth, power, luxury and privileges, belongs essentially to the rich? He or she is precisely not meant by the first blessing. On the other hand, a rich person who utilises his wealth exclusively for the welfare of the community, and who himself and his family live a simple, may be even spartan life, belongs in reality to the poor. The same applies for the blessing of the starving and the crying at Luke. Without repentance, they become, without exception, slaves of the dialectics of richness and misery, hunger and satiety, crying and laughing.

The same applies, for that matter, to the dialectics of effort and reward, suffering and bliss. Who suffers injustice or violence in the consciousness of being rewarded with eternal bliss and with belonging to the rulers in heaven for that, has his reward therein forfeited because suffering for the sake of truth *is* bliss, serving out of love *is* the reward. The German poet Franz Kafka (1883-1924) put this thought in the profound aphorism: "Only here, suffering is suffering. Not in a way as if those who suffer here should elsewhere be elevated because of this suffering, but in a way that what means suffering in this world, is bliss in another world, unchanged and only freed from its opposite".[11]

The blessings of the peacemakers, the compassionate and the pure at heart do not require any further comment. Jesus and Gandhi displayed them by the way they lived their lives. That is also applicable to the blessing of those who are persecuted for the sake of justice. For them also applies that they will not be rewarded by admission in the "kingdom of heaven", but that they *are* in the kingdom of heaven. The last blessing is, in my opinion, not Jesuanic. Every sequence tempts you to add further items to the chain. Jesus would at most have said: You are blessed if you are insulted and defamed for the sake of the gospel. Be delighted and jubilant because the Kingdom of God is yours.

ABOUT THE SALT OF THE EARTH AND ABOUT THE LIGHT OF THE WORLD

These powerful words illustrate the principle that we meet again and again with Jesus: *By their fruits you will know them.* Jesus is emphatic about self-awareness and self-change of the individual. He was averse to everything ritual and cultic, everything liturgic and sacramental, and everything institutional and hierarchic. The *real*, not the symbolic conversion of the faithful mattered to him. The mystery of the Holy Communion that was related to his name shortly after his death would have been condemned by him with harsh words as the attempt of obtaining surreptitiously the entry into the Kingdom of God. In this sense, Gandhi also emphasised, after a faithful Christian had explained to him that he did not restrain himself from sinning because he knew himself redeemed through his belief in Jesus Christ: "If this be the Christianity acknowledged by all Christians, I cannot accept it. I do not seek redemption from the consequences of my sin. I seek to be redeemed from sin itself, or rather from the very thought of sin. Until I have attained that end, I shall be content to be restless".[12]

The firm emphasis on self-awareness and self-change should not be understood as if Jesus cared exclusively or only predominantly about salvation of the individual. The change of society is no less important to him than the change of individuals. There is consequently, beside the hermeneutic circle of self-awareness and self-change, another circle that unfolds in the interaction of change of the individual and the society he belongs to. Such a change occurs out of the spirit and the truth. Who wants to study these circular and self-strengthening processes, may be referred to the Jesus community, to Gandhi's Ashram and Gautama Buddha's Sangha.

ABOUT THE LAW AND THE PROPHETS

Jesus does not abolish the law, he also does not toughen or surpass it but he dissolves it in the *stream of ardour of God's and human love*. From there, he takes his radical criticism of externalised cultic and ritual forms of the Jewish religion, its often unreasonable and absurd purity requirements or its exaggerated observation of the Sabbath rest, which makes it difficult to do good on Sabbath, to help the needy or to satisfy basic needs. It is hardly imaginable that the historical Jesus was supposed to have said: "Don't misunderstand why I have come. I did not come to abolish the Law of Moses or the writings of the prophets. No, I came to accomplish their purpose. I tell you the truth, until heaven and earth disappear, not even the smallest detail of God's law will disappear until its purpose is achieved. So if you ignore the least commandment and teach others to do the same, you will be called the least in the Kingdom of Heaven. But anyone who obeys God's laws and teaches them will be called great in the Kingdom of Heaven".[13] The post-Easter character of these words put into Jesus' mouth, are obvious. It might have originated in the circle of the "Hebrews" of the early community in order to fight off the new doctrine of the "Hellenists". Among the main parts of the Torah are circumcision, strict observation of Sabbath, prohibition of images and purity requirements, all commandments that Jesus relativised. It is, however, thinkable that in this text, an authentic saying of Jesus was included which could have read: I have not come to abolish the law but I have come to fulfil it in its true sense.

ABOUT KILLING AND RECONCILIATION

Jesus' words that are introduced by the formula, "You have heard that our ancestors were told, but I say, "have been named "antitheses". The Jewish theologian Ruth Lapide[14] says rightly, however, that they are not antitheses but intensifications, consolidations or, as I would rather say, radicalisations. The antithesis to "You must not kill" ! would be "You shall kill" ! That is, however, definitely not meant. Jesus explains instead, that it is not only the killing but already the insulting word, the hate-filled thought that are evil, because the word results from the thought and action results from the word. Who entrusts himself unconditionally to the will of God, will be released from evil thoughts in the course of time. *Satya* and *ahimsa* will become his second nature.

With the words, "So if you are presenting a sacrifice at the altar in the Temple and you suddenly remember that someone has something against you; leave your sacrifice there at the altar. Go and be reconciled to that person. Then come and offer your sacrifice to God."[15] Jesus wants to inculcate the teaching that every kind of religious service is hypocritical as long as it is not preceded by the reconciliation with those who have reason to hate us.

ABOUT ADULTERY

It is not only about avoiding adultery or fornication but already the lustful look at the wife of another man, may be even at any woman. In relation to verses 29 and 30, I gladly accept Ruth Lapide's interpretation which does not read it as a call for self-mutilation but as the drastic and exaggerating manner of expression of oriental peoples, meant for the purpose of clarification, that we also meet in other sayings of Jesus such as, for example, the camel and the eye of a needle or the beam in the eye.[16]

ABOUT VENGEANCE AND LOVING THE ENEMIES

These paragraphs belong to the core of Jesus' teachings. If we extend them by the love to God, we can even say that they are the heart of Jesus'ethics from which all the other parts are supplied with blood. There have been countless attempts of alleviating these passages as part of the *tendency of alleviation*. Whole generations of theologians have "interpreted" these *Bible* texts with tireless efforts and admirable sagacity in order to understand them "rightly", with the result of deadening the heart of Jesus' teachings. But when the heart does not beat, the body dies, and that is exactly what happened to the body of the Christian churches. Today they are, apart from some individuals and small groups, living corpses. The salt turned tasteless, or, as Martin Luther phrased it so dramatically, "stupid".

"You have heard the law that says the punishment must match the injury: "An eye for an eye, and a tooth for a tooth". But I say, do not resist an evil person ! If someone slaps you on the right cheek, offer the other cheek also. If you are sued in court and your shirt is taken from you, give your coat, too. If a soldier demands that you carry his gear for a mile, carry it two miles. Give to those who ask, and don't turn away from those who want to borrow".[17] I will not go further into the numerous interpretations of this text because after the previous, it is obvious what is meant. The common denominator of the examples given by Jesus is: Overcome evil with good, and not only with the same amount of good but with an *abundance* of good. Utilise the enormous power of the "echo principle" that, in the long run, no man can withstand.

At this point, it is, in my opinion, indispensable to go into a common misunderstanding of these words. Countless Christians have understood it this way: Do not offer any resistance to evil, abstain from defence, submit to the aggressor, suffer willingly violence and injustice that are done to you, and follow Jesus who as sacrificial lamb sustained willingly all tortures in order to reconcile God with men. I consider this interpretation that is based on the Servant Songs in the Second Isaiah, *utterly wrong*. Jesus behaved completely different from a sacrificial lamb "that is led for slaughtering, and from a sheep in view of its shearers".[18] It is precisely not about renouncing resistance. On the contrary, Jesus thinks: *You shall resist evil, but not with evil. You shall resist violence, but not with violence but with non-violence. You shall adhere to the truth whatever may come. Overcome evil with good.*

"You have heard the law that says, "Love your neighbour" and hate your enemy. But I say, love your enemies! Pray for those who persecute you! In that way, you will be acting as true children of your Father in heaven. For, he gives his sunlight to both evil and good and he sends rain on just and unjust alike. If you love only those who love you, what reward is there for that ? Even corrupt tax collectors do that much. If you are kind only to your friends, how are you different from anyone else ? Even pagans do that".[19]

The early Christians understood Jesus quite well when they practised the principle: *Overcome evil with good, hatred with love and violence with non-violence.* There surely was already a relapse into counter-hatred in view of the social and state persecution at an early stage. There was a relapse into violence and revenge phantasies because it seems that there was no way of coping with the supremacy of the Romans by means of violence. Such feelings found their devastating expression, lasting until today, in the apocalypse of John. Generally speaking, however, early Christendom proved itself against the persecution by its adversaries in state and society. It avoided the "vengeance trap", but walked right into the "embracement trap" that an ice-cold, power-hungry, reckless and merciless strategist called Constantine (270/288-337), whom the Christians would later call the Great, had set. From that moment onwards, most Christians and especially the theologians did not understand Jesus any more. They said that Jesus could obviously not have meant it the way it was written! That would be an invitation to suicide. The Jewish theologian Ruth Lapide, for whom I have high respect, is also of this opinion. To the question: "Can an army be justified from a Christian point of view"? she replied: "For defence, yes. To renounce defence would amount to suicide. And nowhere is written: You shall be a suicide. ". . . Jesus did not call for suicide, but, in my opinion, he would have contradicted Ruth Lapide vehemently. If he lived today, he would probably say: Who feels obliged to defend himself with violence, may do so. I will not hinder him from doing so. Who believes in violence, may make use of it, if he considers it necessary for his defence and the defence of his next of kin. But I do not believe in violence. There is one thing, however, that everybody should know who considers violence necessary and justified for self-defence. This belief includes military armament and, ultimately, also atomic bombs, with the risk that humanity will perish in the *self-inflicted apocalypse* of a nuclear holocaust, and the possibility of dragging with it all higher life-forms on earth into the abyss. Who says *A* must also say *B*, with all its political, economical, human, ethical and religious consequences !

It is remarkable that Martin Buber used a similar argument in a letter to Gandhi. He wrote: "I do not want to keep it as a secret. that I would not have been among Jesus' crucifiers but I would also not have been among his followers because I cannot allow being proscribed from resisting to evil when I see that it is destroying what is good. I must resist the evil in the world the same as the evil inside myself. I can only fight for not being forced to do it with violence. I do not want violence but if I cannot avoid evil destroying good by any other means than violence, I will hopefully practise violence and put myself in God's hands".[20] This letter unfortunately never reached its addressee. What would Gandhi have answered? It is not difficult to guess. He would have written to Buber: You must of course react to evil! The question is in what way. I plead in favour of non-violent resistance, which requires a far bigger bravery than violent resistance, because it sacrifices lives without taking the life of others. The promise of being invincible in time and eternity is aimed at the non-violent resistance, even if the non-violent fighter is killed, which is, however, more probable in a violent fight because of the escalation tendency of violently fought conflicts. Apart from that applies: *The good that believes to be obliged to defend itself with violence, has already stopped being good long ago.*

"Who claims that there is only the alternative: Surrender to the will of the attacker or violent resistance, 'suicide' or 'murderer', errs." There is an alternative. We know it already: *resistance without violence, non-violent resistance.* It entails, of course, the willingness to accept violence without hatred or the wish for vengeance. Who holds on to it cannot be defeated even if he is killed in a non-violent fight. On the other hand, who reaches for violence, even if it is only for the purpose of self-defence, will never win because violence is — compared to truth and non-violence — defeat. This is why Gandhi can say: "Self-sacrifice of one innocent man is a million times more potent than the sacrifice of million men who die in the act of killing others. The willing sacrifice of the innocent is the most powerful retort to insolent tyranny that has yet been conceived by God or man".[21]

It is this power of truth, soul and love, *God's power in us* that is also not afraid of persecution and death, which animated the early Christians and in so doing contributed to the unstoppable propagation of Christendom in ancient times. The church father Tertullian (around 150-225) wrote that the blood of the martyrs became the seed of the church. I will later on go deeper into the dilution of Jesus' teachings that began shortly after Jesus' death.

ABOUT THE WRONG AND THE RIGHT WORRIES

Here is another word about the wonderful passage about the worries. It may of course not be understood as an invitation to stop being active. After all, even the birds under the sky are active the whole day long: they look for food, build their nests, incubate their eggs and take care of their hatch. "Do not worry!" means: do not be afraid of the future, do not be afraid of being in need, do not fear being cheated, stolen from or robbed, do not be afraid of going to rack and ruin in the murderous rat-race of our society, do not be scared of having to share what you own with those who own less then you ! Do not hesitate to behave towards others like you wish they would behave towards you! Behave like the children who do, after all, not ask their parents: Have you taken care of us having enough food in future ?

Yet, it is the worries about the future, the worries about our livelihood, our old-age pension and our security that want to force us to take more than what we really need for living. Who, however, takes more than he needs, takes it away from others. The early Christian community of Jerusalem tried to put this teaching into action and practised a "communism" that doubtlessly goes back to the historical Jesus.[22]

As was to be expected, worries settled in again inside the early Christian community too as the story of Ananias and Saphira[23] reveals. To make matters worse to the "delict" who kept a part of the sales revenue of the field for themselves, they added the lie in order to cover it up. Notwithstanding, the punishment reported in the gospels is completely unjustifiable. Instead of meeting with understanding and forgiveness in the spirit of Christian love, they were supposedly sentenced to death by the Holy Ghost. Gandhi, in a similar situation, imposed a penitence fasting upon himself. Peter would have done much better by imposing upon himself such a fast instead of spreading fear and terror by excluding the two "sinners" from the community, which might well have been the historical core of Luke's legend-like embellished report.

God's rule, as understood by Jesus is, therefore, conceived as a *community of the free and equal* that are tied to each other by the bond of love, a love to neighbours that does not only apply to community members but also to outsiders. This is, in my opinion, Jesus' "missionary order", not the words of the resurrected that have long since been identified as falsification: "I have been given all authority in heaven and on earth. Therefore, go and make disciples of all the nations, baptising them in the name of the Father and the Son and the Holy Spirit. Teach these new disciples to obey all the commands I have given you. And be sure of this: I am with you always, even to the end of the age".[24] Unfortunately, this fraud "for the higher praise of God" proved extraordinarily effective in the history of Christendom, instead of the authors being sentenced to death by the Holy Ghost, like Ananias and Saphira, and their lies being revealed.

DO NOT JUDGE . . . . .

"Do not judge others, and you will not be judged. For you will be treated as you treat others. The standard you use in judging is the standard by which you will be judged. And why worry about a speck in your friend's eye when you have a log in your own ? How can you think of saying to your friend, "Let me help you get rid of that speck in your eye", when you can't see past the log in your own eye? Hypocrite! First get rid of the log in your own eye; then you will see well enough to deal with the speck in your friend's eye".[25] With this saying, Jesus directs the searchlight of our attention to our own failure and our own guilt. On a sober consideration, there are so many things to confess, to improve and to make up for that we will find no time at all to take care of the mistakes of others. At the same time, he invalidates the reward-punishment-scheme completely. Who places himself as a judge above others, arrogates a judgement on their acts that God alone can pronounce. But even God himself does not judge. Who does good, rewards himself; who does evil, punishes himself. There is no room for a human or even divine judgement, no room for punishment and much less so for eternal punishment in hell.

Conclusion: With reason, Jewish theologians called attention to the fact that many statements of the Sermon on the Mount can also be found in the Hebrew *Bible* (the First Testament) and in Judaism at the time of Jesus. There is no doubt that Jesus was a Jew and lived in the world of Judaism. He saw himself in the tradition of the prophets. No matter what he might have thought about himself, he was a great *reformer of Judaism* as well as Gautama Buddha was a great reformer of Hinduism and Martin Luther a great reformer of Catholicism. In its concentration on the essential, its pictorial language and because of its outstanding content, the Sermon on the Mount belongs to the most important religious texts of world literature.

WAS JESUS POLITICAL ?

Some priests, theologians and Christians hasten to assure that Jesus was non-political. If by stating that they mean that he did not have party politics or power politics in his mind, they are right. But if they understand political in a general sense of *participation in community life*, then they are wrong. Every word of the Sermon on the Mount is political because it refers to the way in which we should live together. Viewed in this light, religion and politics are inseparably connected, as well as religion and economy, religion and society, etc. That is also what Gandhi means when he says: "I could not live for a single second without religion. Many of my political friends despair of me because they say that even my politics are derived from my religion. And they are right. My politics and all other activities of mine are derived from my religion. I go further and say that every activity of a man of religion must be derived from his religion, because religion means being bound to God, that is to say, God rules your every breath".[26]

In the nineteen hundred thirties, Dietrich Bonhoeffer (1906-1945) planned a trip to India to visit Gandhi, in order to study his theory and practice of non-violence. It is one of the most painful chapters of German history, which is so rich in tragedies, that this meeting did not take place, especially as there was an invitation from Gandhi to him already in 1934. If that meeting had taken place, I do not doubt that many of the topics of this study would have been supported by him in Germany with a far higher expertise and response.

JESUS AS A RELIGIOUS "WORLD TEACHER"

Albert Schweitzer, Gerhard Lohfink and other theologians are of the opinion that Jesus considered to be, i.e., himself sent exclusively to the lost sheep of the House of Israel, that his goal was the collection of the scattered children of Israel in order to lead back the people into the obedience to Yahweh and his law, as a precondition for the beginning of the time of salvation. I do not think so. His good news were by no means restricted to the "chosen people", it was and rather is directed at all people who are willing to take the path of repentance and penitence. He addressed all people, primarily, however, the poor and disenfranchised, the humiliated and despised. It is completely improbable that he, who did not admit any social distinction in the Kingdom of God, should of all things have accepted the social distinction between the chosen people and the other peoples. There is a whole series of sayings of Jesus that support this opinion, but just as many that contradict it. I consider the latter a result of the *tendency of adoption* of the "Hebrews", the majority faction in the early community of Jerusalem, to Orthodox Judaism. The point for them was to bring Jesus back into Judaism just as his relatives tried to bring the "runaway" Jesus back home.

Whether the miracle story about the Captain of Capernaum[27] is Jesuanic may rightly be disputed. It is thinkable that it was quasi composed around the core of an authentic saying of Jesus that could have read: I tell you: Such a belief (like the one of the heathen Captain), I have never found in Israel with anybody. I say to you: Many will come from East and West and will sit down at table with Abraham, Isaac and Jacob in the Kingdom of Heaven; those, however, for whom the kingdom was meant, will be excluded.

The text Luke 13:1-9, however, is of a clear Jesuanic nature: Some people report to Jesus about people from Galilee "that Pilate had murdered while they were offering sacrifices at the Temple so that their blood got mixed up with the blood of the sacrificial animals", whereas Jesus explains: "Do you think those Galileans were worse sinners than all the other people from Galilee? Not at all ! And you will perish, too, unless you repent of your sins and turn to God. And what about the eighteen people who died when the tower in Siloam fell on them? Were they the worst sinners in Jerusalem ? No, and I tell you again that unless you repent, you will perish, too".[28] This admonition is followed by the parable of the fig tree that urges the listeners to utilise the period of grace that God grants them *as long as* they live. With this saying, Jesus rejects the popular belief that illness, disability and misfortune are punishments for committed sins. Jesus argues: No, those who were killed when the tower fell on them or by command of Pilate are not worse than you. It is only that for them, the period of grace ended, while it is still granted to you as long as you live ! *All* Galileans, not matter if they are Jewish or heathens, *all* inhabitants of Jerusalem, Jewish or heathens, are called to repent.

Result: The three groundbreaking achievements that make Jesus one of the great world teachers are :

1. He overcomes the limits of Judaism towards a *universal* religion. He breaks with the chosenness claim of Israel, with the dogmatic fixation on the Torah, namely the exaggerated Sabbath, eating and purity requirements that, if nothing else, enforce the segregation of the people of Israel from the peoples of the world.
2. He overcomes the ambivalent conception of God of an angry, bigoted, cruel, judging, punishing and annihilating God, or a God condemning to eternal agony, on the one hand, and an arbitrarily choosing, preferring, gracious and merciful God, on the other hand, in favour of an image that shows a God of truth and love, of justice, peace and joy (bliss) for all people.
3. He proclaims the *present* beginning of God's rule that is linked to God's rule in the pre-monarchic era of the people of Israel. It is a kingdom in which the rule of men over men and nature has been abolished because God's will happens in it, not because of fear of punishment but because of love, which is, in the end, only the reflection of God's love to man and the whole universe.

God's rule is not a mysterious power that suddenly befalls this world or emerges after a cosmic disaster that destroys the old world. It is God's will that is done on Earth, as the plea in the Lord's Prayers reads: "Your will may be done as in heaven so on earth", not *directly* through the powerful intervention of God in nature and history but *indirectly* through us human beings. That means it is a growth process, in the interior of an individual as well as in the exterior, the society. This growth process is never finished. In this sense, also Gandhi confessed: "In my search after Truth I have discarded many ideas and learnt many new things. Old as I am in age, I have no feeling that I have ceased to grow inwardly or that my growth will stop at the dissolution of the flesh. What I am concerned with is my readiness to obey the call of Truth, my God, from moment to moment".[29]

I am well aware of the fact that many Christians will have good arguments against my characterisation of Jesus' person and teaching. This is why I want to emphasise here one more time: I consider my characterisation probable but not more than that. Jesus was, in my opinion, a great but nonetheless fallible and erring person. May be he was not the one that I take him for, but that does not change the truth of my findings in view of a universally valid religion. They are valid independently of his person.

REFERENCES

1. *Gospel according to St. Matthew,* 5:1–7:29.
2. *Gospel of Luke,* 6:20-49.
3. Gerhard Lohfink, *At Whom Is the Sermon on the Mount Directed*? Freiburg 1993, 50-53.
4. *Gospel according to St. Matthew,* 11:28-30.
5. *Ibid.*, 18:21.
6. Walter Nigg: *Große Heilige*, Zürich 1946, 35.
7. *Young India*, 15.5.1924; CWMG, 27, 414-5.
8. The commandment to respect strangers is found in Lev 19:33 f.
9. Gospel of Luke, 10:25-37. The Samaritans were Israelites who worshipped Yahweh on holy Mount Garizim and who were ostracized by the other Israelites due to that. The Samaritan and not the pious and respected members of his own people turned out to be the neighbour for the man who had become a victim of the robbers.
10. *Gospel of Luke,* 6:20.
11. *Hochzeitsvorbereitungen auf dem Lande*, Frankfurt, 1983, 39.
12. *Autobiography*; SWMG 1, 185.
13. *Gospel according to St. Matthew,* 5:17-19.
14. Ruth Lapide, Henning Röhl: "*Was glaubte Jesus*?", Stuttgart, 2006, 35 f.
15. *Gospel according to St. Matthew,* 5:23 f.
16. Ruth Lapide, Henning Röhl: "*Was glaubte Jesus*?", Stuttgart 2006, 31.
17. *Gospel according to St. Matthew,* 5:38-42.
18. Prophet Isaiah, 52:7.
19. *Gospel according to St. Matthew,* 5:43-48.
20. In: Christian Bartolf (Hg.): *Der Atem meines Lebens*, Berlin 1998, 22.
21. *Young India*, 12.2.1925; CWMG, 30, 248.
22. *Acts of the Apostles*, 4:32-37.
23. *Ibid.*, 5:1-11.
24. *Gospel according to St. Matthew,* 28:16-20.
25. *Ibid.*, 7:1-5.
26. *Harijan*, 2.3.1934; CWMG, 63, 200.
27. *Gospel according to St. Matthew,* 8:5-13.
28. *Gospel of Luke*, 13:2-5.
29. *Harijan*, 29.4.33; CWMG, 61, 24.

16
The Resurrection of Jesus

The question about Jesus Christ's resurrection poses a key question, may be even the key question of Christian faith. In this question, though the average Christian is hardly aware of it any more, decisions are made for almost all other questions of faith and theology.

—Hans Kessler

While explaining the biblical reports of resurrection,[1] I can establish a connection to what I already explained in the chapter "Tendencies". What was it that really happened in the days after the crucification of Jesus in Jerusalem and in Galilee? If we bring, with the help of the subtraction method, the *intensification tendency* of the scriptures of the *Second Testament* back to their real origin, we get the following image: *The reports of the resurrection are simply and plainly visions that are not based on any kind of objective reality in the sense of modern science.* Jesus' body, wherever and by whom ever it was buried, is decayed. We will come back to the question if this was the finishing blow to Christian belief, because the abandonment of Jesus' resurrection in the sense of an objective fact took the ground from under it. For the time being we have to note that this statement plunges the Christian belief into a deep crisis, because it parts from the idea of Jesus' resurrection as an objective fact. Paul stands for countless Christians when he writes: "And if Christ has not been raised, then all our preaching is useless, and your faith is useless. And we apostles would all be lying about God — for we have said that God raised Christ from the grave. But that can't be true if there is no resurrection of the dead. And if there is no resurrection of the dead, then Christ has not been raised. And if Christ has not been raised, then your faith is useless and you are still guilty of your sins. In that case, all who have died believing in Christ are lost ! And if our hope in Christ is only for this life, we are more to be pitied than anyone in the world. But in fact, Christ *has* been raised from the dead. He is the first of a great harvest of all who have died".[2]

For the time being, let us turn towards the question what we can learn from the earliest testimony of Jesus' resurrection in the *Second Testament*, namely the first letter of Paul to the Corinthians that was probably written at the beginning of the fifties of the first century: "Christ died for our sins, just as the Scriptures said. He was buried, and he was raised from the dead on the third day, just as the Scriptures said. He was seen by Kephas and then by the Twelve. After that, he was seen by more than 500 of his followers at one time, most of whom are still alive, though some have died. Then he was seen by Jacob and later by all the apostles. Last of all, as though I had been born at the wrong time, I also saw him".[3] This report is extremely short. We do not learn anything about time and place of the visions. The encounters of the women with the resurrected one are also not mentioned at all. Paul is also silent about the empty tomb which obviously does not automatically mean that he did not know about it. It is only certain that Paul mentions Peter as the first witness of the resurrection and himself as the last, while precisely his experience in Damascus manifests clearly the characteristics of a vision and an audition, even in the manner in which it was reported by Luke.[4] What really happened before Damascus — it was possibly an epileptic fit or a brain stroke —, shall not be discussed any further here.

Paul reports a total of six appearances of the resurrected. Jesus appeared to :

1. Kephas (Peter),
2. The Twelve,
3. More than five hundred brothers,
4. Jacob,
5. All Apostles,
6. Saul/Paul himself.

The appearance in front of "more than five hundred brothers" could be a hint at the Pentecost event though Jesus did not make a "physical" appearance there. Considering the *intensification tendency* we can confidently take away one zero from the number 500. The appearance in front of Jacob can be explained by the state of competition between Jacob and Peter. In the forties of the first century

Jacob, Jesus' brother managed to supplant Peter as the leader of the original Christian community in Jerusalem. For that, it was important to legimitate oneself by a personal encounter with the resurrected, for which Jacob's enthusiastic report about his experience may have led to a collective "experience of resurrection" by the apostles in the way it had happened earlier on with Peter and the disciples.

We have to insist again and again on taking into account that all attempts of an answer to the question: What happened in the days after the crucification in Jerusalem and Galilee, are merely speculative. We have no eyewitness reports by independent people; we do not even have eyewitness reports by people who were directly involved; we only have reports from second and third hand. That does not mean, however, that we are not allowed to think about what might have happened in those days by making use of our common sense. With this reservation in mind, and in accordance with Gerd Lüdemann, I consider the following sequence of events plausible: Jesus and his small community went to Jerusalem, full of high expectations, in order to announce the present dawning of God's rule in the centre of religious Judaism. It was there, as explained earlier, where the plunge into the crucification catastrophe occurred. The disciples, as they were in highest mortal danger as "conspirators", fled to Galilee. They reunited there, probably in Simon Peter's house. In deep sorrow and grief, deprived of all their hopes, depressed by feelings of guilt because they had abandoned Jesus in the hour of distress — that applies especially to Peter who was, on top of it, the one who had denied him — they experienced a second dramatic turn. Peter experiences Jesus' *presence*. He experiences the crucified as the one he had been during his life, a man passionately fighting for the "damned of this earth", an unconditionally loving and forgiving man who even forgives him his treason. He experiences Jesus' presence quite directly. It is quite possible, yes even probable, that he *sees* Jesus *personified,* which is not seldom the case among people who are moaning the sudden loss of a close relative. In a state of great agitation, he hurries towards the other disciples and reports to them about his experience, wild with excitement, trembling and stammering. As their emotional situation is quite similar to his, his enthusiasm is contagious. This leads to a collective outburst of enthusiasm, of being filled with the spirit.

It almost speaks for itself that, in the *context of early Jewish resurrection belief*, this experience had to take the shape of an encounter with the resurrected Jesus. The disciples return to Jerusalem and report the good news of Jesus' resurrection to the women who had stayed back in Jerusalem. The encounters with the resurrected, his "Ascension" and the Outpouring of the Holy Spirit at Pentecost embellished in the form of legends by Luke in the Acts of the Apostles, take place in Jerusalem, then.

But very soon sceptical contemporaries started to ask questions: What happened exactly? Who saw the resurrected one at first and where? As the disciples had not stayed in Jerusalem and, as a result, had neither witnessed the crucification and Jesus' death nor the days after that, they could also not testify to the resurrection on the third day "according to the scripture".[5] At this point, the women come in. They become witnesses of the resurrection, which, in turn, complicates the matter, because women have only a low value as witnesses (in court). In order to shut the mouth of the sceptics, all kind of legends are made up to "prove" the *physical* resurrection of Jesus: The open tomb, the men (angels) in or at the tomb, the women who want to embalm Jesus' body on the day after Sabbath,[6] and finally even Matthew's "cock-and-bull story" of commissioning and bribing the tomb guards.[7]

In order to understand, why the incarnate resurrection of Jesus was so important for the early Christians, we have to take a closer look at the widespread ideas of the nature of man and spirited beings in early Judaism. To present the variety and complexity of these ideas cannot be the object of this study. I am exclusively concerned with the three forms of appearance of the *biological body*, the *resurrected body* and the *immaterial body* in early Judaism.

The *first* of the mentioned forms of being refers to men of flesh and blood who are born, grow up, age and die. The *second* refers mainly to the Egyptian cult of the dead. The resurrection of the dead is, for all intents and purposes, considered in its material form. Insofar as they are pharaohs, they become hybrids of man and God. They have quite earthly needs in common with men, such as eating and drinking, entertainment, game and hunt; with the gods, however, they share immortality. As a result, their body is different from a biological body. It is a 'transfigured' body. The *third* concept refers to mere spiritual beings such as angels, devils and demons.

From there it becomes clear why the corporeality of the resurrected was so important to the early Christians. All that mattered to them was to make it clear that Jesus did not appear as a bodiless spirit (ghost) but as a transfigured body that one could touch, whose wound marks one could feel[8] and with whom one could eat and drink.[9] For this very reason, Jesus' tomb too had to be empty. This makes it clear that Jesus' resurrection or reawakening did happen in the minds of the resurrection witnesses. There was, in all likelihood, no objective event that could have been the cause of these experiences. What remains, is surprising enough namely that "big bang" announcement of Jesus' resurrection and his proclamation as the Messiah and Son of Man who, in the imminent future will return on the clouds of heaven in order to erect his kingdom on behalf of God.

Is this the end of Christendom? Is the Christian revelation empty; and the Christian faith meaningless? I do not think so. What is not sustainable, in my opinion, is the attempted rescue that Rudolf Bultmann carried out with the famous formula that Jesus resurrected into the *Kerygma* (the Mission Sermon) of the early Christian community. What does he mean with this formula? Did he think of something like the words of consolation that Gautama Buddha uttered to the mourning disciples from his deathbed: that he would always be with them through his teachings? Or did he think of the survival of great historical personalities in their oeuvre? In an interview with the German magazine Der Spiegel his reply to the question: was Jesus, like Goethe resurrected in his works and continued living in them?, he said "One can say that Jesus was resurrected like Goethe if one considers Jesus' life and work as a phenomenon of intellectual history. Because in intellectual history, people and works of great men continue to remain effective and this also applies for Jesus. But if one understands Jesus as an eschatological phenomenon, and that means — according to Romans 10:4[10] ". . . . as the end of world history, as far as its course is available for objective examination, then his presence is not made by his impact on intellectual history but occurs only in Christian revelation and in belief, respectively. To believe in Jesus' resurrection then means. . . . . to believe in revelation and to respond to it by believing in it".[11] What does he mean with these gloomy words? If I understand them correctly, he wanted to say: Jesus' presence is of a different nature for Christians than Goethe's presence in his oeuvre. It is of basic significance for those who derive their trust in salvation from the belief in him as God's only begotten son – and that is eventually a *question of faith.*

Bultmann withdrew, as Joachim Jeremias expressed it, into the "unassailable fortress" of Kerygma, the proclamation of Christ. We have to ask, however, if this fortress is really unassailable. Who talks to religious fundamentalists or even only to pious Christians, will again and again experience that critical questions are rejected with the laconic statement that it is a question of faith. But what does that mean? All kinds of things can, after all, be a question of faith: that Jesus walked on water, that he raised the dead or that a cock laid golden eggs on the altar of a church and whatever such "miracles" there might be. What can we, enlightened people of the twentieth and twenty-first century, make out of Mary's Immaculate Conception or her physical assumption, what of the Dogma of Christ and the Trinity Dogma? Can critical questions really be dismissed with the formula that we are dealing with a question of faith? Are there questions of faith that are simply nonsense and superstitions and others that are intangible to the aqua fortis of critical reason and, if yes, where is the borderline?

Rudolf Bultmann did a lot more for the demythologisation of the tradition of the *New Testament* than anybody else. Yet, didn't he, in the end, revert to the *myth* of Jesus' resurrection? Is it not time to follow through the path he treaded on consistently and to carry out a second demythologisation which *recognises the Christian dogmas as myths in the guise of antique philosophy?* That much is sure, anyhow, that the solution offered by Bultmann, not to declare Jesus' resurrection but the *faith* of the early Christians in Jesus' resurrection as the original date of Christianity, is not convincing. Based on this approach, he was quite consistent by throwing out the historical Jesus, more or less rudely, as a Jewish prophet and rabbi in his book *Theology of the New Testament* by declaring him one of the "pre-conditions" of the theology of the *Second Testament*. The Easter belief of the early Christian community in Jesus' resurrection is an indisputable historical fact, insofar as historical facts can be indisputable at all, a problem already mentioned by Lessing. It would, however, be a wrong conclusion to deduce from the reality of the faith of early Christians in Jesus' resurrection the reality of this resurrection. A sentence by Albert Schweitzer in the *History of the Life-Jesus-Research* shows how obvious such a wrong conclusion is: "Jesus is in our world important, because an enormous intellectual movement emanated from him and also runs through our time. This fact can neither be shaken nor strengthened by historical understanding".[12] That sounds convincing, but is not, especially if, by referring to the "enormous intellectual movement", one does not only consider the bright side of Christendom, but also the dark side in form of inner-church quarrels and power struggles, schisms, crusades, religious wars, persecution of Jews, and the burning of heretics and witches. No reasonable person will conclude from the fact that millions of people believed in the raciology of the Nazis, that their doctrine was the truth. Or, in order to choose another example, no person in his right mind will conclude from the fact that millions of people assumed it to be true, that Marx' interpretation of history was the truth. In the same manner, the conclusion that the reality of the resurrection belief would imply the reality of the resurrection, howsoever one may define it, is inadmissible. That much is sure, the unstable suspension bridge that Bultmann forged over the "terribly broad trench", to use the aptly put term by Lessing,[13] between the *historical Jesus* and the *biblical Christ* with the formula: *Jesus resurrected into the Kerygma of the early Christian communities,* does not sustain the weight because the biblical Christ turns out to be a *myth* — from the point of view of the historical-critical research. One of the two supporting pillars of the bridge collapses.

Is Christianity, therefore, finished as a religion, as is the opinion of Gerd Lüdemann? Insofar as it is a religion built on the foundation on the Christian dogmas, it is indeed finished. The impressive dogmatic buildings in the shape of the Christian churches collapse, but under the debris, a treasure or a pearl of immeasurable value can possibly be found, which is worth getting at any price: I mean the good news of the historical Jesus about *God's rule on Earth*. Wherever people confide unconditionally in God's will in the sense of Gandhi's words: *"Devotion to this Truth is the sole justification for our existence. All our activities should be centred in Truth. Truth should be the very breath of our life",* God's rule then begins to take shape.

As for the last two hundred years, the historical-critical research and the Christian Creed, science on the one hand and faith on the other, are still standing irreconcilably opposed to each other today. In a letter of the Professor of Theology Theodosius Harnack to his dogma-critical son Adolf (1858-1937), we find an almost classical phrasing of the Christian Creed: ". . . . . Christendom stands and falls with the fact of resurrection, with it, Trinity appears to me also as steady as a rock".[14] In the same sense, the famous theologian Jürgen Moltmann comments: "Christendom stands and falls with the reality of Jesus' resurrection from the dead by God".[15] And Hans Küng confesses: "Christendom, insofar as it is the confession to Jesus of Nazareth as the living and powerful Christ, begins at Easter. Without

Easter, there is no Gospel. Without Easter. no faith, no proclamation, no church, no church service, no mission" ![16]

Apparently there is no solution for the problem of the *incompatibility* of science and faith. Yet, I dare to offer one. It is a solution of striking simplicity. We know it already. It is *axiomatics*. In the chapter "The ontological paradox", we saw that each religion and each philosophy is based on axioms, on settings that cannot further be derived. The axiom on which the scientific-technical-industrial philosophy is based, that now-a-days dominates the world, reads: *All that can be perceived by the senses and be understood by the mind is real.* From this axiom, everything that we know now-a-days or that we believe we know about the historical Jesus can be derived from this axiom, because scientific results are always open to criticism. They can never claim or reach absolute validity. Nobody can prevent us from choosing other axioms, for example: *God is the first and last reality*, the world of what is perceptible by the senses and of what is intellectually understandable originates from him, and returns to him. As everything that surrounds us is ephemeral, he is the only existence. Applied to the question of Jesus' "resurrection": *For me, there is no shadow of a doubt that Jesus became a part of the immortal and indestructible existence of God thus far as he made God's will his own.* The same does not only apply to him but also to every person who tries to walk on the path of truth and love (*satya* and *ahimsa*). From that point of view, everything that was mortal in Jesus died and ceased to be, like everything that is ephemeral. But what was immortal in him goes on existing in God because God cannot die because he is eternal life.

The overwhelming realisation that Jesus lives, *because God was in him*, was granted to Peter. In the context of early Judaic belief in resurrection it had to take the shape of a *vision of resurrection*. It is, therefore, true in its core but wrong in its form. The wrong form led to the myth of Jesus' *physical* resurrection.

The battle cry of the reformers and humanists of the sixteenth century was: *Ad fontes*, back to the sources! What they meant was: Back to the Holy Scriptures as the source of revelation. They regarded the *Bible* as God's pure and simple word. So: away with everything that had polluted this pure source in the course of the centuries through church tradition and erudite interpretation. Together with tradition, much of value was also surrendered, but the attempt itself does not seem wrong to me. It is time to renew the battle cry of Reformation in contemporary adaptation. *Ad fontem*, back to the source, back to the *historical* Jesus, the man from Nazareth because he has a lot to tell us. What still appeared as an entity to the reformers, namely God's words in the *Bible*, equipped with an unconditional authority, (*sola scriptura*), looks similar to us now-a-days as theology and church of their time did to the reformers. *Ad fontem* means: *Back to the teachings of the historical Jesus and the example of his life, away with all the legends of the physical resurrection that have become unsustainable, away with Jesus' majestic titles, away with the dogmas!*

In the first-three centuries after Jesus' death, there was a process of *ritualisation*, *mythologisation* and *dogmatisation* of his message about the Kingdom of God, the process of the *historical Jesus* to the *biblical Christ* (Messiah) and eventually to the church dogma of *God-man*. This process has to be passed through backwards in order to get to its origin, the teachings of Jesus and the message of his life. *That is the future of Christendom, if it has a future.*

With reason one will ask if today we still would know anything about him, if he had not become a subject of faith and worship, if the *annunciator* of God's rule had not turned into the *announced one*, if the *believer* had not turned into the *believed one*, if the *man* Jesus from Nazareth had not become the *God-man* Jesus Christ. — No, we would probably know about him as much and as little as we know about the countless unknown and unnamed people who had lived a life of love to God and men in silence. But it is not sure at all that the teaching of Jesus and the example his life would have been forgotten. This is evident in the fate of Gautama Buddha, Socrates and others. That much, however, is sure: What Christendom made of him has little to do with the historical Jesus, the man of flesh and blood from the village of Nazareth in Galilee. On the other hand, historical-critical research, too, went astray often enough. A much-quoted passage by Albert Schweitzer reads: "A strange thing happened to the life-Jesus-research. It set out to find the historical Jesus and thought it could then place him in our time the way he is, as a teacher and redeemer. It loosened the ties with which he had been tied to the rock of the Church doctrine for centuries, and was pleased to see that life and movement returned into the figure while they saw the historical man, Jesus, coming towards them. But he did not stay but walked past our time and returned to his own. That was precisely what scared the theologians of the last decades that they could keep him neither with quibble nor force in our time but were forced to let him go. He returned to his era with the same need with which the freed pendulum returns to its original position".[17] The Jesus that Albert Schweitzer had in mind while writing these sentences, namely the apocalyptic, the hidden Messiah and Son of Man, does not exist. The historical Jesus was a different one. We may still hope for his "resurrection".

The conclusion of this analysis is quite shocking: Jesus carries the title Christ (the Greek version of Messiah) that in the course of time turned into his last name, wrongly. He himself would have rejected it, possibly even in hard words. Only the early Christian community of Jerusalem made him the Messiah once he could not contradict any more.

REFERENCES

1. To a large extent, I follow the analysis presented by the Göttingen the *New Testament* scholar Gerd Lüdemann in his book: *Die Auferstehung Jesu. Historie, Erfahrungen, Theologie*, Stuttgart, 1994.
2. *First Letter to Corinthians,* 15:14-19.
3. *Ibid.,* 15:3-8.
4. *Acts of the Apostles*, 9:1-9; 22:6-11; 26:12-18.
5. *Prophet Hosea*, 6:3.
6. *Gospel of Luke*, 24:1-12.
7. *Gospel according to St Matthew,* 27:62-28:15.
8. *Gospel of John*, 20:24-29.
9. *Ibid.,* 21:1-15; Acts 1:4; 10:41.
10. "For Christ has already accomplished the purpose for which the law was given. As a result, all who believe in him are made right with God".
11. Cited according to Gerd Lüdemann: *Die Auferstehung Jesu,* Stuttgart, 1994, 203, Anmerkung, 5.
12. *Geschichte der Leben-Jesu-Forschung*, Tübingen, 1928, 632.
13. *Werke.* Published by Gerhard Stenzel, Salzburg, 1040 f.
14. Cited by Gerd Lüdemann: *Die Auferstehung Jesu,* Stuttgart, 1994, 205, *Anmerkung*, 22.
15. *Ibid.*, 21.
16. *Ibid.*
17. *Geschichte der Leben-Jesu-Forschung*, Tübingen, 1926, 632.

17
Jesus' Elevation to God (Apotheosis)

From decade to decade, Jesus' tradition evolves more and more into the miraculous.

—*Karlheinz Deschner*

Never before in human history, one man went in for such a career as Jesus of Nazareth: From the son of a carpenter and child of poor people from the little place of Nazareth in Galilee to the ruler over the universe (pantocrator). This phenomenal rise of the *biblical Christ* corresponds with a likewise phenomenal descent of the *historical Jesus* and his teachings. The English philosopher Bertrand Russell (1872-1970), in view of Gandhi's effective history in India, stated unemotionally: *"The independent India turned Gandhi into a saint and ignored all his teachings"*.[1] In principle, the same applies for Jesus of Nazareth: *Christianity turned Jesus into God and ignored all his teachings.* That applies at least for the Christian churches as institutions and the vast majority of Christians. There were exceptions at all times, mostly in the early days of Christianity before the Constantine shift in the year 313 A.D., even if the number of martyrs was by far exaggerated by the church for propagandistic reasons. There were and still are today Christians who are persecuted, tortured and killed because of their faith or for speaking up for the poor and disadvantaged. These Christian witnesses to the truth, from Stephen up to Dietrich Bonhoeffer, Martin Luther King and Oscar Romero are nevertheless faced by the millions and millions of people who were forcibly converted, persecuted, tortured and killed in the name of God and Jesus Christ. Christianity owes its unstoppable rise in the Roman Empire that went parallel to Jesus' apotheosis to the testimony of the faith of the martyrs. That was unfortunately only one side of the astonishing process of propagation, its bright side so to say. Its dark side consisted of the process of degeneration that was soon setting in, the first step of which was to proclaim Jesus' as the Messiah and Son of Man by the early Christian community of Jerusalem. It manifested itself in that *biting intolerance* that originated from the belief in Yahweh and was soon directed against all other religions and cults of the Old World from which the early Christians nonetheless adopted a lot. This intolerance, however, also hit dissidents and dissenters from among themselves with the same or often even with a stronger force. The curses and maledictions that Paul launched against those who did not accept Christian faith or who promulgated a "different gospel"[2] than he did, bear compelling testimony to this. Here, the religion of God's and human love reveals its other face, which, if nothing else can be ascribed to the influx of the concept of God of the *First Testament* that Jesus, actually, had just overcome.

Very soon after Jesus' death, that conflict-laden process of mutual assimilation between Christianity and Roman Empire began, which eventually ended in the elevation of Christianity to become the state religion. *In the course of this process, the Roman Empire became Christian and Christianity became Roman.* The church changed from being persecuted to being persecutor, from serving to ruling, from humble to triumphant and from poor to rich, more specifically it became the church of the rich and mighty as an instrument of domination over the souls. The structural adaptation of the church to the Roman Empire brought with it the formation of a strictly centralistic hierarchy along the lines of the Roman administration in the West of the Roman Empire as well as the introduction of the canonical law along the lines of the Roman law. In 1972, the church critic Karlheinz Deschner published a book with the title: *The Cock Crew Again : An Unmasking of Christianity from the Evangelists to the Fascists* which describes church history as a history of betrayal of Jesus' life and teaching. In its basic statements, it is still applicable today.

Let us now consider with due brevity the stages that the biblical Jesus went through on his way to become the Ruler of the Universe and Judge of the World :

1. The early Christian community of Jerusalem,
2. "Hellenists",
3. Paul,
4. Synoptics,
5. Gospel of John, and
6. Arian dispute.

THE EARLY CHRISTIAN COMMUNITY OF JERUSALEM

The first and probably decisive move on the way to Jesus' elevation to God was made by Peter and the early Christian community of Jerusalem. It was them who raised the resurrected one to be Yahweh's *Adopted Son* as the anointed King of Israel (Messiah) in terms of the psalms 2 and 110, to *David's Son* in terms of Nathan's prophecy, to the eschatological *Son of Man* in terms of Daniel 7:13, to *Son of God* in terms of a righteous person in Wisdom Literature and to *Servant oj God* in terms of the Songs of Second Isaiah. Jesus' apotheosis to God-man in the sense of the dogma of Christ was still far away, but the soil on which this doctrine could grow had been prepared. The ancient world was obviously full of a basic *fear of death* and *desire of salvation* to which the gnosis, the myths of the dying and resurrecting God, the mystery cults and the emperor cult tried to give an answer. In the end, Christianity defeated them all, though by surrendering almost everything that Jesus had taught and died for.

"HELLENISTS"

The Stephen's circle of the early Christian community was mainly formed by Jews of the diaspora who had grown up as faithful Jews in a Hellenistic environment, and who, therefore, represented a kind of cultural hybrids. The transformation of the Jewish Messiah into the dying and resurrecting God of the Hellenistic gods' myths and consequently into Lord (*kyrios*) and Redeemer (*soter*) can be primarily ascribed to them. Through them, the Jewish ritual of breaking the bread during the evening love-feast had already been merged with elements of the mystery cults, insofar as we can rely on Paul's report. In the first letter to the Corinthians we read: "On the night when he was betrayed, the Lord Jesus took some bread and gave thanks to God for it. Then he broke it in pieces and said, "This is my body, which is given for you. Do this to remember me". In the same way, he took the cup of wine after supper, saying, "This cup is the new covenant between God and his people — an agreement confirmed with my blood. Do this to remember me as often as you drink it".[3]

To orthodox Jews, these kinds of "innovations" were a blasphemous horror because they invalidated the hierarchy between Yahweh as the absolute ruler and man, whose purpose was unconditional obedience towards his commandments. For the

"Hellenists", the resurrected one already oversteps the line between God and man, he becomes God-man. By eating the divine body and drinking the divine blood in the holy act, the adept gains a share of God's existence in a magical way. He becomes *immortal*. No wonder, therefore, that the Jewish orthodoxy, to which also Saul/Paul belonged, went with the strongest rigour against the Jesus sect, because it raised the man, who had been crucified by the Romans, not without their cooperation, to become God, Lord and Saviour. It probably took the "Hebrews" considerable efforts to distance themselves from the "Hellenists" in order to save them from the fate of Stephen and his followers, death or expulsion. As reported by Luke in the Acts of the Apostles, they got away with a whipping[4] but were allowed to stay in Jerusalem. The "Hellenists", however, flew from Jerusalem and "were dispersed in the areas of Judaea and Samaria"[5] and later as far as Phoenicia, Cypres and Antioch, as well as to Damascus where Paul, who was seriously ill after his "Damascus experience", was accommodated by one of them and nursed back to health.

A considerable part of the rocket like rise of the historical Jesus to the God-man Jesus Christ has already been covered by the "Hellenists", but it is only through Paul that he gets the thrust that catapults him into orbit.

PAUL

Paul is the main responsible for the transformation of Jesus' proclamation of the *present begin of God's rule* into a *religion of redemption* that turns the *preacher* into the *promulgated one*, the *believer* into the *believed one* and the man *Jesus* into the Son of God *Jesus Christ*. He, not Jesus, is the real founder of the religion. Depending on the point of view under which we consider his work, the finding turns to be positive or negative. If we consider it from Jesus' point of view, as I understand him, it appears basically as an adulteration of Jesus' life and teaching. If, however, we regard it from the point of view of Christianity, of how it took its final shape in the fourth century, then it was him who laid the foundation for the triumph of Christianity in the ancient world, for what he has to be given great credit.

What we encounter with Paul is the superb attempt of a synthesis of Jewish and Hellenistic religiosity. *This attempt failed superbly*. His proclamation is full of contradictions and inconsistencies. This is why it is so difficult to understand it. It is a mirror of his great but internally divided and torn personality that longed for redemption and found it by believing in the resurrected Jesus. Let us try to name the heterogeneous elements that entered his proclamation: There is, on the one hand, the bigoted, angry, judging, punishing and annihilating God of the *First Testament* who demands the sacrifice of a completely innocent victim, his son, in order to be reconciled, so that justice is served and his anger is appeased. Paul even adopts the demonical characteristics of this concept of God in the shape of the doctrine of predestination.[6] Should anybody come up with the idea of asking: If I belong to the castaways by God then I am innocent? Why am I punished with eternal agony? Where is God's justice? He will be sent away with the statement from the *First Testament*: "Who are you that you want to argue with God? Should the thing that was created say to the one who created it: "Why have you made me like this?" Is not the potter the master of the clay? Doesn't he have a right to use the same lump of clay to make one jar for decoration and another to throw garbage into?" In other words: You will be punished with eternal agony though you are innocent, kindly accept it !

This concept of God is also confirmed by the following quotation: "There is a certain order (of resurrection). Christ is first, then, when he comes, all the others that belong to him follow. After that, there is the end, when he has destroyed all power, violence and force and forwards his rule to God, the Father. For, he has to rule until God places all his enemies at his feet. The last enemy that is disempowered is death. If not, he would not have placed everything at his feet. But if it says that everything is submitted, that obviously excludes the one who submits everything to him. When everything is submitted to him, he himself, the Son, will also submit to the one who submitted everything to him so that God rules over everything and in everything".[7] This *Bible* passage that is used to justify the claim of Christianity for religious world domination is soaked in the spirit of violence: Jesus *destroys* all (worldly) power, violence and force. He surrenders his *rule* to God, the Father. He must *rule* until God has placed *all the enemies at his feet*. Everything must be *submitted* to him so that he, to whom everything is *submitted*, can now himself *submit* to the Father so that God *rules* over everything and in everything. That means that also Paul's concept of God matches the image of God of the oriental despot whom we encounter again and again in the *First Testament*.

After all, it is also Paul who, in the Epistle to the Romans, puts in motion the disastrous dialectic see-saw of the doctrine of justification.[8] *The thought of justification as such is wrong, no matter if out of faith or out of works.* A defendant must exculpate himself before the judge. The God of Jesus, however, is not a judge. This is also the reason why Jesus is, on principal, opposed to judging: Do not judge so that you are not judged! Who judges, eventually judges himself. The God of Jesus is the God who searches for the lost sheep and is happy when he found it; the widow who searches the lost drachm and makes a feast when she found it.[9] He is the loving father who hastens to meet the son that returns to him, not to judge him or to reproach him but to receive him as his son.[10] Paul, on the contrary, goes as far as to say: "Do you not know that we will judge angels"?[11]

From the early Christian community, Paul adopts Jesus' resurrection as well as his proclamation of being the eschatological Messiah and Son of Man. From the historical Jesus, he adopts his love ethics. That much about Jewish religion. The following elements come from the Hellenistic cultural background: the doctrine of the Redeemer and Saviour from the Gnosis, the myth of the dying and resurrecting God (in turns of the seasons) from the Dionysus, Heracles, Asclepius, Attis and Osiris cults, and the mystery of baptism and the Eucharistic Supper from the mystery cults.

SYNOPTICS

About the Synoptics about which much has been already been, I can restrict myself to a few comments. On the one hand, they proceed treading on the footsteps of the "Hellenists" and Paul on the path of Jesus' elevation to God in human shape by portraying him as the master over the elements, over illness, demons, Satan, sin, death etc.; on the other hand, they save the Jesuanic tradition of the early Christian community of Jerusalem from falling into oblivion. If we did not have them, we would hardly know anything about the historical Jesus and his teachings. Within the group of the Synoptics, we can observe a further *intensification tendency* regarding Jesus' revelation as Messiah and Son of Man. In Mark's Gospel, it is still treated like a secret, while Matthew and Luke consider it already as understood, whereas Jesus' self-revelation gains centre-stage in the Gospel of John.

GOSPEL OF JOHN

In the work of the evangelist John, Jesus is already quite close to the culmination of his career. He is the pre-existing Son of God who came into the world in order to redeem those from the prison of this world who believe in him and worship him "in the spirit and in the truth".[12] In John's Gospel, Jesus is already named the *one and only* Son of God, the same as later in the credos of the church. In his writings, we already find a classical phrasing of Christology: "And as Moses lifted up the bronze snake on a pole in the wilderness, so the Son of Man must be lifted up, so that everyone who believes in him will have eternal life. For God loved the world so much that he gave his *one and only* Son, so that everyone who believes in him will not perish but have eternal life".[13] "I am the way, and the truth, and the life. No one can come to the Father except through me".[14]

Now, turning away from God and his commandments is not as much a sin as it was in Judaism, but the refusal to believe in Jesus as the Son of God.[15] Because the Jews refuse to accept this imposition, they become an object of hatred and disgust. They are declared the sons of Satan.[16] This is where Christian anti-Judaism already shows its ugly face. It is also the Gospel of John where we find the text that specifies with great accuracy the difference between Judaism and Christianity. The Jews apparently want to stone Jesus because of his self-revelation as the Son of God: Their reproach: "..... you are only a man and turn yourself into God",[17] whereafter the Johannine Christ manifests himself once more as the Son of God, namely as God in human shape.

The influence of gnosis is palpable in the work of John as it was already in Paul's. The Manichaean worldview, the metaphorics of light and darkness, spirit and flesh, God and Satan, the "ruler of the world",[18] is present at every turn. The same applies for the influence of the mystery cults. The famous "I am" words that phrase the essence of the Johannine Christology, so to speak, have nothing whatsoever to do with the historical Jesus. He would not only have discarded them, he would have rejected them as *satanic temptation.*

APOCALYPSE OF JOHN

The elevation of the carpenter's son from Nazareth to God and ruler of the universe has already been completed in the Revelation of John, which supposedly originates from the time of the Domitianic persecution of Christians in the years 95/96 A.D. On the other hand, the degeneration, indeed perversion of Jesus' teachings hit its temporary bottom in this "holy" scripture. The visionary John, who is not identical with the evangelist, beholds Jesus as the eschatological Messiah-Son of God whose arrival he is expecting in the near future. We have now returned completely to the world of thought of the *First Testament*, insofar as God is presented according to the image of the oriental despot. To the members of the Christian community in Thyatira, who had not been misled by the wrong prophet "Jezebel",[19] Christ, "whose eyes are like flames of fire, whose feet are like polished bronze", delivers the message: "I will ask nothing more of you except that you hold tightly to what you have until I come. To all who are victorious, who obey me to the very end, to them I will give authority over all the nations. They will rule the nations with an iron rod and smash them like clay pots. They will have the same authority I received from my Father".[20] And to the community in Laodicea, he brings the message: "Those who are victorious will sit with me on my throne, just as I was victorious and sat with my Father on his throne".[21] While the bestowal of power over the peoples and the rule with an iron rod as well as sitting on God's throne was up to then reserved for the Messiah, it is now extended to everybody who triumphs and adheres until the end to the works that Christ commands. The hate-filled defamation of Jews ("Synagogue of Satan") and false teachers, namely the "Nicolaitans",[22] are, of course, not missing in John's work.

It goes on in this style. In the Revelation of John, there is, in fact, a veritable windstorm blowing of imminent expectation of Christ's return as the eschatological ruler. He is the lamb that opens the seven seals of the scroll, in which the events of the last days that were predetermined by God are described. He is the rider on the white horse[23] who judges and conducts war fairly. The apocalyptic John virtually indulges himself in torture and destruction fantasies, in which the ten Egyptian plagues, the apocalypses of the *First Testament* and the eschatological speech of the biblical Christ are surpassed. Even the prohibition of excess such as in an eye for an eye, a tooth for a tooth is forgotten. The "whore Babylon", used as a synonym for the cesspool of vice that is Rome, is not only paid back for her infamous actions in kind, but she is given back twice of what she has done.[24] By this, the apocalypse, with its threat of eternal punishment, that can admittedly already be found in the gospels, leaves even "Lamech's speech"[25] of the First Testament far behind. While the historical Jesus invalidates the principle of revenge on its positive side completely (How often do I have to forgive my brother? Is seven times enough?), the Revelation of John dissolves it with the doctrine of eternal punishment radically to the negative side because the punishment of temporal offences, no matter how terrible they might be, with eternal punishment invalidates the principle of revenge completely.

It is, therefore, obvious that in the Revelation, nothing, absolutely nothing, is left of the historical Jesus, his life, death and teachings. When theologians and clerics contrast and confront the Second Testament, as the good news of God's love to men through Jesus Christ who became human, again and again with the First Testament, then this presentation requires an urgent revision. The last scripture of the *Bible*, the Revelation, takes literally everything back that the great *reformer of Judaism*, Jesus of Nazareth, promulgated and substantiated through his life and death. No wonder that this scripture is one of the favourite reads of all Christian fundamentalists. The mere fact that the Revelation of John was included in the canon of the Holy Scripture instead of ending in any anthology of Apocrypha speaks volumes. Thus, it received the benediction of being Holy Scripture, *Word of God.* So it needed just one generation to reverse the teachings of the historical Jesus in the works of some Christian authors to their absolute opposite.

The man who once said: "You know that the rulers in this world lord it over their people, and officials flaunt their authority over those under them. But among you it will be different. Whoever wants to be a leader among you must be your servant".[26] the man who once said: "Do not judge others, and you will not be judged".[27] has been turned into the absolute ruler and judge of the world. There are bitter truths as well as there is bitter medicine, but both are beneficial. It is high time that *we understand the relation between the elevation of the historical Jesus to biblical Christ and the betrayal of his teachings and the message of his life.* The order of the day reads: End the *disgusting personality cult* of the Redeemer Jesus Christ, and return to the pure source of his good news of the present beginning of God's rule!

ARIAN DISPUTE

At the end of the first century of the Christian era, everything was.

for the most part, already over. The process of Jesus' apotheosis to Son of God and Ruler of the World was finished. It is all the more astonishing that more than two hundred years later some resistance was offered in the person of the Presbyter Arius of Alexandria, who declared in an informal debate, which Bishop Alexander led with his elders in the year 318 A.D.: *"There was a time in which Jesus did not exist* and *he was created from nothingness"*, which he proved with some *Bible* verses. Later, a young deacon of the bishop, Athanasius, reacted vigorously against this teaching. To him, philosophical considerations did not matter, he fought for redemption. Jesus, the saviour of the world and all people, could not be himself a being in need of redemption. If Arius made a creature of Jesus, he took the redeemer away from mankind. Athanasius reinforced his opinion with the first chapter of the Gospel of John.

With this, the two protagonists of the Arian dispute, Arius (died in 336) and Athanasius (around 293-373), have been identified. Although Arius was denied the appointment as a bishop, he attracted many supporters. Athanasius, however, who represented the Trinitarian formula of the triune God, became Bishop of Alexandria after Bishop Alexander's death. It is unnecessary to outline the changeful history of the dispute in detail because it can be looked up in the pertinent manuals. It is sufficient to note that the dispute took hold not only of theologians and priests but also of Emperor and people and led to the verge of a schism.

In the end, this dispute, in which both sides were not sparing each other with condemnations, excommunications and damnations, was about one single letter, the Greek I, that differentiates the words *homousios* (coessential) and *homoiusios* (similar in essence). The party of the Trinitarians insisted on the coessentiality of God Father, God Son and God Holy Spirit. The Arians, on the other hand, took the view that Jesus was clearly subordinate to God, regardless of his similarity to God.

The Trinitarians achieved a victory on the first ecumenical council in Nicaea, convoked by Emperor Constantine in 325, which found expression in the Nicene Creed. Later, the Arians gained the upper hand. The fight continued back and forth till the fifties of the fourth century when the Arians prevailed across a broad front with the aid of Emperor Constantius II (337-361). On the third council of Sirmium (357), a creed was written that advocated a consistent subordination of Jesus to the father. It took until the seventies of the fourth century before the tide turned in favour of the Trinitarians. With the help of Emperor Theodosius (347-395), who came into power in 379 and was baptised as Trinitarian in 380, Gregory of Nazianzus enforced the Trinitarian doctrine. In 381, Theodosius convoked the first Council of Constantinople in which the Nicene Creed was rewritten under the guidance of Gregory of Nazianzus and Gregory of Nyssa.

I remember well when I was in high school, that our teacher of religion entered the classroom and exclaimed enthusiastically: "Is it not wonderful and a sign of the work of the Holy Spirit that in church history, the truth always prevailed"? I did not contradict him then, because I did not know any better. Today I would ask him what he meant with this, because in the respective Christian churches and denominations different truths had prevailed, after all. And in church history: Was Arius right or Athanasius ? My answer will hardly surprise the readers — Arius, of course ! But he and his followers did not succeed in prevailing, considering Jesus' apotheosis that had already taken place in the first century.

How could the connection between God and man be made, a connection that is hardly comprehensible for modern people? In the mythology of the ancient world it was completely natural. Let us remember the sons of the gods Heracles, Dionysos and Orpheus, whose fathers were gods and whose mothers were humans, or Achilles, whose father was a man and whose mother was a goddess. The oriental rulers of ancient times were also often worshipped as the sons of gods. Alexander the Great and, later on, the Roman Emperors adopted the oriental ruler cult and were revered religiously as the sons of gods. In the moment that Jesus was awarded the majestic title of Lord (Kyrios), which was only due to the Roman Emperor, it became clear that he also had to be the son of God and Virgin Mary. The development to the cult of the holy family: God Father, Mother Mary and Son Jesus Christ were, therefore, predetermined, including the veneration of Christ and Mary. The Jewish Prophet Jesus of Nazareth mutated to be the Son of God, to Lord and Saviour Jesus Christ. Thus, the origin of the Christian dogmas is to be found in ancient mythology. For Gandhi Jesus is a man full of the spirit of God. He brings him back to Earth with the realization: "We become godlike to the extent we realize non-violence; but we can never become wholly God".[28]

REFERENCES

1. Cited in Heimo Rau: *Gandhi,* Reinbek 1970, 238.
2. *Letter (of Paul) to the Galatians*, 1:8.
3. *First Letter to the Corinthians*, 11:23-25.
4. *Acts of the Apostles*, 5:21-42.
5. *Acts of the Apostles*, 11:19.
6. *Letter to the Romans*, 9:14-29.
7. *First Letter to the Corinthians*, 15:23-28.
8. *Letter to the Romans*, 9:32.
9. *Gospel according to St Matthew*, 18:12-14.
10. *Gospel of Luke*, 15:11-32.
11. *First Letter to the Corinthians*, 6:3.
12. *Gospel of John*, 4:23 f.
13. *Ibid.*, 3:14-16.
14. *Ibid.*, 14:6.
15. *Ibid.*, 15:22 f.
16. *Ibid.*, 8:21-47.
17. *Ibid.*, 10:33.
18. *Ibid.*, 12:31.
19. Jezebel was the wife of King Ahab, who encouraged the idol worship of Baal in Israel. *First Book of Kings*, 16:31; *Apocalypse of John,* 18:4.13. John uses her name as a pseudonym of the "false" prophet in the community.
20. *Apocalypse of John,* 2:18-28.
21. *Ibid.*, 3:21.
22. *Ibid.*, 2:6.15.
23. *Ibid.*, 19:11.
24. *Apocalypse of John*, 18:5.
25. *Genesis (First Book of Mose)*, 4:23 f.
26. *Gospel according to St Matthew*, 20:25-27.
27. *Ibid.*, 7:1.
28. *Harijan,* 12.11.38, CWMG, 74,130.

18
Jesus and Paul

Christianity is the religion founded by Paul that replaced the gospel of Jesus by a gospel about Jesus.

—*Wilhelm Nestle*

Paul was a contemporary to Jesus. He came from a wealthy Jewish Orthodox parental home in Tarsus, a town on the Orontes in Cilicia (Asia Minor). He held Roman citizenship. Being a young man, he came to Jerusalem in order to 'study' with the Pharisee Gamaliel. He is a fanatic follower of orthodoxy, a 'bigot for God' and he persecutes the Jesus sect recklessly, something he deeply regrets after his conversion. His conversion occurs before entering Damascus, where he falls off his horse and loses his eyesight temporarily because of an epileptic fit or, what seems more probable, a stroke. Later, he interprets this experience as an encounter with the resurrected Jesus. In contrast to Paul himself, who restricts himself to a few comments in his epistles, the experience is described by Luke in the most vivid colours in the Acts.[1] Many things suggest that Paul was an epileptic since Damascus. He speaks mysteriously about a "sting in the flesh".[2] It is also conspicuous that he dictates his epistles, and only signs them by his own hand in order to certify their authenticity. It is quite probable that a visual impairment remained from the temporary loss of his eyesight. All the more admirable are the passion, the courage and the perseverance with which he dedicates his life from then onwards to the proclamation of the resurrected one as the Son of God, Lord and Redeemer, and to his vocation of preaching about him to the heathens.

First of all, however, he is led, blind and helpless as he is after falling off his horse, to Damascus, where, equipped with letters from the High Council, he wants to arrest Jesus' followers, who have fled there, and later transfer them to Jerusalem.[3] He, the most bitter enemy of the Jesus community, is hosted and nursed back to health by a "Hellenist", of all people, named Hananiah.[4] Not much of an intuition is required to imagine the effect that this experience must have had on Saul. He was outright overwhelmed by this altruistic act of loving kindness. A fervid Christian hater turned into a no less fervid missionary of Jesus Christ the Redeemer. His missionary journeys led him to Asia Minor, Greece and Rome (as a prisoner), where he lived for several years and was later executed, probably in the year 64 A.D., in the course of the persecution of Christians under Nero, to which, presumably, also Peter fell victim.

It was very important to Paul that he had received a revelation that was independent from the early Christian community of Jerusalem. This should not be forgotten when the conflict between him and Peter, and even more so with the circle around Jacob, the brother of the Lord, comes up later on. Contrary to the account in the Acts of the Apostles that tells of a visit of Paul to Jerusalem shortly after his conversion, Paul's own account in the Epistle to the Galatians seems much more reliable. There, he writes that he only returned to Jerusalem three years after his conversion in order to meet Kepha (Peter). He stayed with him for fifteen days. He did not meet any of the other apostles, only Jacob, the brother of the Lord. It must have been a memorable meeting between the simple fisher from the Lake Kinnerat, who had absorbed Jesus' teaching and the example of his life, and the educated diaspora Jew from Tarsus, who was familiar with Judaism as well as Hellenism. The conversation of the two could have had the following content:

Paul

We both believe, rather we know, that Jesus has risen from the dead. With that, he became again the one he originally was. He was *equal to God* but did not hang on to the fact of being equal to God, but renounced and became like a slave and *equal* to men. His life was that of a man. All that you have related about Jesus with whom you went through Galilee and finally to Jerusalem is, therefore, outdated. It is the flower, nice to look at, but without sustenance. Only the ripe fruit, the risen Jesus, nourishes.

Peter

Yes, for sure. I do not want to brag about it, but I really knew Jesus. His word worked miracles. People were at his feet; they adored him. I myself pushed him to reveal himself as the Messiah. But he reprimanded me sharply. I will never forget his words: "Go away Satan," he said, "get out of my sight. You want to bring me down, because you do not have in mind what God wants, but what people want." That insulted me deeply. Jesus was a great man, but he also had very human traits. He could get very angry, for instance about the rich and mighty and the pious hypocrites in case they refused the call for repentance.

Paul (impatient)

I do not dispute that you knew Jesus. But I *recognised* him as who he is: the Son of God, the second Adam, and the Saviour of the world. I do not care about what he *was according to the flesh*; I care what he *is* as the risen Christ *according to the spirit.*

Peter

In many things, I think as you do, but I feel that you did not really understand Jesus.

Paul (harsh)

There is no point in arguing about it. Stick to your opinion, I will stick to mine.

From the short biographical information in the Epistle to the Galatians, it becomes evident that Paul adopted a gospel in an already Hellenistic form as his faith. Only 14 years after meeting Peter and 15-16 years after his conversion, he returns to Jerusalem for the "Apostolic Council" in the year 48 or 49 A.D., in which the conflict between Paul and Barnabas on one side and the circle around Peter and Jacob on the other side, who stuck to the law, especially to circumcision, was solved by means of a compromise, or may be only by a cover-up. He writes that it had been accepted by Kepha, John and Jacob, who are held in high esteem in the community as "pillars", that the gospel was confided to him for the uncircumcised, while to Peter for the circumcised. They did not impose anything further upon him. Paul and Barnabas were supposed to go to the pagans, they to the circumcised.* They should only remember the poor people in the community of Jerusalem and collect for them.

---

* The religious duty to remove the foreskin of men in Judaism and Islam.

Paul, that becomes apparent from his letters, was little interested in the historical Jesus, the Jesus of flesh, because he did not match the image of the Redeemer, that he deduced from the Hellenistic religions. He was interested in the Jesus of the Spirit, who was with God before the beginning of time, then came into this world, suffered death in place of our sins in order to save those from the divine judgement who believed in him and confessed to him. Paul sees in Jesus the downright antithesis of Adam. The way sin came into the world with Adam, it disappears again through Jesus Christ, but only for the chosen ones who believe in him.

Here, the old children's questions reappear. If that is so, what happens to those who lived before Jesus or did not know about his existence? Are they all lost? Explanations like these do not help: That we should confidently leave it to God, because he is, after all, more intelligent than we all. Obviously, these are evasions. In reality, we have a remake of the chosenness belief of the First Testament when dealing with Paul, only with the difference, that all people who believe in the Redeemer Jesus Christ, no matter if they are Jews or pagans, belong to the chosen ones of the *new covenant*. What can be argued against the *old covenant* of the Jewish chosenness belief, obviously also applies to the *new covenant* in form of the Christian church that Paul comprehends as the community of the "perfect", the "Sons of God", or the "Saints". In fact, Paul was convinced that those who believed in Jesus Christ and formed with him a mystic body, thus became sons of God and were raised, as Jesus from the dead (he significantly forgets the women as daughters of God). But what happens to the others? Does it really help them if one gets baptised in place of the dead?[5] There is only the alternative: We either talk about God of the *First* (and partially also the *Second*) *Testament*, who arbitrarily chooses and discards, or about the God of Jesus, who comes towards every man and woman who decide to return, like the father in the narration about the prodigal son.

That our salvation shall depend on a contingent truth of history such as the existence of Jesus of Nazareth is, as Lessing already realised clearly an absurdity or at least irreconcilable with the idea of a loving and just God. "Contingent truths of history (like the news of a man called Jesus who supposedly lived two thousand years ago) can never become the proof for necessary truths of reason".[6]

Gandhi understood by intuition the transformation of Jesus' message made by Paul. He wrote: "I draw a great distinction line between the Sermon on the Mount and the Letters of Paul. They are a graft on Christ's teaching, his own gloss apart from Christ's own experience".[7]

REFERENCES

1. *Acts of the Apostles*,1-22; 22:1-21; 26:9-23.
2. *Second Letter to the Corinthians*, 12:7.
3. *Acts of the Apostles*, 22:4
4. *Ibid.*, 22:12.
5. *First Letter to the Corinthians*, 15:29.
6. *Werke,* published by Gerhard Stenzel, Salzburg, 1039.
7. *Young India*, 19.1.1928; CWMG, 41, 115.

19
The End of Fundamentalism

Then a third angel followed them, shouting, "Anyone who worships the beast and his statue or who accepts his mark on the forehead or on the hand must drink the wine of God's anger. It has been poured full strength into God's cup of wrath. And they will be tormented with fire and burning sulphur in the presence of the holy angels and the Lamb.

—Book of Revelation, 14:9f

The US based Anglican Bishop John Shelby Spong describes the historical origin of the term fundamentalism as follows: "Between 1910 and 1915, a group of conservative Christians, in a reaction against *Bible* criticism in general and against Charles Darwin's challenge, published a series of pamphlets with the title "The Fundamentals". From these pamphlets, the word fundamentalism found entrance into the religious vocabulary and gained in importance as a description of the literalism of conservative Christians".[1]

Lawrence Meredith summarised the religious beliefs of the fundamentalists in five basic statements (fundamentals) quoted by Spong. They are:

1. "The inspiration of the scripture as God's literally revealed word.
2. The virgin birth as the wonderful and literally to be understood guarantee for Christ's divine nature.
3. Jesus' death acting as reconciliation. His death brought the gift of redemption through the salivific in magic power of his blood.
4. The certainty of Jesus' physical resurrection from the dead. The exactitude of the stories of the empty tomb and of Jesus' appearances according to the tradition in the gospels.

5. Jesus' second coming on doomsday when everybody will be judged according to his life. Heaven and Hell as places of eternal reward or punishment are real".[2]

The gap between the religious beliefs of the fundamentalists and the understanding of modern theology has meanwhile become unbridgeable. While for modern theology, each of these assumptions is considered refuted, the fundamentalists consider anyone who merely questions just one of these basic statements as apostate. This makes sense, because, in the mythological way of thinking of the fundamentalists, each of these basic statements carries and supports the others, and is supported by them just as in an architectonic arch, each stone carries and supports the others and is carried and supported by them. Let us summarise once again the results of the historical-critical research:

1. The *Bible* is not only God's word but at the same time man's word, too. Each and every reader is requested to differentiate the one from the other.
2. Jesus died at the cross, his dead body was buried — how and by whom we do not know — and decayed.
3. Jesus did not consider himself as the Messiah or Christ, as David's Son, God's Son, eschatological Son of Man, Lord or Saviour. He was given these titles only after his death.
4. Jesus was capable of erring and he erred. He believed that Satan had been deprived of power so that nothing was standing any more in the way of the propagation of God's rule over the whole world. Therein he was profoundly mistaken.
5. Jesus did not perform any miracles in the sense of an invalidation of natural laws.
6. Jesus did not consider himself to be without sin.
7. The claim that Jesus was God's only begotten son cannot be sustained any longer. The Christ and Trinity Dogma should be abandoned.
8. The absolute truth claim of Christianity cannot be sustained any longer as little as the one of other religions and philosophies. The Christian religion has no supremacy over other religions.

WHAT DO THE BIBLICAL MYTHS MEAN TO US TODAY ?

The world view and the myths of the *Bible* seem strange and remote to us today. They belong to a remote world that perished with the ancient empires. This does not only apply to the antique and medieval view of the world with its three tiered structure of Underworld, consisting of the Realm of Shades (Greek Hades, Hebrew Scheol) and Hell (Greek Tartaros, Hebrew Gehenna), the World of Man and Nature in the middle, as well as the Upper world that is inhabited by gods and spirits or by God and angelic beings, respectively. It also applies to the biblical myth of the creation of the world in six days and the seventh day as resting day, to the myth of the Fall of Man and the redemption through the sacrifice of a pure, in other words a guiltless and stainless, sacrificial animal. It finally also applies to the myth of Christ, in which Jesus assumes the role of the innocent and sinless sacrificial lamb, whose body is eaten by the believers through the bread, and whose blood is drunk through the wine, in order to become, this way, a part of the immortal being of God. Nevertheless, the Christian fundamentalists frantically hold on to these myths. They refuse to accept their critical review and a contemporary interpretation.

It is true, of course, that the earth in its actual form, as well as the solar system, our galaxy and the whole universe have been formed in a process that lasted billions of years and will be finished in a few billion years. From that point of view, all existence is subject to the principle of becoming and passing away. That has only little to do with the biblical myth of the creation of the world. The question has to remain unanswered, whether an imperishable and indestructible power underlies the universe, a power that creates, destroys and recreates, because this power, provided it exists, is beyond the world that is perceptible by the senses.

The same applies to the myth of the Fall of Man. Without doubt, there must have been a moment of awakening in the history of humanity, a moment in which man accomplished the leap from animal to man. That was possible because in the course of evolution, the anthropological preconditions for that had developed: the enlarged brain, the upright walk, the use of tools and, based on that, language and social cohesion. It was not a paradisiacal life in the Garden of Eden, but a hard fight for survival in a world of numerous threats: dangerous animals and poisonous plants, hunger and poverty, heat and cold, accidents and diseases.

From the religious point of view, one can understand the act of humanisation as the moment in which God released man into the freedom of deciding in favour of or against him. We do not know anything about the time in which man used this freedom to decide *in favour of* the communion with God. It might have been days, weeks, months, decades or centuries. We only know that, at one point, he decided against God and in favour of his freedom, independence and "autonomy". He wanted to be his own lawmaker instead of following the divine law in freedom. The reader will remember that Gandhi described this situation as voluntary slavery in the service of God and His creation. It goes without saying that the turning away from God, described in the *Bible* as the Fall of Man, did not only constitute an individual decision, but created, at the same time, a social reality, and had, from now on, a contagious effect towards other people. Just as it was always possible to turn away from God and the great law that He Himself is, it was also possible, of course, to return to Him at any time. With each sin committed by man, however, the return became more difficult and the way to God longer and more troublesome, because it had become necessary to overcome social circumstances that had been created through injustice and violence. Everything in the world is certainly dynamic, in the positive as well as in the negative. The return to God is, nevertheless, possible at any moment, regardless of whether as an individual or as a community.

Today we know that mankind did not make use of the freedom that it was granted wisely. One may think about God's existence as one likes, but what is indisputable is that mankind is in the process of destroying itself and all higher forms of life on this planet, be it through an atomic world war, through environmental degradation or through mental-psychological destruction and self-destruction due to the existing power and ownership structures.

The myth, however, tells a completely different story. It tells about the Garden of Eden as a perfect world in which there was neither sin nor disease, neither misery nor death, in which the original human couple Adam and Eve lived a plentiful life. After the Fall, after eating the fruit of the Tree of Knowledge, they were expelled from this garden forever because the angels with the flaming sword are guarding the entrance to paradise. With the original human couple, the whole creation fell into sin, and, as a consequence of sin, into death.

In Judaism, a return to God is possible through a strict observation of the laws given by God. In Christianity, man would have lost salvation irretrievably, had not God come down from heaven in the shape of his only begotten son, in order to save him, as Paul and, after him, the Christian churches taught. The Catholic church, beyond that, raises the claim of being the only representative of the New Covenant founded by Jesus Christ, of being the only one capable of forgiving sins and providing participation in the eternal existence of God as imparted in the sacraments. Without faith in Jesus Christ as the sinless and stainless sacrificial lamb, that carries the sin of the world and reconciled God with the fallen mankind through His suffering and dying, nobody can, according to Christian doctrine, be saved. It is not difficult to see that this myth is to be assigned to the angry tribal deity Yahweh, who takes the disobedience of men towards him as a personal offence and who must be reconciled through an animal or human sacrifice. But God, as we know by now, is different. He was not created in the image of man, or, to be more precise, in the image of the oriental despot, but it was man who was created in the image of God. The way of a return to God is open to every man and every community, if they make an effort in the right way. But God's grace is not cheap to get. God requires of us a constant effort of striving for truth and non-violence, as well as the release from everything that ties us to this world in selfishness and sensory enjoyment. A mediation by the church is not required for that.

The difference between the two religious ways becomes clearly manifest in the encounter of Gandhi with a Plymouth Brother.[3] The latter had assured him that he had no scruples about sinning because he knew himself to be redeemed through his belief in Jesus Christ. Gandhi replied: "If this be the Christianity acknowledged by all Christians, I cannot accept it. I do not seek redemption from the consequences of my sin. I seek to be redeemed from sin itself, or rather from the very thought of sin. Until I have attained that end, I shall be content to be restless".[4]

WHERE ARE WE TODAY ?

Jesus' and Gandhi's call for a turn around went unheard — apart from a few exceptions. May be a turn around would still have been possible after the end of the Second World War if mankind had gathered its wits and had decided on a turn around, considering the victims of the massacres of two world wars, Auschwitz and Hiroshima. Jesus had hoped for such a turn around from his people, the Israelites,

Gandhi from India. Their peoples should proceed on this way, respectively. The chance was not taken. Today it is too late, the point of no return already overstepped. That is the bad news. The good news is: Wherever in this world individuals and communities decide on a turn around, they will reap the fruits of their deeds. That still applies when the goal, the kingdom of God on Earth, has become unattainable, because this effort carries its sense and its reward in itself.

The Indian mythology knows the figure of the *avatar*. An *avatar* is an incarnation of God that descends in a moment of utmost crisis for a last rescue attempt. May be Buddha, Socrates, Jesus and Gandhi were such *avatars*. They achieved a lot, but, seen as a whole, they did not succeed in persuading mankind to turn around.

REFERENCES

1. John Shelby Spong: A New Christianity for a New World. Why Traditional Faith is Dying and How A New Faith is Being Born. Harper Collins Publishers, 17.
2. *Ibid.* 17 f.
3. Follower of a Christian sect.
4. *Autobiography*; SWMG, 1, 185.

20
What does Jesus mean for Gandhi?

Although I cannot claim being a Christian in a sect like sense, the example of Jesus' suffering is after all a factor in my unshakable belief in non-violence that determines all my activities, the spiritual and the profane ones.

—Mahatma Gandhi

Gandhi, as we have learned already, questions the Christian dogmas in principle. He is simply not interested in Jesus the Redeemer. Whether Jesus had lived or is a product of literary imagination is ultimately irrelevant to him. The Sermon on the Mount, however, holds true for him, as true as the doctrines of other teachers of mankind, because it contains eternal truths. He apparently does not notice the difficult passages that it contains, such as, for example, the threat of eternal agony, because they do not pass the three filters (truth, love and reason, insofar as the things are accessible to reason): "I may say that I have never been interested in a historical Jesus. I should not care if it was proved by someone that the man called Jesus never lived, and that what was narrated in the Gospels was a figment of the writer's imagination. For the Sermon on the Mount would still be true for me".[1]

The opposite position is phrased by Paul, for whom his salvation and the salvation of all Christians depend on Jesus' historical existence and resurrection: "And if Christ has not been raised, then all our preaching is empty, and our faith is useless".[2]

For Paul — and most Christians will follow him therein —, the salvation of his soul depends on Jesus' life, death and resurrection. Behind this, there is the perception that mankind is doomed to sin and death through Adam. Even the greatest saints and prophets have been infected with it and are thus at the mercy of death. However, as God raised Jesus from the dead, the resurrection from the dead begins with him. He is the first, but those who believe in him and confess to him will follow. Paul: "For, it is by believing in your heart that you are made right with God, and it is by confessing with your mouth that you are saved. As the Scriptures tell us, anyone who trusts Him will never be disgraced".[3] (Meaning, of course Yahweh and not Jesus in the *First Testament*). Through the mystical union with Jesus Christ, they suffer death with him and experience the resurrection as the sons of God. In case they are already deceased, they shall be risen from the dead, in case they are still alive, they shall be covered with the "spiritual body" and carried away towards the Lord. Paul: "But let me reveal to you a wonderful secret. We will not all die, but we will all be transformed! It will happen in a moment, in the blink of an eye, when the last trumpet is blown. For when the trumpet sounds, those who have died will be raised to live forever. And we who are living will also be transformed. For our dying bodies must be transformed into bodies that will never die; our mortal bodies must be transformed into immortal bodies. Then, when our dying bodies have been transformed into bodies that will never die, this Scripture will be fulfilled: Death is swallowed up in victory. O death, where is your victory? O death, where is your sting" ?[4]

The expectation of Paul and the early Christians did not become real, as is well known. The second coming of the resurrected Christ as the Messiah-Son of Man was not only delayed but failed to materialise. The yearning expectation of this event among countless Christians in the past and in the present cannot hide that fact. It will also not become real in the future, to the detriment of many fundamentalists who take the *Bible* literally. Truthfulness rather demands labelling it as what it was and is — a *delusion*. What finds expression in it is the conscious or unconscious perception of a world crisis that never happened before in the history of mankind.

Although for Gandhi, Jesus' existence is irrelevant for the salvation of his soul, he nevertheless never doubted that he had lived. Because of his life and teachings, he recognises him as one of the great teachers of mankind. He recognises a *satyagrahi* in him, a non-violent fighter, indeed a "prince of satyagraha". He calls the early Christians, who were ready to accept persecution, suffering and death for their faith, *satyagrahis*. If we recognise, with Gandhi, a non-violent fighter for truth, love and justice in Jesus, then the devastating distortion of his image through the Servant Songs becomes evident in the first place. The preacher of God's rule on earth as an empire of justice, peace and joy becomes a sacrificial lamb that allows itself, passively and silently, to get slaughtered on the altar, as expiatory sacrifice for men. Here we catch hold of the root of that Christian misunderstanding that equals activity with violence and passivity with non-violence, instead of recognising in it an active power of the highest potency to overcome violence.

What Jesus meant for Gandhi, he summarises in a text that I reproduce as a whole because of its beauty and truth :

> "The message of Jesus, as I understand it, is contained in his *Sermon on the Mount* unadulterated and taken as a whole, and even in connection with the *Sermon on the Mount*, my own humble interpretation of the message is in many respects different from the orthodox. The message, to my mind, has suffered distortion in the West. It may be presumptuous for me to say so, but as a devotee of truth, I should not hesitate to say what I feel. I know that the world is not waiting to know my opinion on Christianity".
>
> One's own religion is after all a matter between oneself and one's Maker and no one else's, but if I feel impelled to share my thoughts with you this evening, it is because I want to enlist your sympathy in my search for truth and because so many Christian friends are interested in my thoughts on the teachings of Jesus. If then I had to face only the Sermon on the Mount and my own interpretation of it, I should not hesitate to say, "Oh yes, I am a Christian". But I know that at the present moment if I said any such thing I would lay myself open to the gravest misinterpretation. I should lay myself open to fraudulent claims because I would have then to tell you what my own meaning of Christianity is, and I have no desire myself to give you my own view of Christianity. But negatively I can tell you that in my humble opinion, much of what passes as Christianity is a negation of the Sermon on the Mount. And please mark my words. I am not at the present moment speaking of Christian conduct. I am speaking of the Christian belief, of Christianity as it is understood in the West. I am painfully aware of the fact that conduct everywhere falls far short of belief. But I don't say this by way of criticism. I know from the treasures of my own experience that although I am every moment of my life trying to live up to my professions, my conduct falls short of these professions. Far therefore be it from me to say this in a spirit of criticism. But I am placing before you my fundamental difficulties....

> I claim to be a man of faith and prayer, and even if I was cut to pieces, God would give me the strength not to deny Him and to assert that He is. The Muslim says He is and there is no one else. The Christian says the same thing and so the Hindu, and if I may say so, even the Buddhist says the same thing, if in different words. We may each of us be putting our own interpretation on the word God — God who embraces not only this tiny globe of ours, but millions and billions of such globes. How can we, little crawling creatures, so utterly helpless as he has made us, how could we possibly measure His greatness, His boundless love, His infinite compassion, such that He allows man insolently to deny compassion, such that He allows man insolently to deny Him, wrangle about Him, and cut the throat of his fellow-man ? How can we measure the greatness of God who is so forgiving, so divine? Thus though we may utter the same words they have not the same meaning for us all. And hence I say that we do not need to proselytize . . . . . through our speech or writing. We can only do it really with our lives. Let them be open books for all to study. Would that mean that I could persuade the missionary friends to take this view of their mission? Then there will be no distrust, no suspicion, no jealousy and no dissensions".[5]

The parallels between Gandhi's texts and the *Sermon on the Mount* could easily fill a whole book. His whole life and work can even be understood as the *incarnation of the* Sermon on the Mount. That this sets a standard, measured at which we all fail to a greater or lesser extent, does not change its validity. This is, nevertheless, no reason to despair. The destination remains unreachable for all of us, no matter if we travel a few steps or many miles on the way there. The Jesus, in whom Gandhi recognised a "brother in spirit", has little to do with the Jesus whom the Christian missionaries proclaimed as God's only begotten son in India and other parts of the world. In an article of the year 1927, he replied to the enquiry of an American who considered herself a lifelong friend of India. In her letter to Gandhi, she had written among other things: "Believing that Christ was a revelation of God, Christians of America have sent to India thousands of their sons and daughters to tell the people of India about Christ. Will you in return kindly give us your interpretation of Hinduism and make a comparison of Hinduism with the teachings of Christ? I will be deeply grateful for this favour."

I am quoting Gandhi's reply almost in its entirety, because it links his criticism of missionary Christendom with his confession to Hinduism as understood by him: "I have ventured at several missionary meetings to tell English and American missionaries that if they could have refrained from "telling" India about Christ and had merely lived the life enjoined upon them by the *Sermon on the Mount*, India instead of suspecting them would have appreciated their living in the midst of her children and directly profited by their presence. Holding this view, I can "tell" American friends nothing about Hinduism by way of "return". I do not believe in people telling others of their faith, especially with a view to conversion. Faith does not admit of telling. It has to be lived and then it becomes self-propagating. Nor do I consider myself fit to interpret Hinduism except through my own life. And if I may not interpret Hinduism through my written word, I may not compare it with Christianity. The only thing it is possible for me, therefore, to do is to say, as briefly as I can, why I am a Hindu.

Believing as I do in the influence of heredity, being born in a Hindu family, I have remained a Hindu. I should reject it, if I found it inconsistent with my moral sense or my spiritual growth. On examination, I have found it to be the most tolerant of all religions known to me. Its freedom from dogma makes a forcible appeal to me inasmuch as it gives the votary the largest scope for self-expression. Not being an exclusive religion, it enables the followers of that faith not merely to respect all the other religions, but it also enables them to admire and assimilate whatever may be good in the other faiths. Non-violence is common to all religions, but it has found the highest expression and application in Hinduism. (I do not regard Jainism or Buddhism as separate from Hinduism.) Hinduism believes in the oneness not of merely all human life but in the oneness of all that lives. Its worship of the cow is, in my opinion, its unique contribution to the evolution of humanitarianism. It is a practical application of the belief in the oneness and, therefore, sacredness of all life. The great belief in transmigration is a direct consequence of that belief. Finally the discovery of the law of *varnashrama* is a magnificent result of the ceaseless search for truth. I must not burden this article with definitions of the essentials sketched here, except to say that the present ideas of cow-worship and *varnashrama* are a caricature of what in my opinion the originals are".[6]

The extraordinary appreciation of Jesus' person and teaching, especially of the *Sermon on the Mount*, could lead to the wrong conclusion that Gandhi had taken his *satyagraha* doctrine from the *Sermon on the Mount*, that he had essentially been an "anonymous Christian" (Karl Rahner). That is definitely not the case as the following quote shows: "Though I admire much in Christianity, I am unable to identify myself with orthodox Christianity. I must tell you in all humility that Hinduism as I know it, entirely satisfies my soul, fills my whole being and I find a solace in the *Bhagavad Gita* and *Upanishads* that I miss even in the *Sermon on the Mount*. Not that I do not prize the ideal presented therein, not that some of the precious teachings in the *Sermon on the Mount* have not left a deep impression upon me, but I must confess to you that when doubts haunt me, when disappointments stare me in the face, and when I see not one ray of light on the horizon I turn to the *Bhagavad Gita,* and find a verse to comfort me; and I immediately begin to smile in the midst of overwhelming sorrow. My life has been full of external tragedies and if they have not left any visible and indelible effect on me, I owe it to the teaching of the *Bhagavad Gita*".[7]

REFERENCES

1 *Young India*, 31.12.1931; CWMG, 54, 330.
2. *First Letter to the Corinthians*, 15:14.
3. *Letter to the Romans*, 10:10.
4. *First Letter to the Corinthians*, 15:51-55.
5. *Young India*, 8.12.1927; CWMG, 40, 372 f.
6. *Young India*, 20.10.1927; CWMG, 40, 290 f.
7. *Young India*, 6.8.1925; CWMG, 32, 195.

21
Splendour and Misery of Christianity

I am of the firm opinion that Europe now-a-days does not represent the spirit of God or Christianity, but the spirit of Satan. And Satan's successes are the greatest when he emerges with God's name on his lips. Europe is now-a-days Christian in name only. In reality, it worships mammon.

—*Mahatma Gandhi*

What was the spark that set off the wildfire of Christianity in the Roman Empire? If I see it rightly, it was two elements: *Welfare*, the *active charity* (diaconia) that Christians practised not only within their communities but also towards outsiders, and their *steadfastness in the face of persecution*. The complete reversal of Jesus' message, in the way it is present in the *Book of Revelation* by John, initially referred only to a small minority within the rapidly spreading Christianity. Jesus' message of the *present* begin of God's rule was, in the beginning, definitely understood by the early Christian community of Jerusalem and the emerging Christian communities. They saw themselves as *germ cells of the kingdom of God*, where the inhabitants of this kingdom were linked to God, to their fellow human beings and — so we may add — to extra-human nature through the bond of love, a love that ultimately was nothing else but the reflection of God's love to men and to universe in which he himself is present. It was this spirit of altruistic, active love and commitment even towards strangers and enemies that made the early Christian communities so attractive — regardless of many insufficiencies and weaknesses. Their members shared their possessions, took care of elders and sick people, widows and orphans, and celebrated the abolition of all social differences in their communion, which was soon to become ritualised.

The fascination of the early Christian communities consisted above all in their way of life that was based on a *transvaluation of all values* (Friedrich Nietzsche, 1844-1900), as it had been practised and taught by Jesus. In a world that was, like our own, consumed by voracity for money, wealth, power, security, recognition and enjoyment, in other words, by the reckless "fight for existence", the young Christian communities looked like a heavenly appearance. They did not only encounter enthusiastic approval, of course, but also a sharp, hateful denial that found, very soon, expression in persecution, suffering, and — though less frequently than often assumed — in martyrdom of their members. It accompanied the young communities, with occasional breaks, since their beginnings, as already reported in the Acts of the Apostles. As the commandment of love of one's enemies excluded every thought of revenge — if we ignore the *Book of Revelation* and its affiliated movements for a while —, it is precisely the honest and fearless confessional courage of some Christians that intensified tremendously the appeal of their message. The blood of the martyrs became the seed of the church, as already realised by church father Tertullian (around 150 to about 225).

In the course of the first century A.D., this element of a practical way of life out of the spirit of truth and love retrogressed more and more behind the cultic, sacramental and institutional character of Early Catholicism. One cannot emphasise enough: While Judaism and the early Christians postponed the kingdom of God into the *future* after doomsday, and while the late Christians transferred it into an imaginary *hereafter*, all thoughts and energy of the historical Jesus was aimed at implementing it *in this world*. In this sense, there is a continuity in the form of the community of the equal and free ones between the reality of life of the pre-Easter community of Jesus and the reality of life of the post-Easter community, their members were widely *equal* with regard to their rights and obligations, as well as with regard to the balance of social differences, *free* in the sense of freedom from concern and fear of death, dread and greed, friendship and enmity, egoistic love and hatred. Jesus' way of life and the way of life of the early Christian community, therefore, present an astonishing continuity, that has to be highlighted considering the, in my opinion, disastrous discontinuity that turned the preacher of the kingdom of God into the proclaimed one. Through the *inversion of perspective* from the present to the future or the hereafter, Jesus' message was deprived of its social, political and economical explosiveness. It was downright sterilised and herewith acceptable for the rich, mighty and respectable, indeed useful because of the illusory "community in Christ" that it created. It is, however, a fact that with the exception of a few outsiders, the Christian churches and theologians stuck to the identity of the *historical Jesus* and the *biblical Christ*. Out of the choir of the countless voices announcing that as their credo, we will only single out the voice of Günther Bornkamm (1905-1990) here, *New Testament* scholar from Heidelberg. In 1988, in the 14th edition of his book "Jesus of Nazareth", he wrote: "Through the events at Easter and the certainty of Jesus' resurrection from the dead, the preacher of the coming kingdom of God. turned into the proclaimed one; the one calling to faith became the subject of faith. Jesus' word and the gospel of Jesus Christ became an entity. Many will see this process as the great Fall of Christianity. It is said that from then on, the simple proclamation of Jesus was overgrown by mythology and dogmatics, so that it became already unrecognisable in the work of Paul. "Back to Jesus!" became, therefore, the great slogan. One should, nevertheless, not agree to this slogan too fast, and one should not take it for granted that this way, allegedly so safe, ends with Jesus. The example of the Life-Jesus-Theology might scare us".[1]

I am, as a matter of fact, among those who consider the step from preacher of the kingdom of God to the proclaimed one, from believer to believed one, from man to God to be the great Fall of Christianity, and who, therefore, demand a consistent return to the historical Jesus and his message. Jesus belongs to his time, the errors and imperfections of which he shared. The basics of his message however, are *timelessly valid*. He does not address us in a less immediate and exciting, thrilling and inspirational way today than he did to his contemporaries. When in the Eastern Church, during the Easter vigil, the communities burst out rejoicing: 'Christ has risen' ! I would like to join in this rejoicing with the words: "Jesus (meaning the historical Jesus) has risen from oblivion" ! That is still more a wish than reality. But the hope remains that it might become reality, even if it is only the one of a mustard seed.

That much about the splendour of Christianity that even today has not yet faded out completely. Now to misery: Jesus' kingdom of God and the kingdoms of this world, which were represented by the Imperium Romanum at the time of Jesus and early Christianity, react towards each other like fire and water. Where they meet, it sizzles and steams. The elements fight against each other; either fire wins over water and it evaporates, or water wins over fire and extinguishes it. Seen from the outside, one could say that fire won over water. The Roman Empire became Christian, initially with the edict of toleration of Emperor Constantine in 313 A.D., and finally with the appointment to official religion in 380 A.D. by Emperor Theodosius. Under closer observation, it was, however, the other way round. Water won over fire. Christendom became Roman, meaning dogmatic, intolerant and violent, both inwardly and outwardly. The intolerance was, however, not directed against *political* liberation movements, as with the Romans, but against *religious* ones. To say it more clearly: The Roman Empire became Christian *in name* and Christendom became Roman or Byzantine, respectively, *by its nature.* The church, that had proved itself tolerably in persecution, succumbed to the strategy of embracement of Emperor Constantine, a power politician as cold as ice who acted on the maxim: *Embrace the enemy that you cannot defeat!* Now, after the "victory" of Christendom over the secular power that was in reality a complete defeat, the Christian history of persecution of non-Christian religions and cults in the ancient world began, accompanied by a Christian mission that insisted on the absolute truth claim towards other religions. This truth claim later became the foundation of the claim of superiority and power of the Christians towards people of other religions, especially Jews and Muslims, and it also became, in modern times, in secularised guise, the basis of a claim of superiority and power of Europeans towards non-Europeans as well as the white race towards coloured races.

In the inside, a broad trail of blood runs through the history of Christianity in the shape of the extermination of dissenters and people of other religions, be it ancient or medieval heretics, protestants of the modern era and innocent women, who were tortured to death as "witches" in their thousands, with the consent of the church and often enough also with its active support, or who were burned at the stake, not to mention the victims of religious wars. And did the absolute truth claim of Christianity not also provide the fertile soil for the totalitarism of the twentieth century? The church is with reason proud of its martyrs, though it did not rarely defame them as heretics, as for example the great scholar and martyr Origins (around 185-254). Arthur Drews estimates their number at roughly 15,000 in the first three centuries.[2] The blood witnesses, who died for their belief, however, contrast with millions and millions of people, who were bereaved of their cultural roots through mission or forced conversion in the name of Christ and in the name of God, or who were persecuted and killed as dissenters. To the one who takes Jesus' teaching and life as his benchmark, it is crystal clear: He sees the damage that Christians have done in the world. He can only feel deeply embarrassed about it. It is high time that, as a European, North American or Australian, one puts himself in the position of an African, Asian or a Native American or Australian, and regards the history of our culture from the point of view of the victims.

Other peoples, religions and cultures certainly also have their list of sins. But the one of the Christian Europe surpasses them all by far. There are not only the crusades of Charlemagne against the Saxons and later the crusades for the liberation of the "holy land", where the Christian knights of faith rampaged terribly among the Muslim population; there is "Europe's birth out of the spirit of violence",[3] there is the conquest of America with the annihilation of indigenous peoples that was accompanied by Christian missionaries; there is the ineffable "triangular trade" between 1550 and 1850 to which around 40 million black people fell victim; there is the colonialism and imperialism of the European peoples with its unimaginable cruelties as well as its reckless exploitation of foreign countries and peoples, that goes on till the present times; and there is eventually the phenomenal development of weapon technology up to the atomic bomb that has brought mankind to the verge of self-destruction from which we are only a few steps away. Many a reader may ask angrily what all that has to do with Christianity. In order to understand that, Martin Niemöller's (1892-1984) experience on a lecture tour in Japan could be helpful. Niemöller had been submarine commander in the First World War, then concentration camp prisoner for seven years for being an opponent to Hitler, and after the War church president of Hessen-Nassau. In a debate following one of his lectures, a Japanese listener talked bitterly about the 'Christian atomic bombs' that had been dropped on Hiroshima and Nagasaki. In disgust, he fervently rejected the connection between Christendom and atomic bomb. He stated that atomic bombs were not Christian, but they were the negation of everything that Jesus of Nazareth had taught and lived and died for. Later on he said, however, that the longer he had thought about that, the more he had understood the terrible truth of this reproach. We are not only responsible for what we do but also for what we allow to happen. And, it were the Christians who allowed production and use of those weapons, even if they did not take an active part in their development, production and use. *The existence of these weapons is constant blasphemy.* The only chance to save the world from nuclear holocaust consists in the elimination of these weapons and their proscription under international law. Every woman and man can figure out for her or himself how probable such a development is, that would amount to a "return to life".

Conclusion: If we make up an unemotional balance of what the religion of love and truth turned into in the course of its history, then we as Germans, Europeans or Whites can only ask the countless victims of this inhuman civilisation for forgiveness on our bended knees, like the German Chancellor Willy Brandt did in Warsaw in 1970 in respect of the victims of National Socialism.

REFERENCES

1. Günter Bornkamm: *Jesus von Nazareth*, Stuttgart 1988, 166.
2. Quoted in: Karlheinz Deschner: *Abermals krähte der Hahn*, Reinbek, 1972, 347.
3. *The Making of Europe : Conquest, Colonization and Cultural Change, 950-1350*. Allen Lane, The Penguin Press, London, 1993.

22
"Necessary Farewells"

> *The way of Christianity towards a "religion of scripture" based on the Bible, on dogmas and confessional documents were wrong. . . . . All religions of the world shall be allowed to testify to God or the Absolute based on authentic perceptions.*
>
> —*Klaus-Peter Jörns*

In the year 2004, the theologian Klaus-Peter Jörns published a book with the title: *Necessary Farewells: On the Way to Authentic Christianity.*[1] Therein he says farewell to:

1. The idea that Christianity is the only true religion,
2. The idea that the *Bible* is God's word, pure and true,
3. The idea that a single canon can replace God's universal perception of history,
4. The ideas of chosenness and condemnation,
5. The idea of a reciprocal likeness of God and men,
6. The idea of vilification of our fellow creatures,
7. The idea that death is the 'payment for sin',
8. The understanding of Jesus' execution as expiatory sacrifice and of its sacramental use in a sacrificial meal celebration.

The book is a milestone in the theological and ecclesiastical discourse to which I agree on all crucial points. I only wonder why Jörns takes very little account of the results of historical-critical *Bible* research. There is, after all, a difference if a saying of Jesus was with some probability pronounced by the historical Jesus himself, or if it was invented by the evangelists like, for example, the I-am-words of the Gospel of John, or if it was — as some believe — inspired by the resurrected Jesus or the Holy Spirit. The latter is, as we know by now, a *question of faith*. But then again it is not, provided one succeeds to prove that there is *an inner correlation* between *Jesus' elevation to God and the degeneration, or even perversion of his teachings*. I believe that I have been able to furnish this proof. If this is the case, then all *tendencies* that amount to a dilution, distortion and perversion of the life and teaching of the historical Jesus are subject to criticism. It is a wrong kind of tolerance if we say: It is a *question of faith* if we take the *Bible* literally with everything that we read in the Apocalypse of John. It is a wrong kind of tolerance if we say that everyone should seek heaven in his own fashion. Where faith is misused to justify violence and coercion, oppression and humiliation, the way it happens all over the world in *Bible*-believing, fundamentalist circles, protest and resistance, non-violent, of course, are called for. The same applies for the *Tanakh*, i.e., the Hebrew *Bible*, and the *Koran*.

No matter how painful it may be for many people, *there is no absolute truth in this world.* This is not to claim that there is none at all; this shall be mentioned once more. I think that it exists. But it is beyond the access of our sensory perception and our intellectual understanding. *The absolute truth is God.* We can only approach this *absolute* truth by the realisation of the relative truth in our life that we know, we cannot reach it. "We assimilate God to the extent that we put non-violence into practice, but we do not become God himself".[2] The aspiration for truth is, nevertheless, worth the effort. To say it with Gandhi one last time: *"The commitment to truth is the only justification for our existence. All our doing should be centred in truth. Truth should be the breath of our life"*.[3] Judaism knows this idea as the commitment to the *fulfilment of the divine law*, and Islam — the word Islam in itself means nothing else but "commitment" — takes it as the *epitome of its religious practice*.

Gotthold Ephraim Lessing expressed this thought in his inimitable way when he wrote: "If God kept hidden in his right hand all truth and in his left hand the only, ever active desire for truth, though with the addition that I would err for ever and ever, and if he said to me: chose! I would humbly take his left hand and say: 'Father, give! The absolute truth is only for you alone, anyway' " ! This is a great word to which I can only agree, though with the small addition that there is not only the alternative: *absolute truth* or *eternal error* but also that existential approach to the absolute truth that I explained in the chapter about existential hermeneutics.

In the work of the Athenian philosopher Socrates, there is a striking parallel to Lessing's comment. Socrates endeavoured all his life to expose the (alleged) knowledge of his compatriots as ignorance, not in order to accommodate himself comfortably with their ignorance, but, on the contrary, to awaken in them a *passionate quest for true knowledge*, Eros: the pursuit of that knowledge that is synonymous with existence. Our thinking and feeling, our talking and acting emerges from this existence, like the plant emerges from the seed and the animal from the fecundated ovum. Socrates dissolved the solidified, alienated knowledge that had been separated from existence into the *stream of embers of striving after the true knowledge* that is, however, never reached. It did not matter to him to know what is good, but to *be* good, he did not care about knowing what virtue, what efficiency is, but about *being* virtuous and efficient. Therewith, Socrates turns out to be the "third in league" with Jesus and Gandhi. He even shared their fate as martyrs of the truth.

There are Christians who consider the imposition of abandoning the absolute truth claim of their religion as synonymous with the imposition of surrendering their faith. There is nothing of the sort, of course. On the contrary, the abandonment of the absolute truth claim means the liberation from the narrow prison of dogma. It is this very small, inconspicuous step from the relative to the absolute truth claim that turns truth into untruth. Who turns a screw only a half-turn too far destroys the whole thread. Here, too. Who thinks that he possesses the absolute truth holds a Pandora's Box in his hand from which immeasurable suffering and disaster wells up. Because that much is certain: For the one who considers himself in possession of the absolute truth, be it of religious or ideological nature, people of other religions or dissenters are inevitably in possession of the absolute untruth. That applies equally inwardly towards deviant confessions, as well as outwardly towards the followers of other religions and philosophies. Where the absolute truth claim bonds with the power of definition of an institution like the Catholic Church or the government of a totalitarian regime, the smell of burning at the stakes, on which the bodies of delinquents are delivered to Satan for the salvation of their souls, or the smell of gun powder of the death squads is in the air. It was not always that bad, but coercion and violence in the name of religion, in the name of God, remain a crime against God and men at all times.

The abandonment of the absolute truth claim turns truth *owners* into truth *seekers*. It opens our eyes, ears and hearts for what members of other religious orientations, religions and philosophies have to tell us. It creates a solid basis for the *interconfessional*, *interreligious* and *intercultural* dialogue in which all participants grow in insight and understanding. Jesus loved to speak in parables not without a reason. This is why I also want to have a try at this genre: There is a mountain that we are all required to climb because God lives at its peak in the clouds, far away and unreachable. As long as we seek truth and non-violence, we will go up. We do not only come closer to God but also to each other, regardless of the point at the bottom of the mountain from which we have started. If, however, we resort to coercion, violence, lying and cheating, we will go down. We do not only withdraw from God but also from each other.

I am aware of the consequences of the demand to abandon the dogmas, as it refers to the core of Christian belief: the *Christ Dogma* and the *Trinity Dogma*. Can and may a person who contradicts them still call himself a Christian? I would like to answer the question with Gandhi: "If I had only the Sermon on the Mount and my own interpretation of it at my disposal, I would not hesitate to say: 'Yes, I am a Christian' ". But I do not care about names. I would rather come a step closer to that absolute truth that is God.

Now that the two central dogmas, the Christ Dogma and the Trinity Dogma, have collapsed under the attack of historical-critical biblical studies like the Twin Towers in New York on September 11, 2001, the question arises irrefutably: Is Christianity, therefore, finished or is it possible that we find a treasure among the debris, incomparably more valuable than what we have just lost? — This is the case, as a matter of fact. The dogma turns out to be a hard nut, the shell of which must be broken in order to get to the nourishing and tasty kernel. The truth that is hidden in the dogma consists of the fact that in one and the same process (*uno actu*), the man or woman, who is progressing on the path of existential implementation of the truth recognised by him, i.e., on the path marked by the five monastic vows of the Asian religions, *rises* to God, while God at the same time *descends* into the world. God incarnates in this man or woman, he emerges in the world. He becomes viewable, hearable, and experiencable in him or her, though never absolutely, but always in a relative way. I, therefore, have no scruples in recognising that *God* was *in Jesus,* and *Jesus* was *in God*. I deny, however, the formulation of the dogma: *true* man and *true* God, meaning entirely man and entirely God. For Jesus, on the contrary, applies what applies to all of us: *We are all called to return.* There may well be huge differences in the distance that we cover on the way to the truth that

God is. The bigger the distance the more alike we become to God, but we will never be equal to God, as long as we live. The presbyter Arius of Alexandria was, therefore, right against Athanasius! Jesus was *similar to God* but not *equal to God*. With this, Jesus returns to the human race after seventeen hundred years; and he returns to Judaism. He becomes a prophet, a reformer of Judaism and a teacher of mankind. If he lived or arose from the imagination of a poet, is irrelevant for our salvation, because the life-task of returning to God, the return to (eternal) life, that is at the same time a coming back to paradise, into the Garden of Eden, is the same for all of us. Jesus is not the redeemer, who gives the people who believe in him and identify with him in this manner, quasi a piggyback ride on his back carrying them to heaven.

With that, the "children's question" finds also an answer: What becomes of the people who could not know of Jesus because they had lived before him or who never knew anything about his existence? The same conditions apply for all of us. *Christians have no advantage over the believers of other religions or atheists.* The sentence: 'I believe *with* Jesus, not *in* Jesus" originates from Martin Buber, and Shalom Ben Chorin adds: "It is *Jesus' belief* that links us, and the *belief in Jesus* that separates us". There were truly enough precursors of the afore-mentioned, so that one can only wonder why they did not prevail against dogmatic Christianity. Thus the liberal theologian Adolf von Harnack (1851-1930) demanded already at the beginning of the twentieth century: "It is not about believing *in* Jesus, but believing *like* him, which means believing in God's paternal love and the infinite value of the human soul". It was, after all, already Lessing who differentiated between *Christ's religion* and *Christian religion*, meaning the same as the previously mentioned: "It is incomprehensible how these two religions, Christ's religion as well as the Christian one, can exist in Christ as one and the same person"

Gandhi goes one step further when he considers representative suffering to be realised in Jesus in its pure form, which eliminates enmity, violence and injustice, in one word evil. He sees his own indefinite fastings that were misinterpreted by his enemies as blackmailing manoeuvres in this perspective: "Fasting cannot be undertaken mechanically. It is a powerful thing but a dangerous thing if handled amateurishly. It requires complete self-purification, much more than is required in facing death without a thought of retaliation. One such act of perfect sacrifice would suffice for the whole world. Such is held to be Jesus' example. . . . . But whether the Jesus tradition is historically true or not, I do not care. To me it is truer than history because I hold it to be possible and it enshrines an eternal law — the law of vicarious and innocent suffering taken in its true sense".[4]

If it is true, and I am deeply convinced of it, that there is no absolute truth in this world, then this does not only apply to Christianity but to all religions and philosophic doctrines. That puts an end to fundamentalism and dogmatism of all shades. The wall that separated Judaism, Christianity and Islam, comes tumbling down like the walls of Jericho at the sound of the trombones. The Jews' *Yahweh*, the Christians' *God* and the Muslims' *Allah* prove to be one and the same. If we add Gandhi's assurance that the Hindus, too believe in the one god, *Devadideva,* the god of gods and his interpretation of *nirvana* as one of the many forms of appearance of God; and if we eventually add the god Apollo of Socrates, the eternal, indestructible being of Plato, and the philosophic truth that is God, then it becomes clear that in the end, all religions and even philosophies 'believe' in one and the same truth.

Let us summarise what links Gandhi and Jesus throughout all differences in space, time and cultural background, and what makes them brothers in spirit :

1. The unconditional devotion to that God, who is the absolute truth and Who penetrates all their existence and reshapes it from scratch, which often results in a terrifying radicality of thinking, talking and acting.
2. The quest for truth (*satya*), non-violence (*ahimsa*), renunciation (*brahmacharya*), lack of possessions (*aparigraha*) and non-stealing (*asteya*).
3. Loving devotion to the poor, sick, handicapped, disadvantaged, deprived of their rights, and despised by the rich, mighty, respectable and pious hypocrites.
4. Uncompromising rejection of all forms of hierarchy, whether based on power, possession, reputation or knowledge. A vision of a world in which the people live in harmony with God, their fellow human beings and extra-human nature (Ramaraj — kingdom of God).
5. A confident dealing with tradition and convention.
6. Emphasis on the unity of theory and practice; and teaching and life.

REFERENCES

1. Gütersloh, 2004.
2. *Harijan*, 12.11.1938; CWMG, 74, 130.
3. *From Yeravda Mandir*, SWMG, 4, 213.
4. *Harijan*, 2.10.1946; CWMG, 92, 345 f.

23
Credo

Do we, as Christians, need a new credo? If we take the questions discussed in this book seriously, the answer can only be yes. I attach a proposal of how it could read. In the era of historical-critical science, a credo cannot be phrased only positively. It must review the traditional formulas, keep what has proved successful and eliminate what is obsolete.

I believe in God, the Almighty, Omnipresent and Omniscient primal foundation of the universe. I believe that God is invisibly present in the world, and at the same time, he is beyond the world. His presence in this world results from his omnipresence.

I do not believe that God interferes immediately with natural phenomena and history through miracles. God wants to work in this world, but *through us*. We are supposed to be his head and heart, his hands and feet. If miracles happen, it will be through us.

I believe that God is neither man nor woman; neither father nor mother; neither person nor spirit; neither this worldly nor other worldly. He is all these at the same time. He is truth; He is love; He is the greatest good. He is eternal, immortal and indestructible. He is, however, also the nothingness (*nirvana*), in which all ideas and sensory perceptions expire.

I believe *with* Jesus, not *in* Jesus. Nevertheless, I believe that Jesus was a Son of God, but not the "only begotten" one in the sense of the dogma. I rather believe that God had many daughters and sons, yes; we are all his beloved children, even if we turn away from him in order to go our own ways (sinning).

I believe that the man Jesus became similar to God in the course of his short life, but not equal to God. He was a man, capable of erring and errant. He was fathered by a man (Joseph) and borne by a woman (Mary). He suffered under Pontius Pilate, as far as we can get certainty about historical facts, was crucified, died and was buried.

He suffered the physical death, the first one, like all living beings. He was spared from the spiritual death, the second one.

I believe that the Holy Spirit is the spirit of God. He is as little as Jesus, a separate matter of faith.

I do not believe in one of the Christian churches because the church is not a matter of faith. It is the *imperfect* community of those who are on their way to God, sometimes unfortunately also in the opposite direction.

I believe that there are truth and untruth, success and failure, good use and terrible misuse, holy and diabolic matters in all religions. It is our task to implement the truth that we perceive in our life and to free us with God's help from untruth, as far as we recognise it.

I think that it is possible not only to get forgiveness for our sins but also to be released through God from the compulsion of sinning and, therefore, escape from the second, the eternal death. With the liberation from sin, its consequences will also disappear — fear and greed, (selfish) love and hatred, affection and repulsion.

I do not believe in the resurrection of the dead. I rather believe that, thus far as we realise the truth that we perceive in our existence, we receive a share of the eternal, indestructible existence of God.

Conclusion: What is essential is a return to Jesus' life and teaching. What is essential is a reformation of head and limbs of Christianity. What is essential is the dialogue of the denominations, religions and philosophies while abandoning any absolute truth claim. What is essential is following Jesus' call: *"The time has come; the kingdom of God has dawned."*

What unites Gandhi and Jesus despite their distance in time, space and cultural background ? I know no better answer than the five principles that Gandhi recommended as the subjects of daily prayers or daily meditation :

"I want to adhere to the truth.
I do not want to bow to injustice.
I want to be free of fear.
I do not want to use force.
I want to see, first of all, the good in everyone".

Index